Reflections of the One Life

Daily Pointers to Enlightenment

Scott Kiloby

NON-DUALITY PRESS

REFLECTIONS OF THE ONE LIFE

First edition published 2009
This edition published October 2014 by NON-DUALITY PRESS

© Scott Kiloby 2014
© Non-Duality Press 2014

Edited by Kevin Prince

NON-DUALITY PRESS | PO Box 2228 | Salisbury | SP2 2GZ
United Kingdom

ISBN: 978-1-908664-47-1

www.non-dualitypress.org

This book is written from love to love. It is a daily reminder of what you already know. Everything is a perfect expression of nothing, which is to say that the boundary between everything and nothing is not real. There is only 'what is.' That is love.

Special thanks to
Chad, Jolinda, Mom, Dad, Mark, Teri, John, Jeff, Kevin,
Laura, Mandi, Candice, and Ken and for so many others that
have contributed—too many to name.

JANUARY

There is no greater mystery than this, that we keep seeking reality though in fact we are reality. We think that there is something hiding reality and that this must be destroyed before reality is gained. How ridiculous! A day will dawn when you will laugh at all your past efforts. That which will be the day you laugh is also here and now.

—— Sri Ramana Maharshi

This moment is ever fresh and new

As this New Year begins, it is tempting to actually believe that you are entering a New Year or that this is the end of something and the beginning of something else. That is a wonderful story, but is it truly real?

The human mind has been telling quite a story. The notions of minute, hour, week, month, and year are conceptual. Time is a movie being projected from the mind. No matter how hard you look, you will never walk outside your door and pick up or touch anything called, "hour," "week," "month," "year," "new year," "past," "future," or "time."

The existence of the thought-based, time-bound self is dependent on the illusion of time continuing to be supported through incessant psychological identification with thoughts of past, present, and future. Although the mind has a tendency to go "into" time for a sense of self, do you notice that past and future are merely presently-arising thoughts? In fact, even the word "now" is a thought. Do you see that you are here regardless of whether these thoughts are arising or not?

This moment is ever fresh and new—where the concepts of beginning and ending, me and my life, and my past and my future are seen as stories. There is only the timeless space in which concepts about time arise and fall.

The story of you

Yesterday's reflection stated that the story of "you" is a time-bound, thought-based illusion. What does that mean?

The story is thought-based in the sense that its content is purely conceptual. When there is no thinking, there is no story of you.

The story is time-bound in the sense that it lives in time only. Your identity is determined by whatever thoughts of past arise in present awareness. Your name, job title, family role, childhood memories, and every other aspect of your history are determined solely through memory. Thought is memory (past).

That story of past is incomplete by its very nature. Because it exists in time (past), it relies on more time for its completion (future). As long as there is dependence on memory (past) for your sense of self, there will be projection towards a future completion of that story. This keeps you locked in the cycle of seeking.

Living solely through time is essentially the same as living solely through thought. Time is thought. You cannot touch past or future except through thinking.

Presence is the timeless awareness that sees the story of you. Past and future are merely thoughts arising in present awareness. If you can see something, it isn't you. It is an object appearing in awareness, an illusion you take to be you. Realize the awareness in which the story of you arises. Seeing the story as it arises frees you from its grip.

The false idea of future awakening

If the story of you is a thought-based, time-bound illusion, the natural tendency is to devise ways to be free of it. Many spiritual practices are undertaken in the name of getting rid of the ego. But only the story of you would be interested in getting rid of the story of you. The entire movement to "get rid of" or "be free of" ego is a movement towards future. Whenever there is effort towards future, the time-bound story is running the show. The cycle of seeking continues....

In discovering that the movement towards future awakening is just more bondage to the time-bound ego, the possibility for a timeless seeing arises. This timeless seeing emanates from awareness, which cannot be sought in the future because it is what is awake right now. Future is merely a thought arising in it. It can be quite a blow to the time-bound story to realize that all its grand plans for future enlightenment are just self-centered thought patterns. In those patterns, the underlying plot is, "When will my enlightenment arrive?"

'Your' enlightenment will never arrive. No time-bound story ever reaches enlightenment. Enlightenment is realized to be the timeless awareness that sees the time-bound story arising and falling. In that effortless noticing, the story is seen to be a dream that was never real. There is nothing to get rid of. Only that seeing is needed.

Timeless awareness (conceptuality v. actuality)

No matter what words are used to point to timeless awareness, the pointers are only concepts. What is being pointed to is not conceptual.

These reflections are not inviting you to start buying into a new set of "enlightened" concepts. It is easy to go around thinking and talking a lot about "presence" or "this moment" while missing completely the immediately accessible non-conceptual awareness that is being pointed to here. In that case, presence becomes the new conceptual story of the dream self. The script in this story is "I am present" or "I am working towards being present."

But the words "timeless awareness" are pointing to the fact that there is no person to be, or work towards being, present or aware. The "person" is a conceptual, time-bound story arising in the timeless awareness that is awake now.

"Timeless awareness" is also only a concept and, as such, the mind can confuse the concept with the actuality to which it is pointing. The words are not that which they describe. So, although "timeless awareness" is a concept, it is pointing sharply to an actuality. The pointer "timeless awareness" is pointing to the actual, non-conceptual space in which all concepts (including time and self) arise and fall. It points to that which is looking in (and as) the space of this moment before an interpretation about the moment appears. The catch is that every concept is an interpretation.

The self-centered nature of thought

The self-centered nature of thought remains unseen for most people. If it is seen, it is often taken for granted and considered normal. But as awareness becomes aware of the content of thought, it becomes increasingly obvious that the content is largely self-centered and that this self is ultimately a fiction.

The mind filters every experience through the question, "What does this mean for me?" It interprets reality and its surroundings in a way that places the self at the center. Don't believe what is being said here. Simply notice thoughts. Notice that, according to the mind, everything centers around you: your wife, your pet, your job, your house, your friends, your bad day, your good day, your feelings, your street, your city, your country, your religion, your race, your experiences, and even your God or your enlightenment.

In one sense, we could say that you are not the center of life. But it is closer to the truth to say that there is no "you" to be at the center. When you realize your true nature as awareness, self-centered thoughts start arising in the light of awareness and are seen as empty. You stop interpreting reality in a way that creates and maintains a "you" at the center. Self-centeredness is replaced with unconditional love. "You" cannot achieve unconditional love because "you" are the self-centered story. Unconditional love is realized when that story is seen as an empty fiction.

Confirming awareness

The difficulty in pointing to awareness is that it is not an object or concept. In fact, the concept "awareness" arises in actual awareness. The word "awareness" is like a sign pointing back to its actual source. In these reflections, it is sometimes stated that awareness is who you really are. But even that is merely a pointer. Your true nature is an unbounded mystery. No word can capture it. Awareness is a sharp pointer because it points the mind away from identification with temporary thoughts and back to the source that gives birth to them. This source is always and already changelessly present (it does not come and go). It is timeless (the story of past and future arises and falls in it). It is non-dual (dualistic ideas and judgments arise and fall in it).

In your direct experience, confirm awareness— the simple fact that you are. That confirmation reveals your true nature beyond the limited time-bound story of thought. Confirming awareness means getting a permanent felt-sense of your own I-Amness so that you don't take yourself to be any story placed after the words, "I am . . . ." This frees you from identification with the past, the future, the body, your history, emotions, roles, titles, and every other object that arises and falls in awareness. This disidentification allows the peace, love, and joy of your true nature to arise. No temporary story can provide that clarity.

More on confirming awareness

Yesterday's reflection invited you to confirm awareness. If confirming awareness is made into a time-bound practice in which you believe that you are working towards a future moment of awakening, the pointer "confirm awareness" has been misheard. It has been usurped by the dream self (ego)— the thought-based, time-bound "me" involved in the illusion of seeking.

Confirming awareness is not about working towards future awakening. Future is a thought arising in timeless awareness. If the thought arises, "I am working towards enlightenment," it's the dream self talking.

The pointer "confirm awareness" is an invitation to realize the timeless space in which everything arises and falls. In that way, awareness is an end in and of itself, not a practice to reach some future end. You are simply noticing what you already are. You are not the dream self that lives in thoughts of past, future, and resistance to this moment. That dream arises in the awareness that is naturally at rest in the present moment.

Even if you repeatedly confirm awareness, you are still not engaging in the time-bound practice of seeking if you recognize that awareness itself is timeless. It is the space in which doing, including seeking, arises and falls. Seeking happens only when awareness becomes fixated in that movement. Confirming awareness means noticing what is right here, right now. It means noticing that which never entered the search in the first place.

The inseparability of awareness and thought

The last few reflections have been pointing directly
non-conceptual awareness. In confirming awareness,
is tempting to deny or suppress thought or to treat conce
as undesirable. Just notice the tendency to deny or suppr
thought. That is the dream (mental) self doing what it d
best— controlling. The mind is seeking a state that is fre
the mind. Can you see the futility of that?

Confirming awareness simply means recognizing—
repeatedly—the space in which concepts arise and
This awareness has its own quieting mechanism. Tim
non-conceptual awareness is already free of thought and
It is the vast, inward space in which time and thought
The space is naturally quiet and still. It is the emptines
which everything—every movement of thought—com

That is the amazing thing. It is the space from whic
concept arises, which means the concept is none oth
the space from which it comes. In this seeing, though
to be empty, just as the space that gives birth to it.
no longer has the power to cause suffering and seekii
remains there to serve its practical functioning. Th
allowed to flow freely and naturally from its source
is no longer identification with it. This dance bet
source and its manifestation is one dance—One Life
as many, non-dual awareness appearing as dualistic

How will you know?

The last few reflections have discussed confirming, and repeatedly confirming, timeless awareness until it is seen that awareness is who you really are and that you are not a separate self.

How will you know that awareness has been realized? It is unmistakable! Your questions and seeking dissolve away. It is not that your questions necessarily get answered. It is not that you "find" anything. You realize that the awareness that is behind your face and animating the body is the same awareness behind every face and animating every body. It is realized that all there is, is this awareness. It is the awake space in which everything arises and falls—all bodies, thoughts, emotions, events, experiences, states and objects. All your questions arise and fall in that space. The seeking arises and falls in that space. When it is seen that this space, this opening, is who you really are, it is realized that you cannot find yourself in time. It is seen that there is no separate you to find anything. There is only this timeless awareness and you are That. Everything is That.

When awareness is realized, there is an undeniable knowing. Seeking stops because it is seen that the seeker is merely a series of thoughts arising and falling in awareness. There is no seeker there. There never was. There was only mind movement, which was mistakenly taken to be a separate self.

The traps after the realization of awareness

It takes no time to realize awareness because awareness is timeless. However, even once non-dual awareness is realized, the complete falling away of the sense of being a separate self may not happen all at once. The conditioning of the separate self has a momentum of its own. There are all sorts of traps that the mind can fall into once timeless awareness is realized. For example, there may be an unconscious attachment in the mind to a particular interpretation of non-duality, a subtle belief that only "my" interpretation is correct and that all other interpretations are incorrect. The self creates and maintains conflict and division between its fundamentalist interpretation and those that do not agree with that interpretation. Another trap is that the mind can start to believe that a state of pure awareness must be maintained, a state free of concepts. It begins to deny form, deny thought. This state is still dualistic. A subtle identity arises as "pure awareness"—arrogantly separating itself from "all the others" lost in thought or stories.

In allowing each of these traps to be seen, awareness self-corrects them all. This allows for a true resting in awareness. This resting is not a fundamentalist position. It is not a dualistic identity. It is awareness appearing as everything—every thought, opinion, emotion, experience, and state. It is genuine Oneness, a living realization characterized by love, humility, peace and inclusiveness.

Confusing non-conceptual awareness with denial of concepts

No concept will get you to non-conceptual awareness because you are already there. Awareness is a seeing that who you are is beyond form and time. No amount of thinking or future will reveal it. In fact, if the mind is constantly engaged in seeking and intellectualizing non-duality or presence, there is likely identification with thought happening, a little "me" that is looking for its own absence. It's futile. The goal of that stream of thought is to avoid its own absence.

However, it's easy to confuse non-conceptual awareness with a total denial of concepts. Without concepts, how could we ever point to awareness? How could math or science ever be communicated? How could you tell your kids you love them?

'This' is a seeing beyond attachment to concepts (not a denial of them). In that seeing, it is realized that who you really are is this non-attached, non-conceptual, timeless seeing or being. But concepts are expressions of that non-attached, non-conceptual awareness. Nothing is appearing as everything. To deny form is to deny the formless. To deny time is to deny the timeless. To deny the intellect is to deny its very source.

Walking around totally identified with emptiness is a dualistic split between form and formlessness. Notice that non-conceptual awareness is your essence. Then be who you are totally, including embracing fully, without attachment, everything that arises from, and is not other than, awareness.

Stuck in emptiness

It is easy to get stuck in the idea of emptiness. As yesterday's reflection stated, "Walking around totally identified with emptiness is a dualistic split between form and formlessness." To be totally identified with emptiness means to make a separate identity out of it.

The realization of non-conceptual awareness reveals your own absence. It reveals that the thought-based, time-bound self you took yourself to be is a total phantom. This is a powerful seeing. It reveals the illusory nature of personal suffering and seeking. But the more the mind subtly buys into the dualistic idea of "no self," the more it gets turned into a belief. When your unconscious story, or belief, is "I am pure awareness," or "I am emptiness," there can be a tendency to deny form and thought.

With even a little taste of what the word "awareness" is pointing to, the mind can use the *idea* of non-conceptual awareness to deny concepts, or use the *idea* of emptiness to deny form. This is not non-duality. It is still dualistic. Words like "nonconceptual awareness" and "emptiness" are pointing to a wordless, actual space. That actual space, once it is realized directly, is a doorway into a seeing that even the boundary lines between conceptual and non-conceptual, emptiness and form, and space and objects are illusory.

Words like "awareness" and "space" are stories

We've been using the word awareness to point to who you are beyond thoughts, feelings, states, and experiences. You are an actuality, not a concept. Therefore, the word "awareness" is merely a pointer. The word is not the thing it describes. We could just as easily use the words "opening" or "space" instead of the word "awareness." As soon as you think a word captures your essence, there is a tendency to get stuck on the word. There is no word that captures who you are because you are not a concept.

The mind is telling a story of self. This story consists of one thought after another thought. It may be a victim story, a seeker story, a story of being a successful businessman, or a story of being a failure. No matter what the content of your story is, the story is not who you are.

It is easy to become attached to words like "awareness" or "Oneness" used in non-duality teachings. These are just little stories. They are ultimately no closer to who you are than any other story. But these words "awareness," "opening," and "space" are pointing you out of attachment to thoughts, emotions, states, and experiences. They are pointing to the absence of things. When it is realized that every thought, emotion, state, or experience arises and falls within who you are, the whole movement to define yourself dies. Freedom is revealed.

Direct knowing

You cannot know life directly through thinking. Trying to know life directly through thinking is like trying to pet your dog by stroking a piece of paper that has a drawing of a dog on it.

Quietness is a portal to the end of seeking

Allow awareness to rest into the quietness in the room. Notice that the same quietness that is "out there" in the room is also "in here" in the body and mind. Just rest into that quietness. The quietness is a portal to the pure awareness that is who you are.

What are you seeking? You may believe that you are seeking more money, a better relationship, a better drug, a new job, or enlightenment. But what is it that you really want? If you are really honest, you will discover that you already know those 'things' outside you will not provide the permanent contentment you are seeking. Even if you get the new job or the new lover, at some point the newness will wear off and the seeking for something more or something better will begin again.

If you are really honest, you will discover that what you are really seeking is the end of seeking itself. But if you listen into the quietness that is already here in this moment, that silent stillness already contains peace. That peace is who you already are. The notion of seeking into future to find what you already are is insanity. Just rest as awareness in this moment. The end of seeking is already here in the quiet stillness of awareness.

Oneness seeking oneness

Yesterday's reflection spoke to the quiet stillness that is already here in this moment. It permeates everything. That stillness is a portal to your true nature as non-dual awareness. The spiritual search is a cosmic joke. Out of the non-dual awareness, a movement of seeking arises. A misperception happens. The misperception is that you need to seek or to do something in order to be what you already are. If you can see the futility of that right now, all seeking comes to an end.

From that quiet stillness, the movement to seek arises. What you are ultimately seeking is the end of seeking. The end of seeking only comes when you realize who you are. Who you are can only be realized now in the quiet stillness of non-dual awareness. Can you see the cosmic joke yet? Quietness is seeking quietness. Stillness is seeking stillness. Peace is seeking peace. Out of Oneness comes a movement of energy called the "separate self" who is seeking Oneness. Oneness cannot be found in time. It is already here. To see the futility of seeking is to rest in the non-dual awareness, the quiet stillness that is already here right now.

Choice and freedom

What is the next thought you are going to think? If you observe the mind in this way, you see that you cannot know what thought is going to arise next. Thought arises involuntarily and spontaneously. Seeking arises involuntarily and spontaneously as a dream of thought. You aren't 'doing' the thinking or seeking. It just arises without choice or control.

If you have no control over the next thought, what does that say about your search for future enlightenment? Most people believe that having choice provides freedom. They believe that they are choosing their own path and bringing about future results including future enlightenment. If you can see right now that you have no choice as to what thought is going to arise next, there can be a seeing that all your future plans are illusory. The spiritual search is a dream of thought. In that seeing, real freedom is possible, freedom to allow whatever arises without chasing after a future moment, freedom to simply be what you already are. Seeking can end completely if you see that there is no 'you' doing the seeking. Therefore, there is no 'you' to be enlightened. In that seeing, it is realized that enlightenment is what you already are.

More on the question of choice

Do take this question of choice seriously for one moment. Simply look. What thought is going to arise next? Can awareness know what thought is going to appear before it appears? No, it cannot. Therefore, there is no choice or control. Thinking merely happens. The end of thought cannot be found through thought. The end of seeking cannot be found through seeking. In the story of you, you believe you are going somewhere, to some future moment of awakening. But you are not going anywhere. More precisely, there is no "you" to go anywhere. There is only thought happening. That thought paints a picture of past that you call, "Who you are." It paints a picture of future that you call, "Who you are going to become." But you are not thought. You are not the past or the future. Because you are not thought, you cannot find yourself through seeking, which is a dream of thought.

In seeing that the spiritual search is happening all on its own, there is the possibility that awareness will start to see it for what it really is—a dream of thought. When awareness sees the dream of thought known as "you and your spiritual search" and sees that it is happening spontaneously and involuntarily, all of the mental and emotional effort drops out of the search. There is a natural resting into what is.

Choiceless awareness

To say "there is no choice" is simply to point to awareness itself which is naturally choiceless. Awareness is not dualistic. It does not choose between this and that. It is not involved in the game of seeking or the appearance of cause and effect. Those things arise within awareness. Apparent choice arises within awareness. To the extent you believe you have choice today, then make one simple choice. Choose to confirm that who you are is this non-dual, choiceless awareness. Don't just say it. Realize it. Realize the freedom inherent in it. See that what is looking at these words is a choiceless awareness that is already free of time, thought, emotion, suffering, and seeking.

There is certainly an appearance of choice in the mind. The dualistic mind appears to make choices everyday. But these choices are appearances in choiceless awareness. When choiceless awareness is realized to be who you really are, the individual "you" that is lost in the game of seeking is seen to be a phantom, a dream of thought that is perfectly designed to keep choosing, believing that one day it will reach future enlightenment through its choices. Enlightenment can never be reached in time. Enlightenment is the timeless, choiceless awareness in which the seeking towards future and the choosing of 'this' over 'that' occurs.

Co-creating reality

Thought is memory. It cannot see what is. Only awareness sees what is. Thoughts constitute an interpretation of what is. They are memories. Therefore, no matter what you conclude about what is seen in this moment, the conclusion is not what is. It is your interpretation of what is. Your dream.

Reality is both formless awareness and the forms (interpretations) that arise from it and disappear back into it. In that way, one could say that reality is being co-created. There is 'what is' plus the interpretation of 'what is.' Your mind is interpreting reality all the time. Conflict and separation appear real when you believe that only your interpretation is correct and you do not see that formless awareness is arising as every interpretation. It is arising as everything you see.

When you find yourself in conflict, it just means that you mistook your interpretation of what is happening for reality itself. In reality, there is no conflict. Conflict arises when interpretations clash. Do not seek to be rid of your interpretation. Simply see that it is an interpretation. In that seeing, there is no longer identification with the interpretation, yet there is also not a denial of that interpretation. Thought still arises but it is no longer creating conflict. This is when it is seen that Oneness is seeing itself everywhere, in the broad diversity of life. Formless love is seeing and loving itself in every form.

Chasing concepts

The idea that there is something more that needs to be seen or known in the future before you can be free or enlightened is fuel for the spiritual search. The search is not the answer. It is the problem. The search arises from a misperception that you are not already there. But where is 'there?' What is it? The most the mind can do is come up with a concept to put in place of the word 'there.' It believes that it must reach something called freedom, enlightenment, presence, love, awareness, Oneness, contentment or 'the end of the search.' Each of those is merely a concept.

Like a hamster on a wheel, the mind is chasing its own concepts. The search is perpetuated when concepts are believed completely. This is not about denying concepts, but rather seeing their temporary, illusory nature.

What is being pointed to here is not conceptual. It is the recognition that who you are is inseparable from the space in which these concepts arise. Confirming that you are this space reveals what is being pointed to with words like "enlightenment," and "presence." The words are merely pointers pointing back to the space. Realize that what you have been seeking is what you already are. No matter what idea you have of yourself in the future, see that it is only an image arising in the space of now.

Contraction

The sense of being a separate self is maintained through narrow focusing or contracting around appearances that arise and fall in awareness. Awareness itself is naturally wide open and spacious. Take a moment to sit back and see that the entire experience of now is happening in that open space. Exterior to the body and mind, there are objects such as a desk, a chair, a light, the floor, walls, perhaps heat or cold in the room. Interior to the body and mind, there are also objects including thoughts, feelings, and sensations. All of that is occurring in the wide open space of awareness.

When awareness contracts around an interior or exterior object, the sense of spacious awareness appears lost. The sense of separation between objects appears pronounced, including the sense that there is a self inside the body and mind separate from everything exterior to the body and mind.

In simply noticing this tendency of awareness to contract around objects that appear both "inside" and "outside" the body and mind, spacious awareness begins to realize itself naturally. The tendency to contract around thought and emotion relaxes. You see that who you are cannot be found in the temporary objects appearing and disappearing including the thoughts and emotions. You are the spacious awareness that contains the entire experience happening in the space of now, including the interior and exterior objects that come and go.

No self, authentic self, or true Self?

In various non-dual teachings and other traditions and religions, there are different words for what is realized in enlightenment. For example, it's been called, "no self." It's also been called "authentic self," or "true Self." So which is it? Is there a self or not? Each of these words is pointing to the same realization. Don't get too caught up in the words. The words are not that which they describe. The words are labels only.

Regardless of how you describe the realization, what is being pointed to is an actual seeing beyond identification with a time-bound, thought-based story of "me." The concepts used to describe that seeing are secondary.

Once there is this seeing, there is still an apparently separate body and mind. There are still different interpretations arising in those apparently separate bodies and minds. Some will call it "no self" and others will call it "true Self" or "authentic self" yet they are pointing to the same realization.

If it is a true realization, the interpretation arises and falls in emptiness. This emptiness is not attached to a particular interpretation. It is not identified with thought. If you find yourself trying to convince others that there is no self, and that the use of terms like "authentic self" or "true Self" are wrong, it may be that there is still identification with form. Words are forms.

No point of reference

The moment you have a single point of reference, you have the separate self. You have conflict. Conflict can be a great teacher. It reveals where the mind is stuck on some point of reference.

This is not about trying to reach a place of no thought. Even "no thought" is a point of reference. Non-duality cannot be known through a dualistic point of reference. As soon as you see the mind fixating on its particular view, even if the view is that you have "no view," there is the possibility of seeing that you are coming from a point of reference.

Right and wrong, clear and unclear, good and bad, self and no self, Absolute and relative and all other pairs of opposites arise together and are so mutually interdependent that they are not separate. Right cannot exist without wrong. When you believe your view is right, you have a partial view that exists only in relation to its dualistic opposite.

There is the possibility of seeing that what you ultimately are cannot be found through a single, dualistic point of reference. Call it "non-dual awareness" or "God" or whatever word you like. But remember that every word is a point of reference. What you are is already free of all points, yet it contains all points and arises as each and every point. In that seeing, there is no more conflict.

Oneness

Oneness is the direct experiencing of reality as it is without an experiencer. You are the looking, not the objects being perceived. So any name, concept, emotion, sensation, body, self-image, personal identity, role, title, or historical fact that is perceived is an object in awareness. It is not who you are. This reveals that what is looking is not an object. You are not a separate person. The "separate person" is an object in awareness. You are no-thing—awareness itself.

But no-thing or no self is really only half the story. When it is seen that there is not an experiencer, or that the experiencer is an object in awareness, a more mature understanding reveals itself. This understanding is not conceptual or intellectual (concepts and the intellect are merely objects appearing in awareness). It is not something that can be grasped by thinking about it because it is what you are. This understanding arises when it is seen that the nothingness that you are, the pure perceiving, is not separate from what it is perceiving, from the objects. The entire universe is the Self.

Do not try to live from some conceptual idea of Oneness. A conceptual idea of Oneness is just another object in awareness. Through the direct experiencing of all that is arising in this moment including any image of a separate self, Oneness is revealed to be your true nature.

Millions of words

There are so many words in this book. There are millions of words in the world that have tried to point to enlightenment. Yet no word captures it because it is not a concept. It is not a thing. The words merely point to it. The words point to the very source of all words. If you can see right now that, no matter what word you use to point to enlightenment, the word is not it, then the mind can naturally relax into what is. That relaxation is showing you that what you are is not a concept and cannot be grasped through concepts.

Resting into what is simply means noticing that there is a non-conceptual awareness within you that is already awake and naturally at rest. That awareness notices all objects arising and falling, including all the words that are used to point back to awareness. If what is being pointed to here is really seen, the entire search for enlightenment will be seen as nothing more than a grasping after concepts. If no word can reveal what you are, the entire movement to seek understanding conceptually comes to rest. What is revealed is what you already are. This is what you have always been. It is not a word. It cannot be stated with a million more words. You simply are.

The searching mind

You hear so many pointers to presence that refer to the ego as a thought-based, illusory entity. There can be subtle tendency to create inner resistance to thought. This resistance is hardly detectable. It tends to arise when you notice that you've been "stuck" in a story of past or future. The tendency is to subtly believe that "being stuck in stories" is "bad" or "unenlightened."

In reality, there is no such thing as "being stuck," "bad," or "unenlightened." Those are also just stories. They arise from a mind engaged in a spiritual search. The search is a movement of mind that is trying to bring about transformation. That storyline tends to judge thought as bad. It creates a duality between awareness and thought, preferring awareness over thought. So when excessive thinking about past or future arises, the searching mind judges the fact that "you are lost in a story again."

Thoughts aren't bad or good. They just are. Making thought into a problem creates more seeking as the mind tries to reach a place that is free of thought. It is seeking future. In seeing this movement towards future, it is realized that awareness is already here. It is what is looking. Awareness sees that sometimes thought arises and sometimes it doesn't. It's that simple. Any other view just creates more seeking.

An invitation to unlearn

More than a teaching, non-duality is an invitation to recognize a timeless space. Listening to a teacher or reading a book is insufficient. Non-duality or presence is not about learning new information or repeating memorized pointers. It is a seeing that what you are cannot be found in information and pointers. What you are is the space in which that information and those pointers appear and disappear.

Each pointer is simply an invitation to see that this timeless space is all there is, that the self is a false, thought-based, time-bound construct that comes and goes in that space. Non-duality pointers invite a looking inward to see what is beyond or prior thought. What is here whether there is thinking or no thinking? No matter how grand or insightful a thought is, it cannot tell you who you really are or what is here. Your true identity can never be expressed directly because you are not a thought.

Realization does not come about by making nonduality into a subject that you know a lot about or by repeatedly reminding yourself of what you have been told by teachers. It is an unlearning, an unknowing that happens naturally when awareness no longer contracts around information. This is not to say that information is denied or de-valued, only that there is no longer identification with it.

Detachment

Detachment is sometimes confused with apathy. Detachment is not a state of not caring. It refers to seeing that no experience, thought, state, or other manifestation ultimately affects or changes your true nature as emptiness or formless awareness. Formless awareness is naturally detached from the forms that arise and fall in (and as) it, including states of caring or not caring. It is non-dual.

Awareness sees that positive and negative states are dualistic and temporary. Apathy is a negative, dualistic, and temporary state. States are manifestation. Detachment is not a state. It is an attribute of awareness, which is the unmanifest.

Perhaps a better word than detachment is nonattachment. Detachment assumes that there is a separate you that must detach from something that is arising. But awareness is not a doing. Awareness is naturally nonattached from whatever it sees. To be nonattached simply means to see that who you are is not limited to any particular temporary thing arising in awareness. You are that which is looking. Stated another way, awareness sees that it is appearing as everything that is arising. The unmanifest appears as the manifest but grasps onto nothing that is arising including a temporary state of apathy.

Liberation from suffering, not from pain

Liberation, as that word is used in these reflections, means freedom from suffering, not from pain itself. Suffering is the psychological accumulation of mental and emotional energy over time in the form of a story of "me." Pain is a natural, dualistic occurrence in life that can arise in the present moment.

For example, you are suffering from chronic physical pain in the leg. Liberation will not free you from physical pain. Liberation is freedom from attachment to the psychological story of suffering surrounding the pain. If made completely conscious, the story might appear as "My life is so hard because of this pain." Identification with the mental story, and the emotions that accompany it, creates an overlay placed over the actual physical pain experienced in this moment. The mind is adding time to the pain. The result is psychological and emotional suffering in the form of the story of "me"—the one who is suffering.

Likewise, liberation may not completely free you of anger, sadness, and other emotions and states. These emotions can be natural responses to particular life situations. Liberation frees you from attachment to these emotions and states. In liberation, anger, sadness, elation, frustration, and other emotions and states arise and fall spontaneously in awareness (but with no attachment). Feelings are directly seen and felt and then they naturally die. Stated another way, these states and emotions arise to no one.

No center

When you believe you are a separate self, every state, emotion, thought and event appears to be happening to you. Everything is interpreted as if you are the center of life. Thought is doing the interpreting. Thought is almost entirely self-centered. It dreams in dualism and individuality.

In seeing that the separate self is an illusion, the center falls away. When the center falls away, there is still the sense of the body. There is still the experiencing of states, emotions, thoughts and events. There is still the personality and individual skills and attributes. But it no longer feels as if you are the center of life. When the center goes, the separation, struggle, conflict, and searching go with it. Even if self-centered thoughts still arise, they are seen as empty. There is no longer identification with a totally separate "me." There is a seeing that your real identity is something much larger than the individual body and the dream self you mistakenly took yourself to be.

There are many words for this "something larger" including God, Brahman, the Tao, enlightenment, liberation, reality or Oneness. The word is not the thing it describes. It could just as easily be called 'This.' It is not a concept. When the mind makes it into a mere concept, there is a tendency to create separation between those who get it and those who don't. In that case, the center has returned.

FEBRUARY

Form is emptiness; emptiness is form. In the same way, feeling, concept, mental formation, and consciousness are emptiness.

—Buddhist Heart Sutra

Suffering from illness

As you experience illness, whether chronic or short term, be clear about the difference between the illness and your mental and emotional story about the illness. The latter is the dream self.

The illness, as it arises now, consists only of the present symptoms, pain, and sensations in the body/mind. Your story of suffering, created by identification with thoughts of past, is the time-bound interpretation through which present symptoms, pain, and sensations are being viewed. The story, if made completely conscious, would look something like this: "I have been suffering with this awful illness for quite a while. Poor me!" The time-bound story is unnecessary suffering.

In presence, the symptoms, pain, and sensations are simply allowed to be the way they really are—without the veil of the past. This is not about denial. It is not about pretending that there is no illness or medical condition. Denial would just be another story. This is about noticing that attachment to the story of the "person who is suffering" makes the present symptoms, pain, and sensations appear worse. Notice the identity being made out of the illness. That noticing wakes you up from the story of the one who is suffering in time.

Conflict

We encounter conflict everyday when our ideas are challenged. If there is identification with a certain idea, the mind remains closed, unwilling to take another perspective into account when conflict arises. The dream self hates to be wrong. Because the dream self is a thought-based entity, it sees its death whenever it is faced with being wrong about its thoughts. The degree to which you find yourself in conflict with others will be directly proportional to the degree to which you identify with thought.

If there is openness to hear and consider another's perspective, conflict between two positions can be seen as illusory. It is realized that two points of reference were arising and that awareness contracted around one point and made the other point its enemy. Who you are is the space in which both points arise.

The dream self (i.e, ego) is closed by nature, interested mainly in having its own ideas prevail. Conflict strengthens separation when the mind identifies so strongly with its position that there is no openness to looking at other perspectives. When you identify strongly with thought, it is not about the idea or position. It is about insisting that 'you' are right, which means it is about strengthening the separate self. There is no openness in that insistence energy. That insistence energy is the same energy that fuels war and obscures the natural state of peace, joy, and love.

Partial views

The moment we begin to speak of non-duality, dualism arises. Every word, idea, concept, and belief is a partial view of life. Whenever there is attachment to that partial view, the "me" is created.

Have you ever known someone who presented a sort of fundamentalist approach to non-dual realization? He demanded that only his view was right and that all other views were false? If so, you were witnessing attachment to a partial view. Ego 101. No matter how clearly the mind expresses non-dual realization, the words are still dualistic. It is still a partial view. Words cannot directly express non-duality. Thus, none of these reflections are the truth. They are only pointers. Non-dual pointers are dualistic expressions of an inexpressible realization characterized by non-separation, unconditional love, freedom and peace.

A clear view of non-duality is stated in Buddha's Heart Sutra: "form is none other than formlessness and formlessness is none other than form." Emptiness is appearing as all views, all form. If there is a "right view," it is the one that is the most all-encompassing, loving, peaceful and free of separation and conflict. It is seeing that you are meeting yourself everywhere, in every view. That, of course, is a view. But in seeing the truth to which that view points, attachment to thought is seen through. The "me" and the separation it engenders is realized to be illusory and empty.

Freedom from past suffering

Many come to the spiritual search with intense emotional suffering revolving around past events.

No matter what the content of the story, the structure of suffering is the same: identification with thought and emotion. In other words, regardless of whether the content of the suffering centers on being abused by a parent during childhood, repeatedly being rejected in romantic relationships or some other reason, the suffering is caused by identification with stories about the past and the negative emotions that arise in conjunction with those stories.

When the thought of the past arises, simply notice it. In noticing the thought, you see that awareness is what is noticing. This present awareness is who you really are. You are not the thought of past occurring in awareness. Thought comes and goes. You— awareness—do not come and go.

Once you notice the thought, allow awareness to notice the painful emotion arising in conjunction with the thought. Awareness has no agenda to escape emotional suffering. Only thought tries to escape emotion. The movement to escape suffering only prolongs it, as it remains unfaced. If a thought arises about how you can escape the pain somehow, allow that thought to come and go in awareness too. In resting in awareness, the mental and emotional suffering is allowed to be exactly as it is. When suffering is made conscious in this way, without a desire to be free of it, it transmutes into awareness.

Resentment

Resentment occurs when thought approaches a situation with a preconception about how it is supposed to turn out. When it turns out differently, thought then blames the situation and the people involved. But the cause of resentment is never "out there." Resentment results directly from replaying and identifying with the mental and emotional story surrounding past situations in which your expectations were not met.

In this dream of thought, people are supposed to do what you expect them to do. This is not reality. It is a self-centered mental and emotional story which—if repeatedly played—places 'you and your resentment' at the center of life. This is perfect fuel for the dream that you are separate from life and others.

Don't try to analyze your way out of resentment.

Instead, simply notice the story of resentment as it arises. Notice that what is looking is awareness. Confirm and doubly confirm that awareness so that you see clearly that the story is not you. It is arising in awareness. Awareness is who you really are. Awareness isn't trying to justify, analyze, or escape resentment. It is simply awake to whatever is arising now. In that awakeness, there is no attachment to the thought and emotion that is coming and going. Everything is allowed to be exactly as it is. That is the end of resentment.

Emotional traps

One of the common traps in non-duality or enlightenment is associating it with positive emotions only.

When you attach to a dualistic emotion, regardless of whether it is a painful or pleasurable emotion, suffering is bound to arise. It goes without saying that attachment to a "negative" emotion causes suffering. But attachment to a positive emotion also creates suffering because a sense of "I've lost it" arises as soon an opposite "negative" emotion comes through. That sense of "I got it/I lost it" is common.

Non-duality is not about discarding anything negative or acquiring a new positive story or good emotional mood. It is about seeing that you are non-dual awareness. You are the opening in which dualism arises.

Once you realize this opening as who you really are, there is no longer attachment to anything that comes through that opening. Thus, it is realized that a moment of anger and a moment of pure peace are both formless awareness coming into form. There is a natural equanimity that arises when you see that you are not any of the dualistic thoughts or emotions that appear in awareness. You are awareness itself, which allows everything to arise and fall. Joy, love, and peace are natural attributes of awareness. But those attributes are not dualistic emotions. They have no opposites. Nonetheless, don't become attached to the attributes either. It is a trap to attach to anything that comes through the opening.

Anger

There is an entire self-help industry and a multitude of spiritual programs and techniques designed to help you "get rid" of your anger. They are all based on the faulty premise that you can escape what is. You cannot escape what is. That is impossible. If anger is arising, that is what is arising. Any movement to escape it or get rid of it is a denial of what is arising. It is resistance. When you resist what is happening, you merely strengthen it.

Instead of seeking to get rid of anger, simply notice it. Notice that it arises in a space of non-dual awareness. That space is who you are. The anger is merely a temporary energy movement arising and falling in that space.

Notice the mental stories that feed the anger and the strategies the mind uses to escape it. Let those stories and strategies come and go naturally and effortlessly in the space. This non-dual awareness has no agenda to escape or resist the anger. Spacious awareness is simply present to the anger, exactly as it is. When there is no longer resistance to anger, it is no longer being fed. It disappears back into awareness. Stated another way, nothing appears as everything. So, in this case, nothing (awareness) appears as something (anger) and will effortlessly die back into awareness (nothing) if it is not resisted.

Anxiety

Anxiety arises in the emotional body in conjunction with uncertain thoughts about the future. The thoughts could be anything from concern about finishing a work project on time to the possibility of a tragic illness or event happening to you or someone you love.

Dealing with anxiety through mental strategies or taking medication may provide a quick fix for symptoms. But if anxiety remains un-faced, it tends to lie dormant until the next time a frightening future scenario begins to arise in the mind.

When anxiety arises, it is fueled by unconsciousness. The anxious feeling of fear in the body fuels thoughts about the frightening future scenario. When awareness does not directly see the anxious feeling, it remains unconscious. When it is unconscious, it grows or at least stays around, feeding the energy of thought. As thoughts remain unseen by awareness, they tend to fuel the anxious feeling in the body. This becomes a vicious cycle of suffering sometimes leading to a panic attack.

In withdrawing energy from thought and allowing awareness to directly feel anxiety in the body, awareness is meeting the cycle of suffering. This is not about a quick fix. This is about suffering openly and consciously. When it is realized that timeless awareness is what you are, then there is no longer a thought-based self who suffers in time. That is not to say that fear no longer arises, but rather that it is seen that fear arises from, and is not separate from, awareness.

Fully open

Any movement to escape emotions is seeking. The mind asks, "How can I be free of negative emotions?" You can't. Whatever is arising is what is. Attempting to escape emotions is resisting them. You—the separate self—are that resistance.

Do nothing except notice that the pure awareness that you are in this moment is naturally and fully open to every experience, state, and emotion that arises in that awareness. When any emotion arises, notice that awareness is what sees and feels the emotion directly. "Notice" is not an invitation to witness the emotions as if you are somehow separate from them. Notice is an invitation to be fully open to the emotion and to see that awareness is arising as the emotion.

Notice the tendency to contract against and resist life. To be fully open and awake to life and every emotion that arises in response to life is not a practice or doing in time. It is a present seeing. To be fully open is to be the emotion fully without resistance, without the "person" who would try to escape it. Noticing emotions reveals that emotions are empty. They are made of—and not other than— the very emptiness (i.e., awareness) that you are.

Emotions and thoughts

Negative emotions in the body arise in conjunction with negative thoughts. When you feel guilt, resentment, hurt, or sadness, notice that there are thoughts of past arising in conjunction with those emotions. The mind is lost in a play of memories about how your life hasn't gone the way you wanted it to go. When you feel anxiety or fear, notice that there are thoughts of future arising in conjunction with those emotions. The mind is playing with snapshots of future scenarios in which life does not turn out the way you would like it to.

Suffering exists solely in identification with these thoughts and their accompanying emotions. There simply is no suffering outside of this identification. Past and future exist only in thought. So the story of you—including all these snapshots in time and the emotional suffering that arises with them—is the very cause of suffering. This is why the story of you will never become enlightened. The story of you exists in time, which means that it exists solely in identification with dualistic, time-bound thought and its accompanying emotion.

Enlightenment is the realization that you are the timeless awareness that is awake to these dualistic thoughts and emotions when they arise. You are not the thought-based, time-bound story.

What cannot be objectified?

Everything you see, touch, taste, smell, feel, experience and think is an object. Awareness is what sees those objects. It is not an object. It cannot even be named. To name it is to objectify it. To even call it "awareness" is to make it into a concept and thereby objectify it. It is not any concept or object because it is awake to all concepts and objects. Yet, without this unnamable source, no object can be seen, touched, tasted, smelled, felt, experienced, or thought about. This source, or awareness, gives rise to every object yet the source itself can never be objectified. It is what is looking.

This source is who you are in the most fundamental sense. You are the pure seeing, the knowing prior to or behind the objects. Don't believe what is being said here. Belief is merely another object in awareness. This message is pointing to a direct experience.

In direct experience, you are not anything that you see, touch, taste, smell, feel, experience, or think. If you can see it, it isn't you. So look from the nothingness that sees the objects. What is looking at them? Whatever sees these objects allows them to arise and pass naturally and effortlessly. Experiences, states, emotions and thoughts are realized to be passing objects. You are that which is looking, which remains unchanged while all objects arise and pass.

The inseparability of awareness and objects

Yesterday's reflection stated, "[W]ithout this unnamable source, no object can be seen, touched, tasted, smelled, felt, experienced, or thought about." The source referred to here is awareness itself.

As you are reading this reflection, notice that awareness is inseparable from everything it sees. Without awareness, this page, the words and letters on it and all the other sights, sounds, and smells in the room right now could not be experienced. Without awareness, the internal thoughts, emotions, and sensations experienced while reading this reflection could not happen. Regardless of whether you agree or disagree, or like or dislike, what this reflection is saying, the agreement/disagreement and like/dislike could not be experienced without awareness.

Awareness is inseparable from (not independent of) the objects appearing in it. Can you really tell where awareness ends and objects begin?

Awareness is like the screen on which a movie appears. When you attach only to the objects and characters in the movie, you miss the screen. You miss the source of life—the canvas on which the objects and characters are being displayed. Yet when you fixate on the screen only, and try to deny the objects, you miss the vast beauty and diversity of form in the play of life. Instead of fixating on either awareness or the objects, simply notice that they are an inseparable reality. They are "not two." In that realization, there is nothing left to seek. That is wholeness.

Acceptance

Acceptance of what is takes no effort. You are awareness. Awareness is naturally and inherently accepting of what is.

To realize this, all that is needed is to see what you really are—awareness. To see what you really are, you do not need to add anything to yourself or understand life conceptually. Full acceptance happens naturally when there is no movement to change, neutralize, or overcome experiences, thoughts, emotions, and states. When those experiences, thoughts, emotions, and states are allowed to arise without any effort to change, neutralize, or overcome them, you see that they arise in awareness. In fact, without awareness, none of these things could arise. These things are not independent of awareness. Another way of saying this is that awareness is appearing as each experience, thought, emotion, and state. When you see that what you are is this spacious awareness and that it is appearing as every experience, thought, emotion and state, the need to change, neutralize, or overcome these things is seen as just another movement or thought arising in awareness.

Acceptance is realized when you see that life is living itself. Life takes no effort. You are life. You cannot become or do anything to bring about what you already are. The very movement to change, neutralize, or overcome the present moment is, by its very nature, non-acceptance of what is.

Achievement

Growing up, we are taught that if we put forth enough effort we can achieve any goal. We learn this mindset in school and carry it into virtually every aspect of life. Many of us enter the world of spiritual seeking still conditioned by this belief. We search, read books, listen to teachers or preachers, and engage in methods and practices in an effort to reach some future state of fulfillment.

True and lasting contentment cannot be found in the future. Future is merely a thought-form that arises and falls in present awareness. Form is impermanent. It is always changing. In one moment, it appears that you need more money to be happy. In another moment, it appears that you need a better relationship to be happy. As long as you are chasing these unstable, changing thought-forms, you are seeking. Seeking comes from an inherent sense of lack within. It is a recipe for a life in which you experience a constant background sense of dissatisfaction.

True and lasting contentment can only come through realizing what you are. You cannot achieve what you are. It is not a future discovery. The realization is available only now. Simply notice the alive presence that is reading these words. That presence is already whole, content, and at peace.

Is thought independent of awareness?

Steam appears in space. The space gives rise to the steam and permeates it. The steam appears to be a separate form. But the transparent, spacious steam does not have an existence that is separate from or independent of the space permeating it. Just as the space gives rise to the steam, the steam will eventually release back into space without any need to manipulate it.

Likewise, there is no way to conceptualize one's way into non-conceptual, empty awareness. Awareness gives rise to thought and permeates it. The thought appears to be a separate, solid form. But when awareness is awake to the thought, the thought is seen not to have an existence that is solid or independent of awareness. Just as awareness gives rise to the thought, the thought will eventually release back into awareness without any need to manipulate it.

Everything arises and falls back into its spacious source. If there is a seeing directly of what is being pointed to, all thoughts about enlightenment are seen to be forms that are not independent of awareness itself. Allow thought to arise and fall on its own. In the space that is left when thought releases, your true non-conceptual identity reveals itself. In that recognition, you see that who you are—this spacious awareness—is there regardless of whether there is thinking or no thinking.

What is here?

What is here before each thought? What is here once each thought falls away? There is a space here—a nothingness, a presence. That is who you are. Who you are cannot be described. Once there is a description, including the description in this reflection, the description is a thought that is arising in the presence.

What is here? Instead of trying to find some conclusion—including your name, your story, or some other label or description—just look. Even if you find the greatest conceptual description of what you are or what life is, it is still only a thought. And all thoughts, by their very nature, are temporary. They come and go. What is here when each thought goes?

If a concept arises in response to the question, "What is here," you know the concept is not it. Let it fall and notice that awareness just remains wide open, spacious, and boundless. In this felt sense of boundless awareness, there is a realization of who you really are. You are not a concept or description. You are not a belief or a dualistic position. You simply are. It is that simple.

Conclusions do not see

It is easy to turn awareness into a static mental conclusion. Instead of abiding in and as actual awareness, there is a tendency of the mind to repeatedly play the conclusion, "I am awareness" or "there is only awareness" or some other conclusory non-dual label.

A conclusion cannot see. It just repeats itself. A false sense of mental certainty often comes with this repetition. If any conclusion is repeated enough, it turns into a rigidly held position. Conflict is right around the corner. The need to be right arises directly from egoic insecurity. Conflict arises from attachment to thought—from an attempt to take ownership of reality. No one owns reality.

Actual awareness is not a conclusion. It is a deeply and relentlessly compassionate and loving awakeness to everything that is arising now including to any particular conclusion that may be arising or being held onto as "truth."

The degree of conflict and self-righteousness in your life are good indicators of whether awareness is being treated as a static mental conclusion or whether there is true abiding as actual timeless awareness.

Awareness is naturally secure and confident. It has nothing to prove. This confidence is different than mental certainty. It is a confidence of the heart. It is a confidence with a deep resonance of love, compassion, and pure openness to what is arising now. Conclusions fragment life into pieces. Awareness reveals that the fragments are illusory. It reveals wholeness.

Compassion

There is a tendency of mind to believe that compassion must be cultivated or developed. But only thought would say that. If you notice thought, it is primarily self-centered. Our thoughts about others often say more about ourselves than anything. An outward judgment of someone else is often an inward attempt to build up or maintain the story of "me." For example, if I see other people as flawed, this makes "me" believe that I am not flawed. I get to feel morally superior to the other person.

True compassion is not cultivated or developed through thinking. It is realized to be a natural attribute of awareness. There can be, relatively speaking, a deeper and deeper recognition of this natural compassion as there is less and less reliance on thought for a sense of self v. other. But compassion is an aspect of what we are. All that we can do is recognize, deeply, what we are—awareness.

When someone is suffering, notice the tendency to make judgments about them or even to fix them through thinking about them. What is noticing is awareness. That awareness contains true compassion. Trust it completely. Any necessary response to the person's suffering comes directly from the inherent compassion of awareness rather than from judgment.

Defending the unreal

Defending yourself arises from the fear of death. It may not feel like it at the time, but when you find yourself defending your thoughts strongly, you are defending the sense of self invested in your thoughts. The sense of self being referred to here is the thought-based, time-bound self made up of thoughts of past, future, and resistance to this moment. Who you believe yourself to be depends on the content of that realm of thoughts. When someone is challenging you on the level of the mind, they are challenging some position, belief, idea, or other self-image within that realm. In response to such an attack, the energy behind that self comes to defend itself out of fear of its own death.

When you are verbally attacked or when you meet resistance or disagreement from someone, simply notice the thoughts and emotions that rise up in defense within the body and mind. Feel and face the sense of diminishment of self without rationalizing, judging, reacting, or defending. Allow the emotions and thoughts to rise fully in awareness without telling stories about how they should or should not be happening. These emotions and thoughts burn themselves out when they are simply seen and not manipulated in any way.

Enlightenment is just a word pointing to the seeing of that thought-based, time-bound self as an illusion. When it is seen as an illusion, there is no more psychological need to defend what is unreal.

Stillness and peace

Stillness is a portal to the direct realization of timeless awareness. It reveals what is always and already here, which is a quiet, still, empty, peaceful awareness. Stillness cannot be manufactured because it is already here. It can only be noticed. Awareness is what notices the stillness.

Stillness permeates everything. The space around and within the body and mind is already still. It can seem as if a lot is happening in life—a lot of noise, personal drama, and mental and emotional movement. But we continuously overlook the space in which all of that is happening. That space is naturally still and at peace. In noticing that awareness resonates naturally with that quiet stillness, it is seen that the noise, personal drama, and mental and emotional movement appear from that stillness and disappear back into it. The stillness is revealing the source of all form. When there is focusing only on the forms that arise, the stillness is overlooked. This constant movement of overlooking the stillness creates discontent and seeking. It creates the illusion of the need to search for peace in the future.

Peace cannot be found in the future. "Future" is merely a thought arising in awareness. Peace is just a word pointing to a relaxation of the mind, a seeing that the spacious awareness in which all movement happens is naturally still and at peace.

Inattention is just thought

In realizing your fundamental nature as awareness, inattention is seen as just another object that appears and disappears in awareness. If you look closely, there really is no such thing as inattention. In the moment when inattention seems to occur, what is really happening is that thought is arising. Perhaps there is thinking about what happened three minutes ago or what will happen tomorrow. This feels like inattention only because there is an underlying belief that awareness is supposed to be free of objects, free of thoughts. Therefore, when thoughts of past or future arise, there is the false belief that you are inattentive to what is in the space of this moment.

Do not try to clear away all thought. Let thoughts arise and see them for what they are—temporary, fleeting forms appearing and disappearing in the formless awareness that you truly are.

Simply notice that what you are calling inattention is simply thought coming through, creating the illusion that somehow awareness is obscured. Awareness is never obscured. Without awareness, the very thought creating the illusion of inattention could not be seen. In noticing the thought coming through, it passes as every thought does. Awareness is the screen that allows everything to come and go, including what you mistakenly call inattention. Be clear about that so that you do not fall into the trap of believing that awareness is here only when thought is absent.

Positive stories

It is easy to see that negative stories arise from a false self. It is often overlooked that positive stories also arise from a false self. Be clear that what you are is not any story. If a thought arises, "I am sad" or "I am a victim," see it for what it is—a temporary story arising in awareness. If a thought arises, "I am peaceful" or "I am happy," see it for what it is. It is incredibly limiting to believe that you are whatever the dualistic mind happens to be thinking at the moment.

True love, joy, and peace are natural attributes of non-dual awareness. They have no dualistic opposites. No stories are needed to make them arise, reinforce them, or recreate them.

If you are really "peaceful," or "happy," is there any need to convince yourself of that through storytelling? Often, when we are replaying positive stories, we are repressing negative stories. We are trying to convince ourselves that the positive stories and emotions are true and the negative stories and emotions are not true.

In the realization that you are not any story— negative or positive—the need to convince yourself of anything vanishes. That seeing is non-dual realization. Non-dual awareness is the space in which all stories arise. Non-dual awareness is naturally joyful, loving, and peaceful.

In every death

In every death, there is the possibility of realizing that what you are is beyond the cycle of birth and death. In seeing your time-bound, thought-based story stop, even if only for a moment, there can be the recognition of what you truly are, which is unnamable and unknowable through dualistic stories. You simply are. This is revealed in the space that is left in every death.

In the death of every flower, tree, animal, and person, there is the possibility of seeing that your true identity cannot be found in temporary forms. Forms are impermanent. You may naturally grieve when a form dies. But the death of every form is revealing the vast spaciousness from which the form appeared. That spaciousness becomes apparent again and again in the death of each form.

Space is a portal to what you truly are. Suffering and seeking happen because of identification with form, including your name, body, personal story and even spiritual ideas. Let even your most precious spiritual ideas die to the space. In every death, the space that is left is revealing something extraordinary, which is that what you are is not the thing that died. You are not any of the things that appear and disappear. So the "you" here is not referring to a particular thing including a name, body, story, or other form. You are the source of all things. You are nothing being everything.

A realization beyond words

Intellectualizing Oneness will provide, at best, a good conceptual framework of non-duality. Although it may be helpful to have a conceptual framework, Oneness itself is not a concept. The descriptions are pointing to an actual realization. Oneness is merely a label for realization in the way the word "juice" is pointing to the orange, tangy-sweet liquid you drink for breakfast. The word is never the thing it describes. Incessantly thinking about Oneness is like having your head stuck in a map of Scotland while driving in Scotland, missing the actual territory to which the word "Scotland" is pointing.

Oneness simply is. You cannot think your way into it. The dream self tries to step outside of Oneness and intellectualize her way into it. Don't fall into that trap. Drop whatever concept you are holding onto right now (including the word "Oneness") and simply notice the non-conceptual awareness that is here. Notice the fact that you simply are. Return— again and again if necessary—to the simple fact that you are. That awareness reveals the seeing.

Once Oneness is revealed, see that conceptualization and intellectualization arise within what you are. They cannot provide the direct experience of what you are. They can merely describe it. There is nothing wrong with talking about or describing Oneness. But recognize directly what the words are pointing to first. Then use descriptions to point others to this realization beyond words.

Comparison

In making an outward judgment of another, there is often an implicit inward comparison being made between you and the other, a comparison that is designed mainly to strengthen your sense of being a separate self.

For example, when thought labels another body/ mind as "unspiritual," it splits Oneness into two and creates a duality in the world between spiritual and unspiritual. By making other people unspiritual, you bolster the notion that you are spiritual. Outward judgments are perfect fuel for ego and selfcenteredness.

This is not about believing that all judgment is bad (which would just be another judgment anyway). This is about seeing clearly how dualism works.

Notice that what we call "you" and "other" are really just dualistic thoughts arising in awareness and creating the appearance of two. In seeing that thoughts about "others" often say more about "you" than anything, there is a realization that what you are is not a thought. You are not the story "I am spiritual," nor are others "unspiritual." You are the awareness in which these thoughts arise—in which the comparison between self and other arises.

Outward judgments are an opportunity to see the content of the dream self—to see the specific ways in which a self is being maintained by judging so-called "others." In that realization, there can be a deeper seeing that there is only One here, dividing itself up into a dream called me and not-me.

Unnamable

Many names have been placed on 'This.' We have called it "life," "God," "spirit," "Oneness," "enlightenment," "presence," "non-duality," "awareness," "Brahman,", the "Tao," and a host of others. Yet none of the names are that which they describe. All words are concepts. They are memory. No matter what word you use to describe life, the word is not it.

It is easy to become blinded by spiritual teachings, including non-dual pointers. The ideas are repeated so much that they become conditioning. Then we look at the present moment through the learned ideas, rather than through bare naked presence.

Life is not an idea. Be very clear about that. See that every pointer in this book or anywhere else is merely conditioning. It is some idea put forth to point you to a seeing beyond ideas.

A teacher or book can only use concepts to point you away from reliance on your memorized concepts. Can a concept see? No. It can only point to the pure seeing available through bare naked presence. This seeing is a knowing that is deeper than conceptual knowledge. This knowing reveals directly that to which the words "God," "Brahman," "enlightenment" and all the other words are pointing. There is no separate "I" who knows or finds "enlightenment" or "God." Those are concepts giving rise to illusory separation. There is only this unnamable knowing. No subject. No object. Just 'This.'

Liberation

Yesterday's reflection spoke of the various words that are used to describe the unnamable realization often called "non-duality" or "enlightenment." In the deepest sense, there is only One here but it is appearing as many interpretations. For example, the word "liberation" is sometimes used and often misunderstood. "Liberation" is not describing a person who becomes liberated in the future. It is pointing to the timeless realization that the time-bound, thought-based self who would seek future liberation is an illusion. The word "liberation" simply means "freedom." This is not about the story of a person being free. This is freedom from the false belief in a separate self story that lives in time.

The timeless realization can happen instantaneously or appear to happen gradually. When it appears to happen gradually, what is ultimately realized is that the time-bound self and its story of gradual becoming is an illusion appearing in timeless awareness. In that sense, the words "timeless awareness," "presence," "enlightenment," "God," and "liberation" are all pointing to one timeless essence appearing as separate people living and seeking in time.

If a teaching speaks of "future liberation," be careful to discriminate between the notion that there is a person who becomes liberated in the future, which is a misleading idea, and the timeless realization that the person who is seeking in time is a phantom.

The pointer "no self"

You will often read in these reflections phrases such as "no self" or "seeing through the separate self." Those are good pointers because they express that the time-bound, thought-based story of self is what is seen through in the realization called "enlightenment." However, these words are just pointers. Never mistake the pointers for absolute truth. They are relative expressions of an inexpressible seeing that your true identity is not a story in time, but rather the timeless presence that is awake to that story. When that presence recognizes itself completely, the story is seen to be unreal.

Even though "no self" is a good pointer, it is also misleading. "No self" is not amnesia where you lose all memories of the past. Memories still arise. Thinking still happens. It is just that there is no longer identification with thought.

Even though the words "no self" are used to point, the realization reveals the answer to the question, "Who am I?" That seems paradoxical until it is seen that the answer is not conceptual. The realization of enlightenment resolves the identity crisis because it reveals a deep non-conceptual understanding of who you are. This is why the seeing is sometimes called Self-realization or realizing the True Self.

Don't try to grasp what is being said intellectually. Simply look inward with awareness to where the words are pointing. The simple feeling of presence is the portal to seeing who you really are.

MARCH

*When the witness collapses into everything that's witnessed,
when awareness collapses into its contents, all that remains
is a deep and total fascination with whatever is happening.*

— Jeff Foster

Identity

Yesterday's reflection encouraged you not to try to grasp the message of this book intellectually and instead to look to the simple feeling of presence. The mind tends to over-intellectualize spirituality, getting lost in the game of comparing this idea to that idea and this teaching to that teaching, and trying to think its way into enlightenment. The incessant need for conceptual understanding is a search for the answer to the question, "Who am I?" We are looking to add knowledge to ourselves under the assumption that, if we gather enough ideas or the right ideas or put them into a logical sequence, the question will finally be answered.

Looking for the answer to the question, "Who am I?" with the intellect is like flying to the moon in search of your belly button. The ultimate resolution of the question, "Who am I?" is found through presence, not through thinking. Presence solves the identity crisis completely. Presence is so immediately close as the very life you are right now—the very awakeness that permeates the space of this moment—that it is overlooked each time you try to find it in thought.

Don't misinterpret what is being said here. Realization is not about denying the intellect. Once presence is realized, the intellect is seen to be a wonderful tool for understanding and playing in duality. But your ultimate identity is non-dual and the portal to that seeing is presence.

Love

Love is not something you get from others. It is what you are. When you demand or expect someone to give you love, you are operating on a false assumption, which is that you lack love and must get it from someone outside of yourself.

There is no such thing as "outside" yourself. The One essence of the universe is love itself. Love does not exist only in certain places. It is not a scarce resource. When you meet another, you are really meeting yourself. You are meeting love. This remains unseen because there is a dream of separation that is being played out through unconscious thought and emotion within your body and mind.

The lack you feel within is illusory. It is the direct result of unconscious thoughts and emotions. As long as these thoughts and emotions remain unconscious, they fuel the dream of separation—the story that you need others to give you love before you can be complete.

Notice the mental story of lack and its accompanying emotions when they arise. When awareness shines on that story, the story is seen to be not real, merely conceptual. What is real is love itself. "Love" is a pointer to what you really are. Stated another way, the awareness that sees the story of separation and lack as unreal has, as one of its natural attributes, unconditional love.

Enlightenment is not an experience

You may have heard stories of spiritual teachers who had experiences of Oneness or light or energy before they began teaching. Perhaps you have had some experience or are looking to have some experience. Although such experiences are possible, they are not necessary for enlightenment.

An experience is an individual occurrence distinct from other occurrences "in time." It is form with an apparent beginning and end. Once an experience happens, it is reduced to memory. To say that an experience is an occurrence in time means that it exists in the mind only—as a memory of the past or a mental projection towards future.

The experience of Oneness comes and goes in presence. It is a form. The experience of going to the bathroom also comes and goes in presence. It is also a form.

If the thought arises that some experience you had in the past is enlightenment, let the thought arise and fall. It is merely a thought in the mind. If the thought arises that you need to have some experience in the future in order to be enlightened, let the thought arise and fall. It is only a thought. Enlightenment is not a thought. It is not a particular experience. It is the direct realization that what you are is the unnamable formless presence from which all thoughts, experiences, states and other finite forms come and go.

Approval-seeking and people-pleasing

Approval-seeking and people-pleasing thoughts can easily go undetected. It feels good when others give you approval, acknowledgement, praise or attention or when they seem pleased by what you say or do.

Look closely at what is happening. It is really all about you. It may look on the surface as if you are doing something for others, but approval-seeking and people-pleasing are really about getting something in return for your actions. The junkie who takes a drug expects to get high in return. Getting approval provides a similar high.

To want something from others is self-centeredness. It presumes separation. It places conditions on relationships. The subtle subtext is, "I love you as long as you give me what I need." It's all about personal gratification.

Don't make problems out of "self-centeredness" and "personal gratification" and try to fix them. They are merely concepts pointing to thoughts that create separateness between you and others. Simply notice thoughts that arise that seek to gain approval, acknowledgement, praise, or attention or that seek to please others.

In noticing these thoughts when they arise, it is realized that what is noticing is awareness. Awareness is already complete. It has no agenda to seek something from others. It sees no "other." There is only One here appearing as two. In that seeing, there is no lack and therefore no need to gain something from another.

Boredom

Boredom isn't real. It is entirely mind-created. A thought arises that says that something ought to be happening other than what is happening. That thought creates a sort of vacuum that sucks up the energy inherent in presence. It makes this moment look as if it lacks something. The mental projection towards future that says, "I need something to happen," and the current sense of lack arise together as one movement.

In simply noticing the thought that says something else ought to be happening as soon as it arises, there is a seeing that what you are is the presence that is noticing the thought. Presence lacks nothing. It is totally complete. Presence is not bored. Boredom is an illusion created by believing thoughts of future, which in turn fuel a sense of current lack. Presence is perfectly and naturally in alignment with what is happening right now. Even if boredom arises, presence allows it to be exactly as it is.

Seeing v. doing

In its spiritual search, the mind is looking for something to do. But when it comes to enlightenment, there can only be a noticing of what is already being done. Life is already being done just as it is. Breathing and digesting food is already happening. Thoughts, emotions, and reactions are happening spontaneously and involuntarily. Even the thought that said, "I want to read today's reflection" or "I should pray" or "I need to meditate" arose spontaneously and involuntarily.

Enlightenment is not a doing. It is a timeless seeing. The mind can turn seeing into a doing in time and tell the story, "Once I notice everything, I will be enlightened." It places seeing in time. Seeing does not exist in time. It is timeless. It happens only now. The thought, "Once I notice everything, I will be enlightened" arises spontaneously and involuntarily now. When thoughts are not seen as they arise in the timeless, they are believed. When they are believed, the fictitious story of the doer living in time on a spiritual search is maintained. This is the perfect way to avoid enlightenment.

In its cleverness, the mind may then say, "I'm just going to stop seeking." That too is just a thought arising spontaneously and involuntarily. Your true identity is the timeless space from which thoughts arise. You cannot do anything in time to notice what you are in the timeless. Enlightenment is a seeing of what you already are.

The method of suspending thought

Yesterday's reflection stated, "Your true identity is the timeless space from which thoughts arise." This sentence is just a pointer to the fact that you cannot find what you are through thinking.

Such pointers are often misinterpreted to mean that thought is bad or that enlightenment means the end of thought. Thinking has great value when it is used for practical purposes rather than for self-centered story-telling. For most, thinking isn't being used just for practical purposes. It is being used to answer the question, "Who am I?" and to fixate on the story of "me and my life."

The question, "Who am I?" can only be truly answered by recognizing the source of thought (i.e., the spacious awareness from which thought arises).

To recognize this source, it may be helpful to suspend thought in order to see that you are the timeless awareness from which thought comes. Once you realize that this source is your true identity, there is no longer a grasping towards concepts for a sense of self. When that grasping stops, thinking is released from its investment in the identity crisis.

However, suspending thought is merely a method for realizing timeless awareness. Don't trap yourself into continuously suspending thought once there has been a recognition of your true identity. Once the source is recognized, see that thought is a manifestation of that source. To deny it would be to deny the source.

One Life realizing itself

Although these reflections often invite awareness to notice life happening, the noticing is merely a doorway into the realization that you are that life. There is not a separate person or a separate awareness noticing other separate things called thoughts, emotions, states, experiences, flowers, trees, space, etc. These apparently separate things are just concepts created by thinking.

Noticing these things is merely a portal into realizing that you are life itself. You are this moment unfolding exactly as it is unfolding. You are as vast as the universe—with no boundaries—because you are the universe recognizing itself. Oneness is waking up to itself. Even the words "universe" and "Oneness waking up to itself" are concepts. There is no word for what you are because you are not a word. You are not something separate from everything else. Concepts create the illusion of dualism.

Although noticing or witnessing what is arising in this moment can be a wonderful way of seeing that awareness is awake to everything that is appearing and disappearing, the line between "awareness" and "everything else" is purely conceptual. There is no separate witness. There is no separate awareness. There is One Life being itself. You are THAT.

Vulnerability

Vulnerability is indispensable to enlightenment. The thought-based self is a set of masks—mental mechanisms designed to protect a false self center. We hide behind our roles, identities, beliefs, fixed positions, opinions, and stories. We pretend to know the answers to questions when we really don't. We pretend to be doing better than we really are. We defend ourselves out of fear of being wrong. We avoid rejection at all costs. We point outward at what others are doing, which is a perfect way to avoid seeing what is arising inwardly—within the body and mind. These are all examples of the ways in which the ego-mind avoids exposure to being hurt. Ego is a mechanism of control—mind movement designed to avoid vulnerability.

By simply being awake to what is arising in the body and mind in this moment, we are vulnerable. It is a bit misleading to say that "we are vulnerable." Being awake is not something "we" do. It is what we are. By noticing that we are not the roles, identities, stories and all the other mechanisms of mind that create and maintain a false self, awareness is realized to be our true nature. Awareness is naturally open. In that openness, it is realized that there exists no real threat to awareness. Only a false self image would define itself as "vulnerable" or "under threat." Awareness is simply awake to what is.

The end of seeking

You will know when the realization called enlightenment occurs. Seeking will end. You will stop searching for answers in spiritual books and from spiritual teachers. You will know that, whatever enlightenment is, it is indescribable. Yet you may find yourself trying to express it anyway.

You will know that the sense of being a person separate from the rest of life is a complete illusion. Paradoxically, you will know that, even though there is no separate "you," there is still a relative existence in which there is the appearance of a person that gets up from his bed in the morning, brushes his teeth, and goes to work at his job. You will see no problem with using the word "you" as a linguistic convenience. You will know that, no matter what you say or do, and regardless of whether you use pronouns or not, you cannot step in or out of 'This.' You will see no contradiction in any of that. It is not something the mind can grasp.

The realization reveals that there is only this timeless moment unfolding in a mysterious way. The portal is now. Look within and find the source of the word "you." This immediate recognition of presence reveals that "my future enlightenment" is just an idea appearing and disappearing in presence.

As the seeking ends, laugh heartily at the utter simplicity of the realization that everything occurs within this presence, even the seeking.

The seeing

As you walk around in your house today, notice that what is happening has always been happening.

In every moment (and there is really only this moment), the same thing is happening. Objects appear in what you label "outside" of the body and mind: a chair, carpet, couch, and pet. Objects appear in what you label "inside" the body and mind. These objects are the words "chair," "carpet," "couch," and "pet." The words are pointing to the actual objects in the house.

What is it that is awake to the objects appearing on the "outside" and the objects appearing on the "inside" of the body and mind? Whatever is awake, it is not an object. It cannot be seen like objects can be seen. It is the seeing itself. That seeing is who you really are. It has no name. A name would just be another object.

The notions of inside/outside, every moment/ this moment, past/future and body/mind are objects—dualistic words—appearing in what is awake.

Be clear that your true essence is not any of the objects appearing. In this clarity, it is seen that there is no center. There is no entity to which these objects appear. There is only the seeing.

Non-duality is not a learned subject

Although many words are used to point to enlightenment or non-dual presence, non-duality is not a philosophy or learned subject. Although it is often treated as a philosophy, the word "non-duality" is pointing to life itself. You are that life. You are not a person separate from life who must learn the subject of non-duality, memorize it, and tell the story that you have it or get it. You are "it." The pointers are pointing the mind into a relaxation, an unlearning of all the positions, philosophies, opinions, and beliefs that make up the "me."

The mind likes to make non-duality into a 'something.' It then sets out to understand that 'something,' debate that 'something,' seek after that 'something,' and pretend to get it. That is what the dualistic mind does by nature. Allow that to happen. But recognize that there is an awareness prior to all of that mental movement. This awareness is not of the intellect. It is the screen on which all intellectualizing, debating, and philosophizing take place. Recognizing awareness is the doorway into the realization to which the word "non-duality" is pointing.

As the movement to intellectualize, philosophize, or debate non-duality arises, simply notice that thought movement and recognize the simple timeless awareness from which that movement comes and into which the movement dies. That awareness is the portal into the actual seeing to which the concept "non-duality" is pointing.

Is God a concept?

What is God? Can the answer to that question be anything other than a concept? The mind can only think about God, entertain a conceptual definition of God, or hold a belief about God. Is God a concept?

When God is reduced to a concept, there is automatically separation between you and God. "You" are a mental concept who is looking for a union or a better relationship with another concept called "God." Do you see how the mind can only think of "you" and "God" as separate mental concepts? Can you see how this is a recipe for a sense of separation from God?

Simply notice the concept "God" as it arises. As the concept is seen, notice the spacious awareness that is looking at the concept. Do you see that the mind has reduced God to an image? The timeless awareness that sees that image is your true nature.

There is no separation except in the mind. Do not go to the mind to find God. The word God has always been pointing to presence—the essence of who you are prior to the time-bound, thought-based self you take yourself to be. That essence is already at one with God. They are not two. Another way of saying this is that the concept "God" is not independent of the presence from which the concept appears. That is the end of the illusory separation between "you and God."

The story "I am enlightened"

If you believe you are enlightened, you aren't. "I am enlightened" is just another story of ego. To say "I am enlightened," the mind has to search through thought—into memory—and claim ownership of past experience. Enlightenment is not a story. It is a realization that who you are right now is prior to all past stories that arise in timeless awareness. You are not any story, including "I am enlightened," "I am unenlightened," "I am present," "I am not present," or any similar tale.

Simply notice these stories when they arise. Notice that what is looking at the stories is presence. That presence is already free and at peace. It is already enlightened. The story of the person who is enlightened is a fiction appearing and disappearing in presence. Be clear about what is real and what is unreal. Presence is real. Stories are unreal. They are convenient fictions. Do not deny or suppress stories. Simply notice them and recognize the presence that is prior to them. The truth is in the presence, not in the stories.

Dualistic comparison and separation

Look at the dualistic stories the mind tells in order to create and maintain the illusion of separation. In order for you to be right, someone else must be wrong. In order for you to be good, someone else must be bad. In order for you to be a victim, someone must be the victimizer. In order for you to be unenlightened, someone else must be enlightened. Do you see the game the mind is playing? Your identity as a separate person is entirely thought-based, a creature of mental comparison. "You" only exist in relation to the "other."

Enlightenment is not about getting rid of dualistic stories. It is about seeing them for what they are—self-centered stories based in false separation. The separation that arises from believing these stories is not only false, it is also violent. It is all about "you" and how you are greater than, less than, more spiritual, less spiritual, more successful, less successful, more knowledgeable, or less knowledgeable than others. This illusory, thought-based separation obscures unconditional love.

These dualistic stories are the past in you. They have nothing to do with who you really are now. Your true nature is the timeless presence in which these stories arise. Once that presence is realized, the stories tend to quiet on their own. In that quieting, unconditional love is realized to be a natural attribute of your true nature.

Conscious will

As long as you believe that you have conscious will—the ability to choose—then the spiritual search will continue. The mind believes that it can make choices and exercise control in an effort to bring about future results. The future result could be a "better you," a new car, or even enlightenment.

This belief in conscious will keeps you searching like a hamster on a wheel. The mind is looking for some future moment. Searching is mind movement towards future. It is based on the idea that you can choose to take action now in order to bring about something later. Is that idea true? Can you know what your next thought, emotion, or body movement will be before it arises? If you cannot, do you really have the ability to choose?

There is nothing you can do to reach enlightenment. But you can notice what is already being done. Thoughts, emotions, reactions and body movements are happening beyond your control. These things are a product of your genetics and conditioning. Notice that life is already happening and that you have no choice in the way it happens. Paradoxically, in seeing that there is no free will, real freedom is possible. This is the freedom to be who you are right now and to allow life to happen exactly the way it is happening. That realization ends the search permanently.

Post-shift hopelessness

Personal motivation can drop away completely as a result of the shift in consciousness called enlightenment. This can be quite a shock to the system after years of living with personal goals and a story of "me" who lived in time.

Some experience a sense of hopelessness and entertain suicidal thoughts after the shift. When this happens, it is not enlightenment. Instead, the "me" is still there. It is telling the story of lack again—the story of having lost something. Only the "me" would grief for the loss of itself. Who you really are knows that the "me" is an illusion.

Those that experience hopelessness and suicidal thoughts are stuck in the idea of emptiness or nothingness. Their new story is, "I am nothing" and "I am hopeless." True non-dual realization is beyond the stories of nothing and something and hope and hopelessness. It is not stuck in duality of any kind. It is living freely, naturally, effortlessly, and lovingly from non-dual awareness—not from the story of "someone who has lost something" or "someone who is hopeless."

If the stories of meaninglessness or hopelessness occur, be clear that these are just stories. Stories of any kind have the ability to cause suffering because they are not real. Be clear that non-dual teachings are pointing to presence itself, free from identification from any dualistic stories, including ones that may arise after a powerful spiritual experience.

Uncaused joy

Most people think of joy as the opposite of sadness. When good thoughts or experiences happen (e.g., getting a job promotion), joy is experienced. When bad thoughts or experiences happen (i.e., getting fired), sadness is experienced. The joy that arises only when things are going well is dualistic. It exists only in relation to its opposite—sadness. No matter how much dualistic joy is experienced, the other shoe (sadness) is likely to drop at some point. That is how the realm of dualism works. You can't have one (joy) without the other (sadness).

Dualistic joy is not what is being pointed to here. True joy is uncaused. It arises naturally from non-dual presence. Its existence is not dependent on any thought or experience. It is not there only when you think happy thoughts or have good experiences. It is a natural, non-dualistic attribute of who you really are.

There is nothing you can do to bring uncaused joy about because it is *uncaused*. It arises naturally when presence is realized to be your true nature beyond the time-bound, thought-based story of you that is chasing after positive experiences and avoiding negative experiences. As long as you are chasing the good and avoiding the bad, this joy remains out of reach. The only doorway to uncaused joy is the direct realization of the timeless awareness in which all thoughts and experiences arise. Joy arises naturally in that space.

Within the dream

Persistent self-centered stories arise within the dream of thought, including stories about being a victim, being unloved or unworthy and a host of other stories. The list is endless. These stories are triggered in everyday experiences and relationships. There is a tendency to try to fix these storylines through thinking, mental analysis, strategies or self-help techniques. But thinking is precisely the cause of these stories. The stories are just "me" thoughts entertained on a regular basis.

Spiritual awakening is not about fixing thought-created problems with the same mind that creates the problems. You cannot fix the dream from within the dream. Awakening is available only when there is a seeing of what you are beyond these stories. "Beyond" is such a funny word because it sounds as if you have to find some place "beyond" where you are now—some future moment. That just is not true. "Beyond" means that there is an awareness right here, right now—prior to each of these stories. This awareness is here regardless of whether there is thinking or no thinking. In fact, this awareness is what allows thinking to arise.

By simply noticing the stories when they arise, and resting as the awareness that is looking at those stories, the stories lose their power. It is realized that what you are is already free of the stories. No amount of thinking about thinking can provide that degree of clarity and peace.

Awareness effortlessly allows everything to be

In every moment, there is awareness and the appearances of awareness. That is all that is ever happening. Thoughts are coming and going. Feelings appear and disappear. Sounds, experiences, and states arise and fall. Everything is happening to the nothingness of awareness. The idea that it is happening to 'you' is just one of the thoughts that is coming and going.

This truth is so simple that it is overlooked constantly. The mind is looking for some conceptual understanding of enlightenment or some future awakening or happiness. But "enlightenment," "future awakening," and "happiness" are also just thoughts appearing now. Do you see how simple it really is? If you responded, "Yes, I see," notice that this thought is simply appearing and disappearing. If you responded, "No, I don't get it," notice that that thought is also simply appearing and disappearing.

Be careful not to make noticing into a time-bound practice. Noticing appearances is just a doorway into the present realization that what is noticing is awareness itself. Every appearance is proof positive that awareness is present now. Don't try to suppress appearances. Allow them to be. Notice that only awareness truly allows anything to be. Thought does not allow. It tells stories about allowing. Awareness is what naturally and effortlessly allows every thought, story, emotion, sound, sensation, state, and experience to be exactly as it is.

Victimhood

Everyone has at least a little victimhood in her story. Notice how the mind interprets what is happening in life. Complaining, blaming, criticizing, and judging are often just little movements of the "me"—little stories the mind tells about how life is not happening the way it should be happening.

The mind is projecting this story outward, similar to a movie projector. It is not absolutely true that life "out there" is not happening the way it should be happening. In fact, life is happening exactly as it is happening. Only thought tells the story that it should be different. This thought-based story is the "me." The story is coming from the mind. It is created and maintained through unseen identification with the complaining, blaming, criticizing, and judging voice.

Instead of engaging in self-help techniques, positive thinking, or other mental strategies designed to change negative thinking patterns, simply notice what is arising in thought right now. Notice how the mind is locked into resistance to what is. Just noticing this mental resistance is freeing. It reveals that the presence that you truly are is already free and in complete alignment with what is happening right now. The victim mentality is seen as a thought-based illusion, having no real power at all.

Proof of awareness

Although it may be helpful to recognize pure awareness so that there is confidence that awareness is what you are, enlightenment is not a permanent state of total cessation of thought. The notion of reaching some future state where nothing is arising is a carrot the mind places out beyond your reach. It is perfect fuel for the search. Besides, even if there is an experience of total cessation of thought, it is only an experience. Experiences are temporary. They come and go just like every other temporary form.

Enlightenment is not a particular experience. It is a realization. And every single experience is proof that awareness is already here. The experience of reading this reflection could not happen without awareness. Thoughts, emotions, experiences, states, and all other things cannot happen without awareness. These things arise in awareness. They are not separate from—not independent of—awareness. So every experience is proof positive of awareness itself. Every experience is enlightenment. That is either realized or it isn't.

Enlightenment is the seeing that absolutely everything is arising from absolutely nothing. In that realization, there is nothing on which the mind can fixate, including on the idea of future awakening, the ideas of no self or nothingness, the idea that one must have a particular experience or find some state of total cessation or on any other idea. Yet, paradoxically, it is seen that every idea is an expression of awareness.

Concept replacement

Replacing one concept with another will not get you closer to 'This.' The mind tends to believe, for example, that if the word presence is replaced with being or the word awareness is replaced with Oneness, somehow that will bring you closer to enlightenment. But each of these is only a word. Words arise and fall in what you are. They cannot show you what you are. At best, they are pointers. Notice the mind's tendency to go from one concept to the other in a futile attempt to grasp what cannot be grasped with the mind.

Rather than playing this game of concept replacement, look to where the words are pointing. Each of these words— being, awareness, presence, enlightenment, and Oneness—is pointing to your true timeless nature beyond words. Stick with the simple fact of your existence before you try to grasp that existence with labels. You simply are. Feel into the simple truth of that. Pointers arise and fall in the simple truth of who you are right now. You are not any of these words. You are the source of them. The most pointers can do is point back to their source.

Complaining

Notice what the mind is doing. It looks out into the world and places a conceptual overlay over what is seen. That overlay is quite often a set of complaints including thoughts about how life did not happen in the past the way it should have happened, life is not happening now the way it should be happening now, or life will not happen in the future the way it should happen. These are all just thoughts. 'Your' complaints have nothing to do with reality. 'Your' complaints make up the story of 'you.' This story is projected outwards, just as a movie projector projects a movie onto a blank screen.

Don't try to suppress the complaining voice. Allow it to be. Suppression is resistance. It is more of the story of 'you' trying to control and manipulate life. There is only one change that needs to happen in order to see through this illusory story. Simply notice. Notice the complaining voice as soon as it arises and then notice that what is noticing is awareness itself. That recognition is all that needs to happen. The moment you notice the voice, you see that the voice is not you. It is an object appearing in awareness. You are awareness, not the voice. The false, complaining voice quiets naturally once it comes fully into the light of awareness.

Blaming

R arely will you meet someone who unhesitatingly admits being wrong. Instead, the mind blames others when problems arise. Truth is, there aren't any problems, nor are there others. Life is simply happening exactly the way it is happening right now. The mind-created "me" makes up problems and then blames others when things do not happen according to its dream of how things should happen.

Blaming is perfectly designed to keep the false self alive. As long as there is someone else to blame (the other), there is a 'you' that is right or that is not at fault. Pointing outward and blaming others makes 'you' feel morally superior to those others and fuels the illusory separation between you and the others.

There is nothing to do to bring about the end of blaming. There is only the possibility of noticing what is already being done. Blaming is neither right nor wrong. It is what happens. Awareness blames as a result of being confused about its identity—when it is trapped in the false sense of separation. By seeing the blaming voice, awareness sees that the voice is coming from a false entity known as "me." Seeing the voice for what it is—a false entity—allows that entity to be seen as illusory. In recognizing your true nature as awareness, separation is seen as a figment of the mind. Blaming quiets on its own in that seeing.

When confusion arises

If the concepts in these reflections or in any other spiritual teachings become confusing, it just means the mind is trapped in the idea that presence is something to figure out mentally. It's not. Presence is what you are right now. It is your very essence.

Don't try to grasp presence. You cannot mentally grasp what you are. You can only recognize that you are this presence. This recognition does not happen in the mind.

Be the simple presence that you already are. This is the presence that is here whether spiritual ideas are coming through or not and whether you understand those ideas conceptually or not. This is the presence that never goes away. Presence is never confused. Confusion is a temporary form that comes and goes in presence. Don't fight the confusion. Don't try to get rid of it. To fight or resist confusion in any way assumes there is an entity separate from confusion who must somehow negotiate with it. That is delusion.

Just notice that the very presence you are is awake to that confusion. It is appearing as that confusion. Confusion only sticks around when you believe there is something to figure out or be clear about mentally. Don't fall into that trap. Presence is not intellectual. No amount of philosophizing or intellectualizing will reveal presence.

The intellect

Yesterday's reflection stated that "no amount of philoso-phizing or intellectualizing will reveal presence." This is sometimes misheard to mean that the intellect is bad or that it should be denied. No, that is not what is meant here.

The spiritual search is about finding the answer to the question, "Who am I?" The answer is not intellectual or phil-osophical. The answer is realized when presence is realized. Presence is a word pointing to your timeless essence—the awareness in which the intellect arises. Do not deny the intel-lect or label it as bad. The intellect is a wonderful tool. But it cannot show you who you really are because you are not any concept. Concepts arise and fall in the presence you are.

The pointer "no amount of philosophizing or intellectual-izing will reveal presence" is merely pointing you away from the trap of going to the mind to answer the question, "Who am I?" This is not about denying anything, including thought. It is about seeing that thought cannot solve the identity cri-sis. Presence is the source of every thought. The intellect arises from who you really are—presence. Once presence is realized to be who you really are, the intellect is seen as a manifestation of that source, helpful in many practical ways including everything from reading a simple road sign to designing software.

The seamlessness of reality

Every form is temporary. It appears from vast empty space and disappears back into that space. That is its natural tendency—to appear and disappear. Forms are not independent of the formlessness from which they arise. They are not separate from their source. Planets seamlessly appear from and disappear back into space. Clouds seamlessly appear from and disappear back into the sky. Sounds seamlessly appear from and disappear back into silence. These forms do not need to be manipulated. They arise and fall in the natural cycle of birth and death.

The same is true for thoughts. Thoughts seamlessly appear from and disappear back into awareness. Thoughts, opinions, ideas, stories, and beliefs do not need to be manipulated. They arise and fall naturally and effortlessly. Suffering happens only when there is movement to manipulate, escape, overcome, or neutralize thoughts. When thoughts are simply noticed and allowed to be exactly as they are by awareness, they have no power to harm you. They are quite beautiful in that sense.

Let thoughts arise. Do you really have control anyway? Isn't the notion of control just another thought? Let that thought arise and fall too. Simply notice that your true nature is the awareness in which these thoughts arise and fall and that these thoughts are expressions of (are not separate from) awareness.

Hope and hopelessness

Enlightenment is not about hope. If you have hope, the mind is still locked in its dream of future. The idea that the future will be better has the story "right now is not enough" built into it. Hope arises from a present sense of lack. It's the perfect recipe for continuing unhappiness. Once it is seen that future is just thought arising now, it is seen that living for a future moment (i.e., hope) is just identification with thought. It's the "me" that will never truly be happy because it is always looking for something else in some other time.

Enlightenment is about hopelessness, but not the hopelessness the mind knows. The mind only sees the world dualistically. It's in the business of labeling everything as good or bad. It sees hope as good and hopelessness as bad.

Hopelessness, the way it is used here, means the absence of the need for hope. It is the absence of the need for a projection towards future. It may be more precise to say that enlightenment (i.e., presence) is beyond both hope and hopelessness. This moment is all there is. It is already abundant. When that is seen fully, hope is seen as irrelevant. There is no need for it. "Hopelessness"—as in utter despair—is also seen as just another harmless dualistic story the mind tells. These stories disappear on their own when they meet the light of present awareness.

The spiritual ego

If you hear the suggestion, "Don't think about an elephant," the mind automatically plays the image of an elephant. If you continue to tell yourself to stop thinking about that elephant, the mind just continues playing the elephant image over and over.

In the same way, the mental strategy of "getting rid of" your ego, story, or self just reinforces the very thing it seeks to be free of. It continuously creates and strengthens the image of a "me" who is trying to find freedom from the suffering and seeking of the "me." It doesn't work. The very notion of setting out to accomplish anything in spirituality reinforces the doer—the thought-based, time-bound story that is the very root of all suffering and seeking. This is sometimes called the "spiritual ego."

Seeking enlightenment in the future is the perfect way to avoid enlightenment. There is no future goal except as a presently arising thought. Enlightenment is only a present seeing. In seeing whatever thought is appearing right now, it is realized that what is looking is not a thought. Thoughts don't see. What is looking is who you really are. It is beyond the story. One could call it present awareness or the true Self. But even those thoughts appear to the seeing. In this present seeing, it is realized that the story of "me"—the thought-based, time-bound story—is not real. All suffering and seeking ends in that seeing.

False images

There are many false images of enlightenment floating around. One of the biggest myths is that, when your true nature is realized, you will remain peaceful and quiet at all times, perhaps meditating with your eyes closed for most of the day. That's a false image. It is true that the nothingness of awareness is, in its deepest sense, peaceful and quiet. But that nothingness is the source of all movement and noise. Nothing is being everything. They are flipsides of the same coin. They are not two.

The loudest explosion is none other than the quietness taking another apparent form. Life appears in every form. There is only 'This.' The One Life. It is pure aliveness. The mind often chooses the quietness over noise and the rest over movement because it is seeking pleasure. It seeks to define itself in the pleasure of the quietness and rest. In that self-defining, it often looks to avoid noise, excessive talking, or excessive movement. But to mentally avoid or deny anything in favor of something else is a denial of an aspect of reality—an aspect of your true Self. To be free means to be free even from attachment to the pleasurable peace and quietness.

Life is exactly the way it is including a moment of pure quietness and stillness or a moment of obnoxious noise and movement. Mental attachment to any particular state is the "me."

APRIL

Nobody ever has any truth, just various degrees of falsehood

—Ken Wilber

Love is your true timeless nature

The mind-created "me" that lives in time through thoughts of past, future, and resistance to now obscures the natural, unconditional love that is your true nature in this moment. This love is an inherent attribute of presence. It cannot be manufactured, contrived, gained, or demanded from others. It does not come from others. It is a natural aspect of the timeless presence that you already are. "You" as it is used here, just as in each of these reflections, is not referring to the thought-based, time-bound person. It is referring to your true nature prior to that "me" mental construct.

This unconditional love will never be found in the future. Future is merely a thought arising now. This love does not come from thought. No amount of thinking about love or about presence will bring it about.

Simply recognize the presence that is here right now. The word presence is not pointing to any object that is seen or experienced. It's not the body. It is not a thought. It is not a sound. It is not a feeling. All of those objects come and go. This presence is the pure seeing that is awake to these objects that come and go. Recognizing the loving presence that you are takes no time at all. It is already present in the felt sense of "nowness" and "hereness" that surrounds the body and mind and permeates the body and mind.

Thoughts about presence

Thoughts are thoughts. They cannot reveal the truth of who you are. You are not a thought. You are the presence in which thoughts arise. But even that last sentence is a thought. It is merely pointing to presence. It is tempting to read such a pointer and forget that the pointer itself is just another thought, no matter how clear it is.

Every sentence in these reflections is a thought. The words are merely pointing to the awakeness that is your true nature in this moment. The mind hears these pointers repeated often and tends to mistake the words for that to which they are pointing. Just remember that the grandest and clearer pointers to presence are still just thoughts. They come and go like all thoughts do. Don't mistake them for the truth. Just notice that they arise and fall in presence.

You cannot know what you are through thoughts. You can only know *that* you are. This knowing is not intellectual, philosophical, or mental. This knowing is the direct experience that you are the presence through which words pointing to presence appear and disappear.

Presence is eating potato chips

Presence just means eating potato chips, walking your dog, sitting on the couch, shuffling papers at work, talking on the phone with a friend, listening to your favorite music, or driving down the road thinking. Presence is your everyday existence without the need for something more to happen.

Seeking could be described as eating potato chips while desiring to reach a state of enlightenment or to be an awakened person eating chips or to have some experience other than the simple fact of eating chips right now. Presence is simply eating chips without that desire for some future moment.

Presence is so simple that it is overlooked by the mind seeking something other than what is happening now. In presence, life is simple. There is only the crunch, crunch of the chip, the sensation of it going down your throat, and then biting into the next chip. It's that simple. Just that—the reality of eating chips. It's not about the story of a person eating chips. It's much simpler. It's just eating chips.

The desire for something more than what is happening is the problem, not the road to the solution.

The simple fact of presence

If you believe that you have already awakened or that you will awaken someday, you have placed awakening in the past or future. This means you have placed it in thought. Thought is time. You've placed it in the time-bound, thought-based story of you. The moment you claim to be enlightened or go searching for it in the future, that false story is being believed.

The notion, "I am enlightened" is a thought arising now. It is a label arising from memory. The notions, "I will be enlightened someday" or "I am working towards more presence" are stories of future becoming. This is also memory. How would you know what "enlightenment" or "presence" is without having an image in the mind? These mental images come from second hand sources like this book and other non-duality books. The mind memorizes these images and starts chasing after them. It stays within the mental dream self, chasing carrots out beyond its reach. As long as you are looking for enlightenment in the future, it will not be realized.

Let these images gently point you to the presence that you are right now. The word "enlightenment" is pointing to this presence. Notice the simple fact of presence that is undeniably here. This presence does not come and go. It does not change. Stories come and go in this presence. This presence is here, whether there is thinking or no thinking.

Wisdom

Wisdom does not emanate from thought or belief. It emanates from the direct seeing of reality the way it really is. When life is filtered through the story of "me," reality is not being directly experienced in that way. It is being processed through a self-centered story. When that filter is happening, thoughts, experiences, states, emotions and circumstances are interpreted in terms of what they mean for the central figure "me."

Even knowledge is usurped by this story. Knowledge, in the way it is being used here, means conceptual knowledge. Reality is being interpreted through a set of stored files (i.e., learned concepts). Once there is identification with those concepts, the "me" is born. It's all about being right. That is not wisdom.

Wisdom arises naturally from awareness. In seeing this identification with concepts, the desire to be right loosens its grip. Wisdom is seeing the ways in which there is a sense of self invested in learned concepts. There is nothing to do to cultivate wisdom. Doing comes from the mind. There can only be a present seeing of what is already arising. What is already arising is identification with these learned concepts, including concepts about spirituality, religion, politics, philosophy, and various world views. That seeing is wisdom. It allows the seeing through of this false sense of self invested in ideas.

Problems

What is a problem? It is a negative mental interpretation of a situation. The underlying story of every problem is, "This should not be happening." But how can what is happening NOT happen? Is that possible? To say that something should not be happening is like looking at a chair and believing that it should be a frog. The "me" is the mind that is in resistance to what is.

So how do you accept a situation instead of making it into a problem? 'You' don't. That would just be the "me" again. Acceptance does not happen through the mind.

What is here now that is already accepting of both the situation and the thought that arises to try to accept the situation? Awareness. Awareness has no agenda to accept or reject. It is non-dual. It is neither for nor against the situation. It is neither for nor against the thought arising in response to the situation. Awareness is your natural state.

Awareness sees no problem. Situations, reactions, thoughts, and emotions are coming and going in awareness. There is no grasping towards or fixating on these temporary forms. Life is awake to itself, allowing itself to be just as it is. There is no person who must deal with a problem. In the recognition that you are awareness, not a person who is aware, the response to a situation, if one is needed, comes naturally and effortlessly.

The illusory distinction between non-duality and duality

Thought does not 'do' non-duality. Thought is in the business of making relative, dualistic distinctions where there are, ultimately, no such distinctions. The pointers in this reflection or any non-dual pointer are only helpful to the extent they are relatively and dualistically clearer than other pointers that have been heard. For example, the words, "awareness and phenomena arising from awareness are not two" are clearer dualistically than the words, "Dog ears are blue" if the purpose of the communication is to point to the realization called non-duality. And that is the 'point' of all such communications.

To deny the relative aspect of words is to deny thought. Thoughts are phenomena arising from awareness. The phenomena are not independent of awareness. This is not something thought will grasp because thought's function is to divide reality into illusory fragments (e.g., thought and awareness, duality and non-duality).

To deny thoughts—phenomena—is to deny their very source—awareness. The only thing that would deny thought would be another thought. Instead of trying to grasp non-duality through thinking, simply notice what you are. You are the non-dual awareness from which thoughts arise. See thoughts for what they are—expressions of awareness. They create the illusion of separate things and separate people.

In this realization, the distinction between the concepts of non-duality and duality as well as between awareness and thought are seen as illusory. The distinctions are conceptual.

Relationship

In relationship, there appears to be two who must negotiate with one another. The mind gets heavily involved in that negotiation. It often tries to think about and analyze the other person or play with images about how the other should be different or better than he or she is.

When the identified mind is incessantly thinking about the other, there is no true relationship. Duality is running the show. The false, thought-based story of you is locked in a game of mental analysis and emotional entanglement with the false, thought-based story of the other. These two stories never really meet. They only think about and react against one another, stuck in an apparent trap of separation. These stories obscure the unconditional love that is possible in relationship.

Your true nature is non-dual awareness. In recognizing that you are not anything that arises temporarily in aware-ness—including thoughts, emotions, images, and stories—identification with those temporary things drops away. The "me" is seen as illusory. Simultaneously, when it is recognized that the "me" is illusory, it is also seen that the "other" is illu-sory. The negotiation is seen as unnecessary. The mind quiets its attempts to analyze and change the other. As all that "me" mind movement relaxes, the non-dual presence that remains is unconditional love itself.

Peace

True peace cannot be found in the story of you.

Dualistic thought divides reality into pairs of opposites and then picks a side. It attempts to bring about peace by supporting its side and opposing the opposite side. Even to be against conflict IS conflict. To oppose something is to make an "other" out of it. Conflict is born in the mental division between self and other.

Peace is your natural state. It is not something that one attains through thinking. So it is not something achieved in a time-bound spiritual search (i.e., story). Time is thought. The separate self is a time-bound, thought-based illusion. To say that "I' will find peace in the future is to feed a story of thought. That illusory entity will never find peace because it sees itself as separate. Its goal is not peace. Its goal is separation. In that separateness, it must find an "other" against which to define itself. Conflict is created in that division.

Timeless, non-dual presence is what you really are. It is the pure seeing right now that is prior to the "I" thought. That presence is already naturally at peace. It is already undivided because it is prior to any mental division between self and other. In recognizing that what you are is non-dual presence, the "I" thought no longer has power over 'you' when it arises. Therefore, there is no desire to define that self against or be in conflict with an "other."

Worry

Although worry is predominantly mental, it is an entire mind and body experience. A stressful thought about the future arises. Fear arises in the body in conjunction with that thought. As the thought remains unseen, it fuels the raw energy of fear in the body. As the raw energy of fear remains unseen, it fuels the mental story. This is the cycle of suffering. It is the "me." Therefore, the "me" cannot find a way out of it. The "me" will only make the worry itself into a problem.

There is nothing you can do to stop worrying. There can only be a seeing of what is already being done. What is being done is that emotion and thought are arising but remaining unseen. As they remain unseen, the cycle continues.

Awareness is what you really are. You are not this dream of thought and emotion. The moment fear arises in the body, notice that it is there. Notice the space around the fear. That space is who you are. The fear is just a short term visitor. As you notice that what you are is this space, notice too that the thoughts of future are also just short term visitors appearing in the space of awareness.

By resting in what you are—awareness—the cycle of worry dissipates naturally. This is the false self being seen through.

One

Stop for one moment and just look without thought. In suspending thought for one moment, there is a glimpse into your true nature as the one essence of life. It is realized in that instant that quiet space permeates the universe. It permeates the body and mind and every object seen. The nothingness of this space is appearing as everything.

All words—including these words—divide the universe into fragments, as if space is something that is separate from objects, as if stillness is something separate from disturbance, as if silence is something separate from sound, as if awareness is something separate from thought, and as if you are something separate from the universe. The universe is one mirror appearing as these reflections.

In order for there to be a "me" that lacks something including love, enlightenment, peace, or happiness, concepts have to arise to divide the universe into something called "me" that lacks something separate called "love," "enlightenment," "peace," or "happiness." The thought that creates that separation will never find Oneness.

Believing thought to be reality is what creates the illusion of separation. In taking a moment to suspend thought to see reality the way it really is, the illusion is seen through. As there is confidence gained in the fact that your true nature is this one essence, thought still arises but it no longer has the power to fool you into believing that it is reality.

Questions

Questions arise on the spiritual search. The most an answer can do is point you to presence. Presence is non-conceptual. It isn't an idea. It isn't a conceptual answer. It is the very presence that is alive right now, the presence in which questions and answers arise and fall.

The spiritual search is just mind movement. One question after another arises in this search. If there is an underlying belief that there is some conceptual answer out there that needs to be found in order for Oneness or enlightenment to be revealed, that belief creates the problem. It is fuel for more questions. Conceptual answers do not reveal presence. They appear and disappear in presence. Answers beget more questions. Such is the cycle of seeking.

Allow the questions to arise. Instead of looking for an answer, let the concepts point you to what is non-conceptual—presence. The direct realization of presence reveals that enlightenment is not about getting your questions answered. It is about seeing that they don't matter anymore.

In recognizing that you are presence, it is seen that only the false self is invested in the game of seeking conceptual answers. The false self needs questions so that it can continue its search into future. As the false self is seen through, the game is over. In that seeing, there is a deep non-conceptual knowing that presence is your true identity. Presence has no questions. It simply is.

Conclusions

Non-dual realization cannot be revealed by attaching to a particular dualistic conclusion. There is no such thing as a statement of the truth. There may be clearer ideas, relatively speaking, but only to a central "me" that imposes the label "clearer" on the idea. In non-dual seeing, it is realized that conclusions exist within dualism. Thinking makes the separation between concepts appear real. The idea that there is a "right" that has a separate and independent existence from "wrong" is the illusion. Ideas relate to each other as polar opposites. Right and wrong arise simultaneously and are mutually interdependent. This is true of all opposites including up/down, liberation/bondage, open/close, success/failure, clear/unclear, self/no self. The line between these polar opposites is conceptual.

Presence is the field in which all dualism is playing out. This field is what you are. Presence allows, but sees through, the dualism of all opposites. To attach to any dualistic conclusion is an attempt to deny its opposite. It is actually impossible to deny an opposite because pairs of opposites arise together. An idea does not exist without its opposite. By entertaining the notion "right" you are impliedly inventing the concept of "wrong."

Don't try to think about what is being said. Simply notice what the mind is doing. Presence sees all conclusions and plays in the realm of dualism but is ultimately free of whatever arises and falls.

Just this moment

Look and see that this moment is all there is. There isn't anything other than what is presently happening. 'This' is the smell of dirty laundry, the feeling of warmth in the room, the sound of birds outside, the sensation of pain in the knee, and the thought about what to eat for lunch. All of that is arising now. 'This' allows everything to be just as it is without trying to manipulate, overcome, or escape it. This is the nothingness of present awareness experiencing the everything-ness of life.

When thought believes that something ought to be happening other than what is happening right now, the spiritual search is born. In seeing that it is impossible for life to be happening in any other way than it is happening right now, the search is seen as the problem, not the solution. See that even the search arises (as thought) in this moment. Even the notion that there is a problem or a solution is a thought happening now. Even the notion that there is a "now" is an idea arising and falling. Even the notion that you are reading this reflection is an idea arising and falling in 'This.'

Presence is an opening

Presence is not a particular state, experience, or feeling. If you experience a moment of freedom, peace, or a good feeling, the mind may associate that particular state, experience, or feeling with presence. The mind reduces the state, experience, or feeling to a memory. It reduces it to thought. When that particular event passes, thought seeks to recreate or find that lost state, experience, or feeling. This is how seeking perpetuates itself. Thought is time. "Future" is merely a thought arising now. The thought of the past event is seeking the thought of some future event. Thought is chasing thought. Do you see that the search is purely conceptual?

Presence is not any particular state, experience, or feeling. It is more like the opening through which each and every state, experience, feeling, and everything else arises. There is no way to "recreate" or "get back to" a present opening. There is only this opening—now—and whatever is coming through. The thought, "I need to get back to that freedom I once felt" may be coming through the opening. If that thought is believed, the seeking continues. If the thought is seen for what it really is—a thought arising in the opening—it isn't believed. It is simply allowed to be. In that seeing, there is no seeking.

Anything is possible

It is sometimes assumed that, in enlightenment, anger and other negative feelings no longer arise. Don't fall for that trap. Enlightenment just means presence. Anything is possible in presence. Presence is just a word pointing to the awakeness that is looking right now.

Presence is the opening through which all forms appear and disappear. Any form can come through, including anger. When emotions seem to appear from and disappear back into a story of "me," they accumulate over time, creating resentment and conflict. When it is recognized that the "me" is not real, presence is seen to be what you really are. When anger arises in presence, it does not accumulate into a story of "me." Instead, it appears from and disappears back into a space that is completely and totally free of attachment or identification with what is appearing. Anger, therefore, is no longer seen as a problem. It is just raw energy passing through. The mind is no longer moving to overcome, suppress, analyze, neutralize, or escape that energy. But even if such mind movement arises, that movement itself is just a form passing through the opening.

Suffering and seeking

Suffering and seeking are intrinsically tied together.

Suffering is the past. Suffering happens through identification with thought and emotion. Identification means that you believe that you are the thought-based story of your past and the emotions that arise in conjunction with that story. That story feels necessarily incomplete because it is not reality. It is a story that exists in time. Time is thought. This story is just a set of mental images. Images are, by their nature, incomplete. They have meaning only in relation to other images. The past story of you is looking for meaning—for completion in other images. Those other images are the future.

Seeking is the future. When the past story is believed to be who you are, the mind believes that it must do something to make the story complete in the future. Therefore, it engages in self-help therapy, career movements, relationships, buying material items, seeking enlightenment and a host of other things in order to find that completion.

This story is not really interested in completion. It is interested in continuing to keep the story alive. It does this through seeking. Suffering leads to seeking. Seeking leads to more suffering because future completion is never reached. "Future" is just a thought. It cannot be reached.

Your true nature is the timeless awareness from which the thought-based, time-bound story of you appears and disappears. This seeing ends the cycle of suffering and seeking.

Space and things

Thoughts, emotions, sensations, experiences, and states arise from a basic, natural space. This space cannot be known through thinking about it. We can call it "space," "awareness," "nothingness," "emptiness" or whatever other label we like. But no word is it. Every word is appearing in it.

Thoughts, emotions, sensations, experiences, and states are uncaused. These things appear naturally, automatically, and spontaneously. In just allowing them to be exactly as they are, without moving to manipulate, overcome, learn from, recreate, or escape them, it is seen that these things disappear back into the space.

These things are not separate from this space. One could say that the things appear and disappear from the space. But even that is some attempt to understand through concepts what can only be known through direct non-conceptual realization. In seeing that all things appear and disappear in space, the entire universe is seen to be at rest. It is not that only the space is at rest. The mind likes to associate rest with words like "space," "quietness," "awareness," "presence" and "emptiness." The entire universe is at rest precisely because the things—thoughts, emotions, sensations, experiences, and states—that appear and disappear in space are not separate from that restful space. You are this unnamable Oneness.

Taking things personally

There has to be a person before things can be taken personally. The person is the energy of the body and mind that contracts around the time-bound, thought-based story called "me." That energy will always take things personally. It will always come up to defend itself and attack the other when the other is threatening the sense of "me" that is locked up in that energy. Therefore, to say "I will not take this personally" or "I will stop taking things personally" is a total fiction. It can't be done, at least not to a significant degree or on a permanent basis.

In the moment you feel attacked or find yourself taking something that someone says or does personally, see that it is an image that is being threatened. Presence is your true Self. Presence is not a mental image so it cannot take things personally. It cannot be threatened. Only a false image—a conceptual self—can be threatened. That which notices the mental and emotional reaction when something is taken personally is presence. Rest as what you really are, presence. Presence sees that the image you have of yourself is false. In that seeing, the duality between presence and the image arising in presence collapses.

Self-deception

The mind has an uncanny capacity for self-deception. It can hear a spiritual pointer and forget that it is merely a pointer. So when the pointer, "there is no one to reach enlightenment," or "all there is, is Oneness" or "awareness is what you really are" is heard, it can easily be turned into a belief.

Each of the pointers above, when taken to be absolutely true, becomes an erroneous idea. The pointers in this book and every other non-duality or enlightenment teaching are merely signs pointing to a realization that can only be known through direct experience. Just as the word "pencil" is merely a sign pointing to the tool you use to write a letter, the words Oneness and awareness are pointing to the direct experience of life just as it is, without the filter of identification with concepts.

The moment any pointer is taken to be absolutely true, a new religion is born—a belief system. As with all belief systems, that pointer must be defended. Only a false self would defend a pointer or way of expressing 'This' because the false self is identification with thought.

See all these pointers as merely signs, arising and falling in awareness, and pointing to a realization that can never be known through thought. This realization can only be seen through the direct experience of now. In this direct experience, thoughts are not reality. They are appearing in reality.

Pointing outward into your own dream

Yesterday's reflection stated that the mind has an uncanny capacity for self-deception. This applies not only to spiritual pointers, but also to thoughts arising in everyday life.

When you are in relationship with someone, your thoughts about the 'other person' are 'your' thoughts. They constitute the dream of thought known as 'you.' They have little to do with the other person because "other person" is also merely a thought arising within the mind—within the dream.

When someone does not do or say what you want them to do, see that the mind is interpreting it this way. It isn't absolutely true that the person should not have done or said that. The mind is dreaming a dream that life should not be the way it really is. That's impossible. How can life not be the way it actually is in this moment?

When thoughts arise to interpret an experience as if it should not be happening, or as if it should be different than the way it is, recognize this for what it is—a dream of thought. It's an interpretation. It isn't reality.

To argue with what is actually happening is to take the dream to be reality. It is like pointing outward into your own dream. It is similar to sitting in a movie theater and arguing with what the characters are doing, except this movie is coming from the projector in 'your' own mind.

Being

Right here, in timelessness, there is being. Being is the one thing that cannot be denied. You can say you are this and not that. Those dualistic stories come and go. But being does not come and go. You simply are. That is an indisputable fact. It is not that you are a person. "Person" is one of the stories that comes and goes. Being is much simpler than any story. Being simply is. It is the one and only constant. It is the one thing that is always here no matter what thought, emotion, experience, or state is happening in being.

Although the word "being" is a concept, the word is pointing to an actuality. The mind cannot grasp the actuality of being. Concepts arise in being. The recognition of the actuality of being is not conceptual.

Being is the suchness of this moment before the mind labels that suchness as good or bad or enlightened or unenlightened or in some other dualistic fashion. Being is. Stick with the actuality to which those words are pointing. See the word "being" as merely a sign, then look to where the sign is pointing. The sign is pointing to life itself before the mind tries to mentally grasp it. In a way that can never truly be expressed, and that appears paradoxical to the dualistic mind, the sign itself is an expression of that same being.

Reflections of the One Life

There are many different expressions of non-duality. It is easy to get hooked into one particular way of pointing to it. Each expression, from the clearest non-dual pointer to the most confusing one, is an expression of Oneness. This is not to say that all expressions are equally clear. Some words point more directly and clearly to the realization. But the pointer is never that which it describes.

The One Life is like a mirror. There is only one mirror. However, there are various reflections of that single mirror. Non-dual pointers appear as reflections. The moment there is attachment to any reflection, including a non-dual pointer, separation and conflict happen.

Some pointers in these reflections may seem unclear. If you read a pointer that seems unclear, move on to the next pointer. Don't get stuck. But if stuckness happens, seeing it frees you from its grip.

In the clear seeing that you are nothing being everything, all reflections are allowed to be just as they are. That last sentence is merely a reflection. Use the reflection as a pointer, then let it pass. Reflections, by their nature, have a short life span. They arise and pass. Attachment just means focusing in on a reflection in some attempt to make it into truth or permanence. That is ignorance.

Splitting the One into two

There is only One here, but the One gets split into two in various ways.

There is an internal split in the mind. Pairs of opposites arise in the mind (e.g., good v. bad, nice v. mean). Desirable traits are owned as "mine." Undesirable traits are repressed and projected outward as belonging to "others." That which bothers you the most about other people is a dualistic trait within yourself that has been denied and projected outward as somebody else's trait. This is called "the shadow."

There is also an internal split between body and mind. The mind separates itself from the body. The body is treated as an appendage, as something separate from and subordinate to the mind. Feelings in the body aren't felt directly. Instead, they are obscured by the process of thinking. This is called the "body/mind" division.

There is also a split between "me" and "other" or "me" and "life." This split makes it appear that you are an individual entity who must negotiate with others and with life itself. This is the "separate self" and is the cause of seeking, suffering, and conflict.

To see these divisions and boundaries as unreal, as facets of a mind that has bought into an illusory dualism, is to recognize the non-dual unconditional love that is your true nature.

Splitting the One into two (the shadow)

Yesterday's reflection spoke of the shadow. The "shadow" is a Western psychological term pointing to an internal split in the mind.

What bothers you most about other people? Whatever quality bothers you most about others is a dualistic aspect of yourself projected outward, appearing as an "other." The mind often tells dualistic stories about a self that has only positive traits. Take, for example, kindness. The mind splits non-dual reality into two. The stories, "I am kind" and "I am unkind" are polar opposites that arise mutually and simultaneously and that are interdependent. You can't have one without the other. In believing the story, "I am kind," suddenly it appears that the others "out there" are unkind. This is how thought differentiates a "self" from an "other." In reality, there is no self v. other. The "other" is a shadow of a mind that has bought into illusory duality.

The more you repress a certain undesirable quality, the more it appears "out there" in the other. It appears on the other side of a conceptual boundary that exists only in the mind. By simply owning the voice of the undesirable quality, and seeing it as a dualistic story of self that has been repressed, the shadow "out there" is seen as illusory. In that seeing, the separation and conflict between self and other is seen as unreal—a battle arising from a dream of dualistic thought.

Splitting the One into two (shadows of the victim)

The last few reflections have described the shadow as a split in the mind in which a positive trait is owned as "me" and its opposite negative trait is denied and projected outward as belonging to the "other." The reverse can also happen if the story of "me" centers on being a victim.

A victim has a negative story of self that may include thoughts of being unworthy, inferior to others, lonely, or some other negative mental image. He owns the negative trait and denies its positive opposite. The story, "I am unworthy" arises simultaneously with and is mutually dependent on the opposite story, "I am worthy." As soon as there is a buying into the story, "I am unworthy," the opposite story is repressed and projected outward. Suddenly, it appears that others are "worthy." This feeds the story of being a victim as the mind differentiates between self (i.e., victim) and other (i.e., not victim).

There is nothing one can do about the shadow except notice what is already being done. This mirroring effect in relationship is happening spontaneously. It is already being done, beyond your control. In simply seeing that these opposite stories arise together, and owning the repressed story, "I am worthy," the split is seen as illusory. There is no such thing as a person who is worthy or unworthy. These are stories existing within a mental dream of separation.

The shadow (external pressure is internal drive)

The shadow also shows up in external pressure and internal drive.

Suppose Joe makes a decision to spend more time with his kids by taking them to the amusement park once a month. Instead, Joe gets too busy and is unable to take off work to be with his kids. Yet the internal drive, or story, that he should spend time with them is still there. That drive, however, is forgotten about or repressed.

One day Joe's wife casually says to him, "Aren't you going to take the kids to the amusement park?" In response, Joe gets angry and defensive, "I've been working a lot. I can't just take off whenever I want. Why are you nagging me?!"

Although Joe thinks he is experiencing external pressure from his wife, she is merely acting as a mirror, revealing Joe's internal drive that he dropped—the drive to spend more time with his kids. By making it about his wife, Joe is denying his own drive. That drive—once repressed—appears as a shadow—an "other" (i.e., his wife). If Joe's wife would have nagged him about something for which he has no internal drive, Joe would not have become defensive and no conflict would have arisen between the two.

Repressed internal drive often appears as external pressure. In this seeing, dualistic conflict in these situations is seen as illusory, a product of the mind-created false, repressed self.

The body/mind division

Thought creates a boundary between the body and mind where no such boundary exists. As stated in an earlier reflection, the body is treated as an appendage, as something separate from and subordinate to the mind. This creates a tendency of not seeing and feeling emotions directly as soon as they arise. When emotions are not seen, they remain unconscious, fueling the story of "me" in the mind.

This is not about merging the body and mind. It is about seeing that the division between the two is entirely conceptual. It doesn't exist. To even consider the body separate from the mind, you have to buy into two concepts, "body" and "mind." The concepts themselves create the notion that the mind is separate from the body.

In simply noticing the mind's tendency to conceptually divide reality into two, between body and mind, it is realized that what is noticing is pure awareness. Awareness knows no boundary between body and mind. Simply take a moment to verify this for yourself. Without the thought "body" and "mind" where is the division? Where does one end and the other begin? Are there two there? Where is the precise boundary? Can you find a division? Perhaps you can, but only when you think about it.

The split between self and the rest of life

What you take to be a "you" totally separate from the rest of life is really just awareness contracting or focusing on (i.e., identifying with) phenomena arising in awareness. The phenomena are the body, thoughts, beliefs, ideas, positions, opinions, emotions, sensations, experiences, states and all other temporary forms. As phenomena arise in awareness, there is identification. This identification creates a false center known as "me."

This contracted "me" energy creates the sense that you are a person "in here" (in the body and mind) that is separate from what is "out there" (outside the body and mind). The crux of this separate self sense is the time-bound, thought-based story of past, present, and future. That story is continuously fed by interpreting life conceptually and thinking of yourself as existing along a timeline. You believe you are the past and that you are heading towards future. All of that is purely conceptual.

To see through this illusion of separation between self and life, notice that what you are in the most fundamental sense is unchanging, no-boundary, non-local awareness. No matter what phenomena appear and disappear in awareness, the awareness never leaves or changes. In simply noticing the phenomena, without focusing in on it, the phenomena are allowed to be exactly as they are. They are allowed to pass without identification. In this disidentification, the boundary between self and the rest of life is seen as illusory.

The false division between awareness and phenomena

Even once there is a seeing that the division between self and not-self is illusory, the mind can get apparently stuck in yet another division. This happens when the mind believes that awareness and the phenomena arising in awareness are two (i.e., they are separate).

See for yourself that no such division is there. When a thought is arising, what sees the thought? When a sound is arising, what hears the sound? When an experience is happening, what experiences the experience? When a state is arising, what experiences the state? Without awareness, the phenomena in awareness could not arise. Stated another way, the movie screen is necessary for the movie. The screen and the movie are not two. You can't have one without the other, which is just another way of saying that the two are inseparable.

Phenomena have no existence separate from awareness. To treat awareness and phenomena as being separate is to create a split that is not really there. The division is conceptual. The universe is seamlessly One.

MAY

By thinking of something you create an entity and by thinking of nothing you create another. Let such erroneous thinking perish utterly

— Huang Po

To be like a leaf

Enlightenment is just a fancy word for being totally surrendered. It's like being a leaf. The wind blows you every
which way and you are just glad to go in whatever direction
it takes you. And you know that wherever you are, that is
exactly where you are supposed to be because that is where
you are.

You aren't trying to figure out how to be a better or more
spiritual leaf. But if those thoughts arise, that is fine too. You
are not arguing with other leaves or trying to be heard or seen
above all other leaves. But if that arguing or trying happens,
that is fine too. You are not fighting the wind. And yet if fighting happens, that is fine too. You are just content moving in
whatever way the wind (life) moves you. Even when you are
moving, you are naturally at rest because you are not separate
from the wind. There is no you and the wind. There is only
One Life, appearing as two. You are the One pretending to be
a separate leaf, dancing with your friend "wind."

You are happy being exactly where you are, whether anyone
is paying attention to you or not, and whether anyone thinks
you are an enlightened leaf or just a plain old leaf because you
know that there is no real boundary between those two.

That which sees the false self

Just be what you are right now without trying to change it. The movement to change what you are is a movement of mind. That movement of mind comes from the memorized past, which is the false self. The movement of mind that seeks to change that story of past is the projected future, which is also the false self.

See that time-bound story that moves along a continuum of past to future? That is not what you are. Simply notice the false self when it arises. That which sees the false self is what you really are. Presence.

Look from the space

Look at the world from the space behind your face. As a person approaches you or a situation begins to unfold in front of you, notice that you are looking from that space. Space is what naturally allows the person or situation to be exactly as it is.

When you look in the mirror, you see a form that you call "you" staring back at you. It appears that you are a totally separate person. But when you walk away from that mirror and look at the world, you are looking from a space. From an internal view, you have no head. There is only space looking at whatever is happening.

Do not look at the world from the filter of a concept including the idea that you are a "person," "Christian," "Buddhist," or even that you are "space," "no self," "awareness" or "Oneness." Those are all just concepts. Look from the *actual* space that you are. You are the space in which even these concepts appear.

Don't get stuck in simply witnessing what arises. Once this actual space is recognized, see that this space is immediately intimate with whatever is arising. There is no boundary between the space and what is appearing in the space. This is another way of saying that there is no self separate from the rest of life. This is the realization of Oneness.

The story of 'you' is based in resistance

Just noticing resistance as it arises reveals so much. The story of 'you' is a story of resistance. Separation continues as long as resistance is not seen. Resistance is the mental and emotional energy that arises and contracts against life situations.

Notice the thoughts that say that what happened in the past should not have happened, what is happening now should not be happening, and what may happen in the future should not happen. That is resistance. Notice the emotional resistance that arises in conjunction with these thoughts.

Notice that the thoughts and emotions arise in a space. Actual space surrounds these things. When it is realized that you are the actual space, and not the things arising in the space, there is no longer identification with these things.

The mind tries to develop time-bound strategies to overcome resistance. But strategies involve thought. Hidden within time-bound strategies is the idea that you need more time, more future, to be free. But future is just another thought. That thought is resistance to what is—now.

Instead of buying into mind strategies, simply notice the space in which things happen. You are that space. That space has no agenda, no strategy, to escape or overcome resistance. Space naturally allows the resistance to be as it is. In that allowing, there is no more energy fueling the resistance. Without that fuel, the resistance dies. This is a present seeing, not a time-bound strategy.

Life spontaneously happening

As you sit there right now, thoughts are arising on their own. You aren't choosing them. Those thoughts form a conceptual self. Because those thoughts are arising on their own and creating the self from their formation, who you really are is prior to those thoughts. Therefore, instead of saying that you aren't choosing the thoughts, it is more accurate to say that there is no "you" there to bring those thoughts about. Thoughts are simply happening spontaneously.

Emotions, sensations, states, and experiences are also happening spontaneously. Life is happening all on its own. The suffering and seeking arise when there is the belief that the conceptual self that is formed out of the spontaneously-arising thoughts is in control.

Instead of going into thought to try to figure this out or bring awakening about, just notice the thoughts and everything else spontaneously arising. Notice that what is noticing is not a thought. It is the source itself. One glimpse of this can change everything. The notions of choice and control are seen as illusory in that glimpse. If there is no choice and control, is there a "you" that could bring about anything called "enlightenment" or "awakening?" Aren't those ideas also spontaneously happening? Don't believe what is said here. Just look.

Be-ing

Do not think of being as an object. Thought deals mainly in objects. Through the use of concepts, the mind divides this One reality into separate parts. This is why the spiritual search happens. The mind believes that there is a person (object) separate from being (another object). This creates the misconception that you must take steps in time to recognize being. That is the time-bound spiritual search.

Don't think of being as a noun. Consider it a verb, as in be-ing. What does it mean to just be?

Be-ing is a timeless essence. It has no beginning or end because it is not an object. It is tempting to say that this being permeates everything. But that really isn't accurate. This being is none other than everything. It is an essence be-ing every thought, state, emotion, and experience. The very movement of trying to understand, conceptually, this reflection is being be-ing a movement of thought.

Being is not about a denial of doing things. In being, it is recognized that there is no doer. Doing continues to happen. But there is a realization that there is no person separate from being who needs to find something. There is only being be-ing the *thought* that this finding needs to happen.

Avoiding the negative and seeking the positive

Notice the desire to suppress, deny, avoid, or escape so-called "negative" feelings and states such as anger, sadness, boredom, loneliness, anxiety, grief, lack, and frustration. Also, notice the desire to maintain or recreate so-called "positive" feelings and states such as love, joy, happiness, contentment and excitement.

This movement to avoid the negative and seek the positive is the spiritual search. Whenever that movement is happening, a spiritual search is in place.

Oneness does not deny anything. Everything is included. Oneness is not about reaching a future positive state. It is the recognition that what you are *is* nothing being everything— every state and emotion.

In noticing this movement to avoid the negative and seek the positive in the moment it arises, the movement quiets. What is happening in that quieting is a recognition of what you really are. You are an unnamable, unchanging opening (also called 'being' or 'non-dual awareness') that never moves or changes. In recognizing what you really are, it is seen that these movements are temporary expressions that appear in that opening. These movements, whenever they appear, are included and seen as not other than what you are.

In this noticing, it is realized that there is nowhere to go. There is only this opening and whatever is appearing in it. Everything is allowed to be exactly as it is, whether it feels good or bad. That is the end of the search.

'This' includes everything

As you read about enlightenment or non-duality, it can appear that teachers and books are pointing to a state in which one sits quietly without much thought arising and without much happening. A moment of sitting quietly without thought and action is just a passing state. Although that state is possible, 'This' includes everything.

Almost anything that is said about enlightenment is a trap because it is not a particular experience, state, idea, or feeling.

'This' is a boundless, quiet essence appearing as everything that happens—every form, thought, feeling, experience, and state. 'This' is One appearing as many. 'This' includes obnoxious rock music, creating artistic projects, cooking an elaborate meal, taking a vacation, working all day, engaging in a passionate hobby, walking through the loud city streets with hundreds of people around you, agonizing in pain from an illness or injury and anything and everything else. It is a present realization that includes even the story of being a separate person but one that is ultimately free from attachment to that story. In that seeing, who you really are—beyond your name, form, and history—lives itself fully in this life in whatever way that happens naturally and effortlessly. It may be sitting quietly without thought. It may be feeling totally frustrated at work. Whatever is happening is happening to no one. That is the freedom.

Cause and effect

The question of cause and effect can be confusing if not seen from the proper perspective. The mind deals only in cause and effect. It deals in story, in time. In thought, there is a "you" who has come from the "past" and is going towards a "future." It seems logical to believe that "you" can reach enlightenment, happiness, or something else in the future—that there is action you can take today to reach something tomorrow.

All of that is purely conceptual. There is a timeless awareness here that sees the story of cause and effect as an appearance in awareness. The story of cause and effect arises uncaused. It arises involuntarily and spontaneously.

The notion of a "you" that is coming to some "future state" is merely a product of involuntary, dualistic thought. Thought is not independent of awareness. Without awareness, the story of cause and effect cannot arise. Recognizing timeless aware-ness is the doorway to non-dual realization. Recognizing timeless awareness is not a doing in time. You cannot do something now to reach awareness later. Timeless awareness is not subject to cause and effect. It is not subject to time. Recognizing timeless awareness is an end in and of itself: the direct, present recognition of the awake space from which the story of cause and effect involuntarily and spontaneously arises.

Seamless reality

Stop and look at life for one moment without thought. In just that one glimpse, life does not fall away. There it is in vivid detail. No thought is necessary to describe it. In fact, no thought describes it anyway. What is, is *what is*, before any words come to describe or define it. This one glimpse is Oneness. It is the direct experience of reality without the veil of thinking.

This reality is seamless. Although there are lines, textures, colors, and forms that create the appearance of separation, there is no true boundary between any two things. Every thing seamlessly bleeds into everything else. This glimpse of the seamless Oneness is a glimpse into what you really are. You are this One Life before that life is described and defined.

As thought returns to describe and define what is seen, notice that thought divides the One Life into fragments. It pictures a sky, as if the sky is separate from the earth. It pictures a desk, as if the desk is separate from the floor. This is what thought does. It creates the appearance of boundaries that are not really there.

Reality is one seamless whole. Be clear that thought creates the illusion of separation. Once this is clear, the recognition of Oneness is not obscured by thought as it returns.

You are a mystery

You are not any thought, feeling, reaction, role, identity, title, job position, belief, perspective or any other thing that appears within the field of awareness. You are that which sees those objects. You are what is looking. Notice any and all objects that arise in the field of awareness. See that none of those objects are you. Once you realize yourself as that which is looking, and no longer mistake yourself to be any object in awareness, you know who you truly are.

You also know that no description, concept, thought, story, or belief can ever capture who you truly are—not even the words "awareness" or "Oneness." Even the phrase "you are what is looking" is an object within awareness. The words human being, enlightenment, child of God, Christian, Muslim, Hindu, spiritual seeker or spiritual teacher are little stories or relative truths. They too are objects floating within awareness. You are not any of those thoughts. Thoughts are abstractions. They are signs or ideas pointing to an unnamable presence that is here prior to, during, and after thoughts arise and fall. No matter what you think about life, yourself, or God, that thought is temporarily arising and falling in awareness.

Do you see that you are a mystery? Do you see that even the word "mystery" is an abstraction, a little idea arising and falling in the field of awareness?

Conflict

The ego is unconscious and therefore blind to its own conflict and its habitual tendency to project that conflict out into the world. It makes itself right and others wrong including other people, religions, belief systems, political parties, and countries. The world is a reflection of the egoic mind. The healing of the conflict in the world does not occur through activism if that activism is itself oppositional and based in right v. wrong. True healing occurs through the realization of non-dual peace.

In each instance in which there is attachment to a belief that separates those who buy into the belief from those who do not or that makes you right and the other wrong or your group right and the other group wrong, a separate identity is created. There is a sense of self invested in the belief system. You create an illusory mental boundary between self and other, a self-serving division between right and wrong. In that moment, you are conflict. In seeing the conflict within your own mind in the moment it arises, the mind quiets. You realize your natural state as peace. When peace is realized within, you are no longer projecting conflict out into the world.

Ego

The ego is simply mind movement. It is escape from present awareness into past, future, and resistance to now. It is escape into a mental and emotional dream that creates a center called "you." This center sees itself as separate from others and from the rest of life. In order to keep self-centeredness alive, the dream has to keep dreaming itself. It does this through more escaping. Escape is resistance to what is.

Resistance is your greatest teacher. It reveals the details of the mental and emotional self-centered story. In this moment, when awareness is fully aware of what is arising, you see that there is no separate self. There is no ego. There is only identification with thought and the emotion that arises with it, which creates the illusion of a self at the center of life. That seeing is freedom.

Arguing with what is

In the egoic dream, you believe that life is supposed to be the way you think it should be. Your story of self is being projected out into the world. For example, thought tells you that the car in front of you should be driving faster. In reality, that car is moving at exactly the speed it is moving.

Thought tells you that your spouse should not nag you about picking your dirty clothes off the floor. In reality, your spouse is doing exactly what she is doing.

To argue with what is arising right now is insane. Your thoughts of others seem to be objectively true but they aren't. They result from an interpretation that is entirely personal. This personal interpretation is like a filter through which life is viewed. That filter is constantly arguing with what is. This mental arguing is a recipe for suffering and conflict. It creates a separation that is not really there.

Unconditional love, peace, and freedom are realized when you see this dream of self as it is being projected outward.

Problems

There is no such thing as a problem outside of identification with thought and emotion. In the moment when a problem arises, look at what is really happening. What is really happening is that thought and emotion are arguing with a present situation. Energy is directed at making the situation into a problem. This energy that identifies with thought and emotion is the separate self sense. That self thrives on problems.

The moment that you notice a problem, notice the thoughts and emotions that are creating the problem. This is where your argument with what is manifests itself. Notice that the problem is not "out there" in life. It is "in here" in your mental and emotional interpretation. As awareness sees this energy of problem-making, that seeing sets the problem free. The problem is seen to be just an illusion.

In complete alignment with whatever is happening in this moment, no problems arise. Life flows through you fluidly and effortlessly. You then meet each situation, including challenging situations, with a clarity and level of surrender that a separate self can never attain.

Compartmentalization

Spirituality is not separate from the rest of life. Thought tends to fragment life into illusory compartments, separated by illusory boundaries. For example, to thought, there is a clear distinction between "work life" and "spiritual life." It is very easy to believe that spirituality is happening only when you are meditating, reading a spiritual book, or praying.

There is only one spirit, animating all of life in a beautiful array of forms. Notice the ways in which you are acting as if your spiritual life or practice is somehow separate from your work life, personal life, or family life. Only the mind makes these illusory distinctions. It believes that meditation is spiritual but work is not, or prayer is spiritual but sex is not, or a church is spiritual but a sidewalk is not. These illusory distinctions keep the mind fragmented and lost in its incessant compartmentalization of life into spiritual v. not spiritual and right v. wrong. Thought then seeks those things that it believes will make the self more spiritual. The very act of spiritual searching is a denial of the spirit permeating all of life. In presence, it is realized that the idea that you must practice being spiritual or that spirit is "here" but not "there" is seen as just that... an idea.

Your core story

Your core story is that final illusory barrier between you and this great love called enlightenment. As waking up happens, there may be a sense that you are "not quite there"—a feeling that something is standing in the way of liberation. Trust your instincts. Some bedrock story of self is likely acting as a barrier, whether it is a story that you are a victim or an attachment to your profession, religion or other belief system. The notion of "not quite there" may lead you to believe that you need more time. But time will only give you more mind, more story. Instead, be willing to face your core story directly in this moment. All barriers are thought-created.

Because egoic movement is unconscious, it can be difficult to even see the core story that makes up the self-contraction within that does not want to fully and finally dissolve. Only presence will see it. Even when you are able to see what the core story is, there is often great fear in facing it through pure awareness. After all, this is your core identity. But the divine presence cannot be fully realized in you unless there is a recognition of that deepest story of self that you are holding onto for dear life. The core story is often the last and final frontier. In realizing that your core story is as illusory as all stories, 'This' is revealed to you.

The Search for "truth"

During the spiritual search, the sense of being a separate self (i.e., ego) hijacks the search for truth. It looks to abstract concepts of what God is, how it can become closer to God, what spirit is, what it means to be spiritual, what enlightenment would look and feel like, how to be more present, or how it can become more spiritual in the future. These are all concepts, learned and memorized from the past. This very moment is truth itself.

How can a concept present something truer than what is actually here in this moment? Thought, at its best, can merely act as a sign or a map that points to life. Look around. Life is now. Awareness is looking for itself. Stated another way, spirit is looking for itself. But it cannot find itself in an object. It cannot find itself in a concept. When this is recognized, the search is over. "Truth" is revealed. But it is seen not to be a concept. It is a realization that what is happening right now is all there is. What is happening right now is what is true.

Denial

The search for enlightenment in the future is a denial of the enlightenment that is always and already present. The search is a denial of life itself.

Unless this is seen, the spiritual search can last for years. The search is conceptual. It is one thought (you) chasing another thought (enlightenment). It's like a dog chasing his own tail. The search is designed to just keep going. It is not about finding. It is about continuing to search.

This cycle of thought-chasing-thought leads the mind to believe that there is a "me" coming to enlightenment in the future. When awareness sees this thought stream, that present seeing is enlightenment. The illusion of the person on a search falls away in that seeing. In the seeing, there is no more denial of life, no more denial of what is really happening, no more denial of the fact that enlightenment is what you are and what you have always been. The concept of "you" that is chasing after a future concept of "enlightenment" is obscuring the actual enlightenment that is your true nature in this moment.

Inattention

Notice when thought is referencing past, future, or resistance to now. These thoughts appear in awareness. When these thoughts appear, it *feels* like inattention. In other words, it feels like you are not here "in the now." Is that really true?

Inattention is merely an object in awareness. It is a movement of thought, a dream of past, future, or resistance to now. In noticing that movement, notice that there is often another voice that comments on the inattention. This voice says that you should not be lost in your self-centered story. The voice is trying to convince you that what is happening (i.e., inattention) should not be happening. Is that true? Is it true that something that is happening should not be happening including inattention? Is it true that thought should not arise? Only a thought would say that thought should not arise.

Instead of making a new self-centered story about whether you are or are not "present" enough, just notice what is. Noticing what is—including so-called "inattention"—allows what is to be just as it is. A thought within the time-bound story and the subsequent thought that tells you that you should not be lost in that story are both appearances in awareness. Be clear that you are the awareness. In that clarity, it is seen that no appearance can take you away from what you are.

Listening

Does thought listen? Imagine a friend telling you about the details of her day and, rather that hearing what is being said, noisy thoughts are coming up one by one in your mind. These thoughts may be questioning certain details of her story, agreeing or disagreeing with her assessment of some situation she is telling you about, or even wandering into details of your day or whether you fed the cats this morning.

Thought does not listen. Only awareness does. Recognize that you are the aware space in which your friend is talking. Sense the present awareness of the inner body and mind. That awareness is naturally awake and quiet. It effortlessly listens. If any noisy thoughts arise while listening, simply see them. In seeing them, the inward space recognizes itself again.

When a voice arises that tells you that "you should listen more," just notice that thought. That thought isn't listening. In noticing each thought, the thought is allowed to die its natural death. Every thought arises and falls from the space. As each thought dies, what is left is the space that is truly listening. This space contains true compassion. Therefore, any response to your friend that comes from that space will be naturally compassionate.

Fear

Fear is an actual movement of raw energy within the body. When fear is not seen directly by awareness, it fuels mental storytelling.

For example, you are someone who is horribly afraid of public speaking. Your boss demands that you give an oral presentation next week for your colleagues. As soon as you learn of this assignment, you start worrying about it.

When the mental story of next week's presentation remains unseen, you spend a week in fear, repetitively playing mental scenarios of the speaking engagement. This repetitive mental dreaming keeps you from being at peace now and interferes with your ability to prepare adequately for your speech.

Stop right where you are and look directly at any stories of future that are keeping you locked in fear. Watch those thoughts. Seeing them for what they are—a story of self—allows attention to return to this moment, where life actually is. Take your attention into the actual emotion of fear arising in the body. Simply notice that energy without mental commentary. Do not seek to avoid, escape, or think about the fear. Yet if a movement to avoid, escape, or think about it arises, simply notice that movement.

Notice that the awareness that sees the feeling of fear in the body and the thoughts of future is already at peace now.

Inner body awareness

Bring present awareness into the body and mind throughout the day, especially when you notice thought wandering into the story of self—into past, future, and resistance to now. Notice the awareness in your toes, your legs, your pelvic area, your stomach, your chest, your arms, your fingers, and your head. If any mental commentary arises during inner body awareness, simply see that commentary and bring attention back into the body and mind.

When inner space is aware of itself in this way, thought naturally quiets. It is seen that awareness throughout the body is one flowing energy field without boundaries. In noticing that the space of the inner body is one undivided space, this same undivided space is seen to be "out there"—outside the body. This is the realization that there is no boundary between you and the rest of life. Thought creates this illusory boundary.

Don't think of "inner body awareness" as a practice or doing in time. Thought is what places a practice in time. If the thought arises, "I should continue practicing inner body awareness so that I can become more present," just notice it. That story is a lie. There is no becoming to awareness. Noticing inner body awareness is an end in and of itself. It is a present seeing.

Simple being

As the story of self lodged in thoughts of past, future, and resistance to this moment is seen to be unreal, all there is, is simple being. This realization is so utterly simple and accessible that it is often missed. It is missed because it is looked for in thought or in a particular experience. But being is prior to any thought. It is also the ground of every experience and every thought.

Being does not mean "being a person who has realized something special." It is simply *being* appearing as everything that is happening, including the thought, "I have realized something special" and the thought, "I have not realized anything special." Being is naturally light, loving, and as free as the air. It is unencumbered by any thoughts or emotions arising from it. Yet it pushes nothing away. It does not try to stay in a place of no thought or no emotion. It is not trying to have a particular experience. It appears as a spiritual experience and a moment of frustration, all the same. It is the essence of everything. There is only this simple being, which is in alignment with the flow of the present moment. It is in fact none other than that flow.

Chasing after God

Does your belief system include the idea that you must search for God into the future? Look around. There is nothing outside this moment. There is no presence outside this moment. Can you really argue with that? If there is no presence outside this moment, can there be a presence of God outside this moment?

The separate self is a mental construct in time, contained within the thought realms of past, future, and resistance to now. Thought is mostly self-centered. It is always about you, where you have been, where you are going, and whether you have attained or will later attain a union with the God in your thoughts. Is God a thought?

When you live as if God can only be found in the future, you set yourself up for not finding God. Conceptually, you create a "you" that is separate from "God." This just fuels the spiritual search.

God is looking through your eyes. The presence that is here, now, is timeless. It is eternal. It is outside of time. Therefore, it is outside of the separate self. It is beyond (or not of) personal will and choice. It is beyond (not of) the mind. It is beyond (not of) the conceptual ideas of "you" seeking "God."

The teaching of present moment awareness is simply saying, "come out of the stream of time (self) and into this moment (God)."

One Truth, many expressions

The major religions are pointing to one truth. In Hinduism, Maya is an illusion, a veiling of the true, unitary Self, also known as Brahman. In Buddhism, suffering is transcended and the perfect peace of mind known as Nirvana is realized. In the Tao Te Ching, the Tao is the "Great Way," where man's resistance to life subsides and a harmonization with the Tao is realized, an awareness of one's deep oneness with the entirety of the universe. In Christianity, sin serves as a barrier to having a complete relationship with God and Jesus Christ saves people from their sins, reconciling them with God.

Each religion is pointing to a spiritual transformation where truth is revealed beyond the ego. Thought tends to believe that the truth is contained within the words of whatever religion one is following. But the words are pointing to a truth beyond words. The enlightenment to which this book points is the liberation from attachment to any ideas about the truth into the living realization of that truth.

It sounds pretty heady until you see how simple it really is. In the present moment, the truth to which the words God, Brahman, the Tao, and Nirvana point is realized to be already here, already present, and not at all separate from the very awareness in which the idea of "you" appears as a thought.

This love

As awareness is realized to be what you truly are, the story of you as a separate self falls away. Awareness is unconditional love. This love is that which is looking from your eyes right now. You cannot find this love in time or get it from others. It is what you are. This love loves the whole of life because it is the whole seeing itself through the vessel of the individual body and mind. In that seeing, there is no longer an investment in making things personal.

This love is not like romantic love or other kinds of conditional, attached love. Attached, conditional love exists within the field of opposites. It is all about the separate self. As a separate self, you want someone to give you what you think you need from them. As long as the person gives you what you seek, love is there. But the moment the person fails to give back the personal gratification you are seeking from the relationship, the love turns to an opposite feeling of anger or even hate.

The unconditional love that is being spoken of here is unattached and unconditional. It is already whole. It loves regardless of what happens. It isn't seeking anything from the other because it sees no other. It sees only love. The movement of seeking personal gratification in relationships is the separate self sense. As that movement releases, unconditional love is realized.

Spiritual practices die on their own

Before you pray or meditate this morning, ask yourself this question: Is it true that peace is not already here in this moment? As you begin to ask that question seriously, you may start to see certain beliefs pop up that are keeping you locked into the idea that you are somehow separate from peace, God, enlightenment or whatever it is you are seeking. The idea of separateness is entirely thought-created. You literally think into existence the notion that there is a "you" separate from that which you seek. You dream up the idea that you must do something before you can attain something else. In that way, you give yourself more time, which just means more mind. Time is mind. Investigate this for yourself. Notice that you cannot entertain the thought of future attainment without thinking.

Do you see the thoughts that tell you that you need to pray or meditate in order to achieve something? Those thoughts are the only thing obscuring the realization that peace is all there is. God is all there is. Enlightenment is all there is. Under the movements of seeking towards the concepts of peace, God, or enlightenment, the actual truth to which those words are pointing is already here now. Spiritual practices die on their own when it is realized that there is nothing you could ever do to get closer to the divine. You are not separate from it.

Noticing at work

While at work today, notice space. Notice the space within the body, all around you, and in every room. Notice the space between your fingers and around your arm and hands as you reach for an object.

Notice each step wherever you go, even to the bathroom. Just notice one foot in front of the other. Notice the body as it moves towards or away from something or somebody. Notice each time your thoughts appear to be somewhere else, in some dream of time, while life is here in this moment. Notice that you have no control or choice about any of these things. They just happen.

Notice the breath coming in and out of your chest. Notice your head turn when a co-worker calls your name. Notice any tendency to resist or judge your co-worker while she is speaking to you. Notice that you are the aware space in which your co-worker appears.

Every time you notice what is already happening, attention is here in the space of now. You are recognizing that you are the timeless awareness that is noticing. Don't think of this as a practice in time. Don't believe the idea that you are noticing or being mindful so that you will reach enlightenment later. That's just another thought. Notice that thought. Noticing does not happen in the time stream. Time is arising in the awareness that is noticing.

Beyond words

No matter what concept is used to point to the ultimate truth, the concept is not it. The words 'This,' God, Oneness, non-duality, Brahman, the Tao, enlightenment, liberation, presence, and the divine are merely representations, all of which belong to the world of dualistic form. The truth involves not only form, but also a formless realm that cannot be described. It cannot be described because it is truly without form, meaning beyond or deeper than the level of ideas. It is the transparent essence of life permeating everything. This formless essence appears obscured when there is attachment to words pointing to this essence.

If you stood next to a tree with a paintbrush and canvas and you painted that tree as realistically as you could, the painting would never be the actual tree. It would lack its formless essence. In the same way, no thought about this truth is the actual truth. At best, it is a representation.

In seeing that this truth is not in the words, the mind stops trying to "get it." It sees that no attempt to understand the truth conceptually will actually reveal the truth. In that seeing, what is being pointed to with words is revealed to be none other than what you are. This realization is the indescribable truth to which the words God, Oneness, non-duality, Brahman, the Tao, enlightenment, liberation, presence, and the divine are pointing. Don't get stuck in the words.

The embodiment of oneness

Oneness is not some fancy belief system or grand philosophy. It is beyond thought. It is a truth that cannot be expressed. It is simply lived effortlessly, naturally, and lovingly.

Kabir once said, "Many understand the drop merging into the ocean but few understand the ocean merging into the drop." Beyond the conceptualization and the experience of Oneness, there is an embodiment of Oneness. This is the living truth of Oneness, embodied in the human form. As the old saying goes, you will know him "by his fruits." It is easy to walk around uttering fancy words such as "it's all One" or claiming to have had a Oneness experience. But the degree to which one is living in separation and conflict with others and resisting or escaping from what is in this moment is most telling.

The embodiment of Oneness is an exalted way of pointing to simple presence itself. When life is lived in this moment without resistance, conflict, and separation—when love and peace infuse each action and relationship—Oneness is embodied. The ocean has merged into the drop.

JUNE

To remain or abide as awareness does not mean we get into some state called "awareness" and then find a way to remain in that state. To remain as awareness is to simply recognize that all states and experiences are the continuous flow of awareness.

—— John Astin

Man will not find the truth through an idea

Man will not find truth through an idea. He will only chase after the idea. There are a lot of spiritual ideas out there and a lot of clever ways of pointing to truth. But truth is only ever right now because life is only right now. Truth is timeless. 'This' is it.

When spiritual concepts are heard, there is a tendency to identify with the concepts and store them away as memory. There is nothing wrong with memorizing concepts. That is the mind's natural function. But if the ideas are taken to be truth, there is no looking beyond ideas. Thought tends to stay stuck in a cycle of seeking confirmation of its content. So the Christian goes looking for Christ. The Hindu looks for Brahman. The Buddhist looks for Buddha nature. This is the "me" looking to confirm its story.

The truth to which all these words are pointing is present awareness. You are the presence from which these ideas come and go. Instead of blindly believing spiritual ideas, question them.

See that the word "truth" is, itself, an idea. Ideas are merely representations, abstractions. Let ideas point you to this moment, then let them die. See that the presence you are in this moment is appearing as every idea. In recognizing that even the greatest ideas about truth are forms appearing and disappearing in formless, present awareness, actual truth is revealed.

Searching v. noticing

Searching has the element of time in it. It is based on the idea that there is a "you" that must engage in some method or practice to find enlightenment in time (tomorrow or next year). Be clear that time is mind. The notion of "future" arises only as a present thought. The notion of "you" also arises only as a present thought. Searching happens when this is not seen and, instead, the mind chases after concepts. It's like being on a treadmill. It feels like you are going somewhere but really you are just moving your legs, exhausting yourself.

Noticing has a totally different quality than searching. It takes no time at all. Noticing is the present seeing of what is actually here now. What is here is a timeless aware space in which everything is happening—thoughts, emotions, experiences, states, and situations. This aware space sees the concept "you" searching for the concept "enlightenment" in some other concept called "future." In that sense, time arises in that timeless space. That is just another way of saying that mind arises in that space. So what is enlightenment if it is not a concept? Is it real? Yes! Enlightenment is the present recognition that your true identity is this aware space from which thoughts arise, not the thoughts that arise in that space, and that the thoughts do not have a separate existence from the space.

Truth

Does your search for truth involve only mentally weighing and comparing ideas against one another? In searching with the mind, you pick whatever belief provides mental security and a sense of self. You buy into beliefs in order to protect yourself from having to fully face the fear of the unknown. But truth is not about feeling secure. It is about what is true.

Are you afraid that your core beliefs will be threatened if you question them? Anything that is threatened or destroyed by mere questioning is not real. It is only a belief you are holding onto so that you do not have to fully face your fear of the unknown.

Hidden within every belief is doubt and fear. Doubt is mental uncertainty about your belief that is repressed so that the belief can continue. Fear is like the energetic glue in the body that holds the belief together. In questioning a belief, awareness is finally able to see the hidden mental doubt and the fear that unconsciously fuels the belief. By seeing the fear directly, without the veil of mental analysis, the fear is seen to be merely raw energy. In that seeing, fear dissipates naturally. It is seen that there was a false sense of self invested in that belief. As the belief falls away, there you are—pure presence—free of the need for a false, mind-created self based solely in fear. That is truth.

Simple presence

Simple presence is the total allowing of what is already happening. As you get ready for work or to go wherever you are going this morning, notice what is happening totally beyond your control. Thoughts are appearing. Emotions are happening. Perhaps there is tiredness or grumpiness, but it's just happening involuntarily. You aren't choosing any of these things.

As you are getting ready, notice that your arm involuntarily and spontaneously moves towards the closet to find clothes to wear. You don't have to give the command, "Arm! Move to the closet." The moving of the arm just happens. Notice that, even if there was a thought prior to moving the arm such as, "I need to find something to wear," that thought arose spontaneously and involuntarily also. It came out of nowhere.

Life is happening completely on its own. The mental voice that arises to resist, manipulate, and change what is happening is what creates the suffering and seeking. It creates the illusion that you have control over what is happening. In seeing that even the voice that arises to resist, manipulate, and change happens beyond your control, there can be a natural resting into what is. That is simple presence. No one brings it about. It happens completely on its own through noticing that life is happening to you. You are not bringing it about. In that seeing, the suffering and seeking energy is released.

Awareness

Be clear about what awareness is. Take a moment to pick two objects within your view in the room. Make sure the objects are at least three feet apart. Let's say it's a lamp and a door. When you are looking only at the lamp or only at the door, there is focused attention. For the most part, attention is directed primarily at the object while the surrounding objects seem vague in the periphery.

Now, instead of focusing on one of the particular objects, notice the space that holds or allows both objects but is focused on neither object. This is a gentle space that simply allows. It isn't focused on the lamp or on the door. This space just recognizes itself as that which allows those two objects, and all other objects in the room, to just be as they are. This is spacious awareness. It is what knows the present moment directly. This is what you are.

When these reflections invite you to notice thoughts, emotions, experiences, states, or other objects or movements, it is not an invitation to place focused attention on those objects or movements. It is an invitation to recognize this spacious awareness and see that these things are appearing and disappearing in it. As you become comfortable knowing that this awareness is what you are, it is realized that the objects or movements in awareness are not separate from awareness.

Delaying the simple recognition of presence

It is easy to turn non-duality into a philosophy or spiritual path leading to some future attainment. The mind gets preoccupied in the drive to understand non-duality conceptually or to have a powerful spiritual experience or shift. Turning the realization to which these words are pointing into a philosophy or spiritual path is an act of mental reductionism. These words are pointing to simple presence, which is available only now. This presence is not a thought or a goal in time. Thoughts and goals arise from presence.

Although the recognition that presence is what you are may happen gradually, the only point of entry—so to speak—is this moment.

The recognition is apparently delayed by trying to figure out non-duality through thought and by seeking some future attainment of it. The recognition is only available when focus turns away from trying to mentally grasp spiritual awakening and chase future attainment, and towards the simple presence that is aware of what is arising right now.

In seeing what is arising now, it appears that identification with spiritual ideas and goals delays or obscures presence. This presence is immediately available as the very life that you are before you try to grasp what that means conceptually or reach towards some future experience. In reality, that presence cannot be truly delayed or obscured by anything because it is appearing as everything, including as every thought and goal.

Peace

People claim to want peace. They engage in spiritual methods, adopt belief systems, protest war, express opinions, join groups devoted to bringing inner or outer peace and take other actions to bring about peace in their lives or for the world.

Most efforts to bring about peace involve doing some action now in the hope that it will bring about peace at some future point. Peace cannot be found in the future. "Future" is just a presently arising thought.

The peace that is being pointed to here is so directly and immediately available that it is overlooked each time there is identification with thought, emotion, or some other finite form that is arising including the idea that you must do something now in order to find peace later. Peace is rest and this rest is realized only in this moment in the direct recognition of present, formless awareness. In that recognition, it is seen that every movement comes from that restful awareness and is not separate from it. In that seeing, there is no longer identification with the movement. Everything—every movement—is then allowed to be exactly as it is.

Humility

Thought dreams up a center known as "me." That dream is all about what happened in the past to "me," what I hope will happen in the future to "me," and how I am not satisfied with what is happening right now to "me."

The word humility points to the absence of attachment to that stream of thought. In this realization, thoughts still arise but the energy of attachment to them releases. It is realized that there is no center to life. There is great love and freedom in that release.

You can philosophize for years about the meaning of the word "humility" without ever tasting the real truth to which the word points. To realize humility, simply notice in each moment when thought is in past, future, or resistance to now. Notice thoughts of wanting to be right, wanting to be someone special in relation to someone else including higher, better, smarter, or more spiritual than another. Notice thought's tendency to "one-up" someone, especially in a spiritual discussion.

In being aware of this thought movement, its self-centered nature is seen. The sense of a separate self is seen as a dream of thought. What is left is awareness. Awareness is naturally humble. The story of "you" cannot achieve humility. Humility happens only in the absence of attachment to that story.

Spirituality for personal gain

There are many spiritual methods and belief systems that promise future fulfillment, happiness, money or other success. If you look closely, the whole idea that you can gain something from spirituality is based on a false premise, which is that there is a separate "you" that lacks something.

Although you may be able to employ practices or hold beliefs that make you happier or more successful, mature spirituality is realizing that life is not about you or what you can get. As long as you seek enlightenment, enlightenment is unavailable. In seeking, you act from the false concept that you are a separate self that lacks something. It is that very concept that creates the need for a search.

Enlightenment is the realization that there is no separate "you" to gain anything personally from life. There is only life and you are THAT. No separation. In that realization, your entire resistance to what is vanishes and the deepest truth of spirituality is revealed. This truth is impossible to express. But be clear that it isn't about personal gain. If anything, it is about the loss of something—the loss of the sense of separation. In that loss, there is great freedom, love, joy, and peace.

Rejection is a teacher

Whenever you encounter rejection and the feelings of diminishment that accompany it, notice that a hidden mental story is revealing itself. Rejection is showing you that there is a false image in the mind of who you are. Those who reject you are merely holding up a mirror to reveal who you think you are. Who you think you are is not who you really are. It is a story. Stories are not real. This is why they can be threatened.

Let rejection teach you that you are not any story. You are the awareness from which stories arise. Rejection is always revealing the ways in which the false "me" tries to protect itself from vulnerability by holding onto a false image. A false image of self is, by its very nature, vulnerable. Notice any strategies or analysis the mind uses to avoid feeling vulnerable. Avoidance is resistance to what is. See that awareness is naturally open to whatever appears in awareness including rejection and feelings of diminishment. Avoidance and resistance are also movements that appear and disappear in awareness. These movements are none other than awareness. Everything that arises is a perfect expression of awareness.

Once you know that your true nature is awareness, you see that what you really are can never be threatened or rejected. In this seeing, life is allowed to be just as it is. There is no need for a false image anymore.

Enslavement to spiritual ideas

The greatest spiritual ideas reveal that your true nature is naturally unattached to spiritual ideas. Man has created a string of ideas including Hinduism, Buddhism, Christianity, and Non-Duality. Each of the ideas is pointing to an absolute truth beyond the idea itself.

The real truth to which all these ideas point is inexpressible and cannot be known through the conceptual mind. It has nothing to do with attaching to some spiritual idea or persuading others of some belief. This truth cannot be defended because it cannot be owned on a personal level. It is beyond the time-bound, thought-based story of a person. It is a realization in which the entire world of ideas collapses and the energy that attached to those ideas is released. In that collapse and release, there is a deep knowing that cannot be expressed through dualistic words.

In the willingness to see right now the ways in which you are enslaved to spiritual ideas, complete freedom and unconditional love are seen to be your true nature. This is not something the mind grasps by thinking about freedom and love. It is the direct knowing of what you are beyond ideas about what you are. The words merely point to the recognition.

Relationship is a mirror

Relationship is a mirror. Objects, situations, and people are acting as mirrors in which your story of self is being reflected back to you. When you enter a situation and make a judgment that it should not be happening, that situation is showing you your story of self. In that moment, the story is, "I cannot be happy or at peace until this situation changes." In resisting the situation, you are keeping alive the illusion that you are separate from that situation.

In the moment you make a judgment of someone, you are defining who you are in relation to the other. For example, if you judge someone as attractive, the story of self is that you are also attractive or that you are ugly in comparison to that person. Hidden within thought's judgment of others is comparison between you and the others. The self is trying to be someone in relation to someone else. It is seeking to be separate from the rest of life.

In truly seeing that relationship is a mirror, the movement to define a self in relation to objects, situations, and people quiets. This is sometimes called Oneness because when the sense of a separate self is seen through, it is realized that there is only 'This' and you are not separate from 'This.' It is realized that the apparently separate objects, situations, and people are all reflections of 'This.'

Misinterpreting the message

Does recognizing timeless awareness mean that you follow whatever impulse arises in awareness, including the impulse to cheat on your spouse or hurt others?

To the mind, awareness may look like a state of ignorance, apathy, depression, or nihilism. This view results from trying to grasp the pointers conceptually rather than looking to where the words are actually pointing.

The actual awareness to which these words are pointing is naturally free, loving, peaceful, and open. It is not a particular state, attitude or impulse. It is the ground or essence of all states, ideas, impulses and attitudes. It is a fundamental Oneness and therefore an unconditional love of life. If there truly is no separation and if your true nature is unconditional love, is there a "me" who would desire to harm "myself" or "others?"

'This'

Notice the space of now. It is changelessly present. No matter what happens within the space, the space is always here. In this space, thoughts arise. Feelings are felt. Sensations are sensed. Sounds are heard. Experiences are experienced. But the space never changes or leaves. That space resonates with the awareness that is your true nature. It is not separate from awareness.

Is spacious awareness separate from the things that arise in it? Don't think about that question, just look in your direct experience. Notice that to even say that there is a solid boundary between space and objects, awareness and thought, silence and sound, or formlessness and form is dualistic. There is nothing wrong with dualistic concepts. They also arise in 'This.' But notice that only thought is interpreting a boundary between these dualistic opposites. Without thought, there is only 'This.'

The pointing here is not about reaching a thoughtless state. It is simply pointing to what is so immediately accessible and obvious that it is often missed. It is pointing to the fact that life is simply arising now as One Life and that separation occurs only within a dream of thought. When thought is completely believed, the world appears divided. But when thought is allowed to simply arise and fall without attachment, Oneness is realized.

That which is already awake

Why is there so much seeking for awareness if awareness is always and already here? Awareness, when it is fully recognized to be what you really are, contains within it genuine love, compassion, humility, and peace. When you first hear these words, the words resonate on a level that is deeper than the mind. This resonance paradoxically draws you into a spiritual search for what you already are.

Seeking is based on a misperception that is naturally corrected when it is realized that what you are seeking is what is seeking. Awareness is looking for itself. It tends to look in every object that appears on its screen. In that way, it misses the simple and obvious recognition that awareness is what is looking right now (and always).

The search itself is a complete illusion. The search arises in awareness. If you look closely, the search is comprised mostly of thoughts about future, fueled by a sense of lack. These thoughts arise from awareness and are therefore not independent of awareness. The thoughts will never find anything called "spiritual awakening." Awareness itself is already awake. All that can happen is a recognition of that which is already awake.

Effort

When you first begin your spiritual search, effort seems necessary. There is a pull towards the truth that is completely natural. You may find yourself going to bookstores to look for spiritual books, attending church and spiritual groups, going to meditation, doing yoga or engaging in some other spiritual practice or method. There is nothing wrong with any of that. It is all part of 'This.'

But this book is about the possibility of seeing that effort obscures the real truth of who you are— the loving peace and quietness that lies under all the effort and that is inherent in awareness. When it is realized that awareness is what is looking, the whole movement of effort towards finding awareness is seen as futile. Awareness is naturally effortless. The movement of effort towards what is naturally effortless is seen as ridiculous. It's like a fish swimming upstream to find water.

The spiritual ego

Thought just wants something to hold onto. It is seeking to understand conceptually the unnamable truth to which the words consciousness, enlightenment, non-duality, God, Allah, presence, Buddha, nirvana, 'This,' and spirit are pointing.

There is nothing wrong with any of those words. But they belong to the realm of form and are merely signs pointing to the formless spirit that animates life in every form.

When formless awareness is recognized, attachment to form releases. By simply noticing attachment to spiritual ideas, those ideas lose their grip and a natural surrender happens. It is realized that form is formlessness and vice versa, something thought cannot grasp. That does not mean that the words are no longer used. It means that there is no attachment to them. It is realized that form is an expression of formlessness.

The separate self is attachment to form (to ideas). The self makes its idea (e.g., God, non-duality, Brahman, Buddha) more important than the others' ideas in an attempt to keep the story of a "separate me" alive. This is the spiritual ego. The spiritual ego seeks to have its conception of truth prevail in the world of ideas. The spiritual ego is just as false as any other story of "me." It is bringing conflict to the world under the guise of "spirituality."

Surrender

Surrender is one of the hallmarks of non-dual realization (i.e., enlightenment). At first glance, when you hear about the spiritual principle of "surrender," it may sound as if you need to do or become something or someone in order to be more surrendered. No. Surrender is an attribute of your natural state of presence.

The separate self contraction cannot become surrendered because the contraction is resistance to what is. If there is nothing you can do to gain surrender or be more surrendered, why even discuss surrender? Surrender is what is already here in this moment under all your efforts to obtain something from others, from life, and from the spiritual search. It is what is here in the absence of resistance to what is.

In order for surrender to be realized as an attribute of presence, notice the mental and emotional seeking and resistance that appears to obscure presence. Instead of doing something, notice what is already being done. Notice the ways in which thought and emotion are resisting what is and seeking something from others, from life, and from the spiritual search. In allowing these movements to meet the light of awareness, there is no more attachment to the movements. What is left is the natural rest of surrender. In that natural resting, it is realized that presence was never really obscured. There was merely a misperception happening. You falsely believed that you were the separate self contraction.

Inner body awareness

Notice the space within the body, the awareness that is aware of every sensation, every movement, and every emotion. See that you are that present space. This is not a prescription to do something in order to achieve some goal or end result in the future. It is a present invitation to recognize the aliveness that you are prior to the story in the mind of who you are.

The space within your body is already there. When thought creates the veil of a separate self, with its stream of incessant story-telling, this space within is often missed. You are completely "in your head" with thought, so to speak.

Notice the emotions and sensations that arise within that space, regardless of whether they feel "good" or "bad." Do not try to bring about the end of a negative emotion or sensation. If fear arises, simply notice it and notice the space in which it is arising. See that awareness naturally allows the fear and has no agenda to bring about its end. Only the mind has an agenda to change what is arising. That agenda is the spiritual search.

In the moment of realizing fully this inner body awareness and whatever form is arising within it, you see that the space (formlessness) and the emotion (form) are not two. The emotion is simply the space taking a shape temporarily and then dissolving back into the space from which it arose.

Identification with thought

Thought is not bad. It is a natural and beautiful expression of awareness. Suffering and searching occur when there is identification with thought. This identification creates the sense of a separate self.

The separate self is nothing more than energy within the body and mind that focuses on and contracts around the thoughts that arise. The result is repetitive, unnecessary thinking, most of which revolves around a story of "me." This story consists of essentially three thought realms: the past, the future, and resistance to now. The sense of separation is kept alive by continuously identifying with thoughts within these three realms.

The separate self is a story about how the past is unsatisfactory. The past is "me." The sense of separation is further fueled through resistance to what is happening now and through seeking some future moment when life will be better.

Spiritual awakening is not found in the future. It is a present seeing that the story of the time-bound, thought based "me" is not real. That seeing can only take place right now because time itself is part of the story. In this present realization, the energy behind the "me" story releases. The mind quiets on its own. Peace and freedom are realized to be natural attributes of presence. Thoughts still arise but they are no longer identified with.

Beyond belief

The personal story of "me" is in the business of seeking something from life. Usually it is seeking something to enhance the story. This is often on such an unconscious level that it is simply missed.

At some point along the way, the story may turn to spiritual belief. It may seek enhancement of its personal story by believing this or that doctrine or philosophy or following this or that path.

Enlightenment is not about seeking enhancement of the personal story of "me." It is about realizing that the entire story is an illusion. It is the realization that the endeavor to gain a "more spiritual self" through belief just keeps self-centeredness in place. A belief is just more of the "me" story. Belief welcomes conflict as the "me" insists that its belief is right and that the others are wrong.

What is being pointed to with the word "enlightenment" is beyond belief. It cannot be known through thought. Therefore, no belief will reveal it. It is the natural wakefulness of simple presence. In that wakefulness, unconditional love and liberation are realized. Stated another way, spirit wakes up to itself. This spirit is what is being sought in the spiritual search. It cannot be found in an idea. Ideas merely point to it. They are abstractions. Spirit must be directly recognized as the very life you are. Once it is realized, there is no need for belief.

Seeking pleasure and avoiding pain

The ego's objective is to seek pleasure and avoid pain. But pleasure and pain are two sides of the same coin. They arise mutually and simultaneously as dualistic opposites in the world of form. The concept of pleasure would be unrecognizable without pain, its opposite. The trap within the world of dualistic opposites is that the more you seek pleasure, the more you set yourself up for suffering when the other shoe drops. And the other shoe will drop. Pain will have to be faced at one point or another. Pain and pleasure simply do not exist without each other.

Emotional and psychological pain is a portal to presence. It is telling you exactly where you are identified with some story of past, future, or resistance to this moment. It is telling you what you are trying to avoid. Pain does not truly go away when you try to avoid or escape it by chasing after its dualistic opposite—pleasure (or the absence of pain). It simply goes dormant. This is the other shoe waiting to drop.

In the recognition of awareness, it is seen that awareness is naturally open to emotional and psychological pain in the very moment it arises. Awareness has no agenda to escape pain. In no longer escaping pain, the dualistic cycle of seeking pleasure and avoiding pain loses its strength. Non-dual presence allows all duality to arise naturally. This is radical non-resistance, the denial of nothing.

Piling up

Have you experienced frustration at work or even at home when it feels as though various projects must be done within a short period of time? Do you see how the piling up of projects or things on a to-do list creates a mental barrier to the accomplishment of the task at hand?

The "piling up" of projects, to-do items, tasks, and things is completely a mental story. Whenever time is entered into the picture in that way, the mind appears clouded and distracted. It is difficult to bring attention to the task at hand when thoughts of the various other tasks later in the day are floating in and out of consciousness.

As the story of what you must do later in the day arises in the mind, simply see it for what it is—a thought. Do not judge it. Do not beat yourself up for not being present. Yet if judging and beating yourself up arise, see that those are just thoughts also. In noticing the stories, they are allowed to come and then go. The seeing of the stories is gently reminding you that reality is what is happening now. Reality is the doing of the task at hand. Things "piling up" is a mental story. Even if some practical planning is necessary, notice that the planning itself arises as present thought.

Accumulated negative energy in the body

In the unconscious state, attachment to painful stories of past creates an accumulation of negative energy within the body. This accumulation is essentially stored negative mental and emotional energy lying dormant within your mind and body. The story associated with this negative energy can be based in childhood abuse or trauma, bad relationships or marriages, a victim mentality, or any number of other stories. The energy tends to arise when you entertain that past or in relationships with people with whom you have a history of conflict.

Nothing needs to be done about this accumulated energy except a noticing of the space in the inner body and mind that is naturally aware of the energy as it arises. This space is naturally open to any feelings of fear, frustration, sadness, loneliness, or anger that arise and the corresponding stories that accompany the emotions.

In this conscious space, this accumulated energy is allowed to arise without trying to neutralize, analyze or escape it. Awareness has no agenda towards the energy. Only the mind seeks to neutralize, analyze and escape it. Awareness simply allows whatever arises to be just as it is. This is total acceptance. This acceptance releases the energy, revealing the awake, naturally peaceful presence that is the source of the energy.

The cycle of suffering

You are doing the laundry and a story of yesterday's argument with your spouse arises along with anger about what he said. In the unconscious state, thought grabs a hold of that story and does not let go. You analyze and rehash the details of the conflict with your spouse and formulate a rebuttal that you intend to bring up when the argument continues with your spouse.

Before you know it, this story has a hold of you. You spend half the day thinking about how you are right and he is wrong. You feel resentment towards him as you replay the story. You are in the cycle of suffering.

Throughout the day, various temporary thoughts and emotions, such as the story of the argument with your spouse, arise and fall. Suffering happens only because consciousness gets stuck on some temporary thought or emotion that arises. The "me" does not want to let go. It wants to be right—feel vindicated. The goal of the "me" illusion is to keep the sense of separation and self-centeredness alive.

Notice the temporary thoughts and emotions that arise throughout the day and the 'larger' inward space in which they arise and fall. When you find yourself holding onto a story, simply notice it. Attention returns to the inward space. You step out of the illusion of "me" and into the simple truth. The truth is that laundry is being done. It's that simple.

Waking up from the movie of ego

Imagine you are in a theater watching a movie. It's a suspense thriller. You have attached emotionally to the main character. You have seen the struggles the character has been through. You identify with her story. You are on the edge of your seat, waiting desperately to see how it all ends—to see the grand finale when everyone lives happily ever after. When the movie ends, you know it is not real and that it never was. You are able to walk away, liberated from attachment to the movie.

The personal story of "me" is much like a movie. You have an unsatisfactory past. You are seeking the future to bring some release of that dissatisfaction.

The pointers in this book are about the possibility of waking up from the movie of "me." It is much like sitting back in your chair at the theater and realizing, "This is just a movie. It is not real." In that relaxation, the present moment is realized to be the only true reality. The sense of a "separate me" with all of its suffering and searching in time is seen to be a script in the mind. What is left is unconditional love and unbounded freedom. It is then realized that completion is already here in this moment. There was never anything to seek.

Effortlessness

Enlightenment is the natural, effortless state. Effortlessness cannot be achieved by effort. The person who is trying to achieve enlightenment is actually obscuring the natural, effortless enlightenment that is his true nature in this moment.

The word "person" here refers to that thought-based story in the mind that resists life and believes that it can and must control life and manipulate outcomes. That story is applying effort in an attempt to achieve a future goal—whether it be the resolution of conflict, happiness, romantic love, a better appearance, material success, or spiritual growth.

Enlightenment is realized only in the absence of that entity who is applying effort towards future. Effort emanates from the underlying idea that the person is somehow separate from life and other people and that he therefore must resist life and others in order to bring about change. In seeing that this is just an idea, all the energy behind the effort releases and there is only 'This.' 'This' is the expressible realization that you are not a person living in time. You are the present awareness in which that story arises. That is the end of effort.

Sensitivity is a gift

Sensitivity—if it merely results in egoic reactions that remain unconscious—is a source of suffering. Reacting unconsciously to the hurtful things people say and do strengthens the mental and emotional story that believes it is separate from the "others" that are causing pain. You may find it difficult to function in social situations if you are continuously hurt by what people say and do.

In the proper perspective, however, sensitivity is truly a gift. Instead of creating suffering, sensitivity can be an alarm bell that alerts you to the presence of irritation, frustration, hurt, fear, and anger that arise in your inner body and mind in reaction to outer stimuli. It is a tool that reveals the content of the story of self that separates you from the world "out there" and causes internal suffering.

Each time you are hurt emotionally and mentally by what someone says or does, notice that you are the awareness that sees the thought and emotion. In this way, you begin to see where your psychological and emotional pain lies—what your deepest rooted story of self is. In allowing sensitivity to make the story of self conscious, the story can no longer survive. In that dissolution, you realize that suffering is never caused by the "others." It arises from not seeing the story of separateness in the mind.

Distractions

Notice what appears to distract you away from the present moment. Thought takes off on a line of thinking and, before you know it, you are reliving mentally and emotionally something that happened five minutes ago or five years ago. You are cleaning the kitchen counter and thought gets distracted into what is going to happen later in the day or tomorrow. You are driving down the road and some guy pulls in front of you. After you pass him, thought continues to tell the story for miles down the road about how rude and disrespectful that guy is.

Notice that what you take to be distractions are really just movements of thought. These movements arise and fall in presence, which is what you truly are. In simply noticing the thought, there is a recognition of this presence. It is seen that thought arises from and is not separate from that presence. This reveals that there is really no such thing as a distraction. There is only ever awareness and the appearances of awareness.

The One and the many

Oneness includes the many. Non-duality is not only a realization of the formless realm or non-conceptual awareness, but also a recognition that form is none other than formlessness. Form includes people, jobs, relationships, ideas, feelings and all other things. So what is the difference between living life as a separate self and living life from non-dual realization? The only real difference is that instead of believing that you are a person separate from the rest of life, there is a recognition that what you are in the deepest sense is an unnamable presence. That presence is also the essence of everything you see. In that way, what you are is not separate from the rest of life. This seeing reveals a natural compassion, love, peace, and joy.

Your very essence is spacious awareness. This spacious awareness is prior to the story of being a separate person. But don't let the realization stay there. See that the nothingness of awareness is appearing as absolutely everything.

As soon as the mind starts to associate non-duality only with nothingness, it is holding onto an idea about non-duality. That is not non-duality. Although the word "non-duality" is an idea, it is pointing to reality itself. In reality, form and formlessness are not two. The One is appearing as the many. Don't try to grasp that intellectually. Look to where the words are pointing in your direct experience.

JULY

*Many spiritual seekers get "stuck" in emptiness, in the absolute,
in transcendence. They cling to bliss, or peace, or indifference.
When the self-centered motivation for living disappears,
many seekers become indifferent. Stuck in a form of divine
indifference, such people believe they have reached the top of the
mountain when actually they are hiding out halfway up its slope.
Enlightenment does not mean one should disappear into the realm
of transcendence. To be fixated in the absolute is simply the polar
opposite of being fixated in the relative. With the dawning of
true enlightenment, there is a tremendous birthing of impersonal
Love and wisdom that never fixates in any realm of experience.
To awaken to the absolute view is profound and transformative,
but to awaken from all fixed points of view is the birth of true
nonduality. If emptiness cannot dance, it is not true Emptiness. If
moonlight does not flood the empty night sky and reflect in every
drop of water, on every blade of grass, then you are only looking
at your own empty dream. I say, Wake up! Then, your heart will
be flooded with a Love that you cannot contain.*

— Adyashanti

Depth

To be present is to realize the depth of life. Presence is the direct recognition of what you are and what life is prior to your thoughts about what you are and what life is.

In living entirely within the movie of the thought-based, time-bound self, you miss the depth of life all around and within you. Thought places a flat, superficial name and set of thoughts over everything. The true depth of life is entirely missed. So when you see your friend, "Joe," you cannot see the depth there. You are looking through the personalized lens of your thoughts (i.e., who you think he is or want him to be). The mind is busy playing its story of Joe including his name and the memories you have of him. In that sense, you aren't meeting Joe the way he really is. You are interacting only with your own movie of Joe.

As you notice the movie, allow the noticing to be like a little alarm bell, revealing that what is noticing is presence. That presence is prior to who you think you are. That same presence is what Joe is prior to your thoughts about Joe. Presence has an inherent depth of unconditional love and compassion that no movie could ever provide. As this presence is recognized, thoughts still arise but you are not fooled into thinking that they are reality.

Criticism of others

In criticizing another, no true understanding of the relationship can happen. You are imposing your interpretation of reality on the other. Awareness is looking through the filter of the false self. Hidden within your criticisms of others are unexamined ideas such as, "I am not happy with you. I cannot be fully at peace until you change. If you will simply do what I want you to do, I will love and accept you." This makes love conditional.

Do you see the self-centeredness buried in that criticism? This self-centeredness is missed when the mind is busy pointing outward to the other. You do not see what is happening within. What is happening is a story of separation: me v. you.

Non-duality is not about mentally concluding that there is no "self" and no "other." Those are just conclusions. Non-duality is a seeing. This includes seeing the whole relationship including the unconscious, personalized thoughts arising as you criticize the other. In presence, you are not looking through the filter of me v. you. You are not judging the person based on their past actions. You are not engaging in some thought of what you would like the person to be in the future.

Unconditional love is only possible in this moment through awareness of the entire relationship including your thoughts and emotions about the other. It is then that the division between self and other is seen to be unreal.

Illness and injury

Whenever there is physical illness or injury—whether it is a cold, a pain in your leg, or a long-term illness— notice the personalized mental and emotional story of suffering that often surrounds the ailment. Illness and injury are perfect fuel for strengthening the time-bound, thought-based story of "me." The mind tends to stay stuck in the past, thinking about how long the illness or injury has been around. It also tends to stay stuck in the future, thinking about how long it will take to be free of the illness or injury.

If there is pain or discomfort, see that awareness is the present space around the pain or discomfort. Notice that your true identity is this present awareness. Notice any thoughts or negative emotions that arise in response to the pain or discomfort. See that the thoughts and emotions are not you. They are arising in what you are—present awareness. Notice that even the words "illness" and "injury" are stories of the past (i.e., memorized concepts) arising in present awareness.

Gently bring your attention back to this moment when you notice the story of "woe is me" playing in the mind. Notice any negative emotions that arise in your inner body when the story arises.

Illness and injury are aspects of life. However, suffering isn't necessary.

Childlike Wonder

Childlike wonder happens in the experiential realization that every thought and emotion and every other aspect of life arises spontaneously out of nothing. The heavy burden of "me" is seen to be unreal in this seeing.

From the point of view of the false, separate self, thought measures back into past to claim, "I did that," and measures forward into future to claim, "I am going to do that." But look more closely. Even those thoughts arise spontaneously out of nothing. Are you bringing those thoughts about?

In seeing that you are not the doer, there is a realization that you are being done, that life is being done. It is simply happening whether there is consent or resistance to the way it is happening.

What you think you know is what stands in the way of this liberation. What you think you are in control of stands in the way of this liberation. As it is seen that the story you take to be "you" does not know or control anything, liberation is realized. This is childlike wonder. No separate self can achieve childlike wonder. The separate self is too busy dreaming that it has control and that it knows all the answers.

Childlike wonder appears obscured by the mental movements of knowing and controlling. But even the thoughts that say "I know" and "I am in control" are happening spontaneously. Therefore, there is no obscuration.

Your real identity

If you are thinking and someone says, "Look at that tree," thought has to stop so that awareness can take the sight in directly. Thought does not see. Only awareness sees. In that moment of suspending thought long enough to see what is here in the present moment, you are getting a glimpse of your true nature as awareness. You are that which sees, not the object that is seen.

If you are thinking and someone says, "Listen to that sound," thought has to stop so that awareness can take the sound in directly. Thought does not hear. Only awareness hears. In that moment of suspending thought long enough to hear what is arising in the present moment, you are getting a glimpse of your true nature as awareness. You are that which hears, not the sound that is heard.

Can you see how your true nature gets apparently obscured? You are living life through the filter of the time-bound, thought-based separate self, instead of recognizing that your real identity is the timeless awareness in which everything—every thought, sound, object, state, experience, and situation— appears and disappears.

Paradoxically, as awareness is realized to be your real identity, you see that the objects that appear in awareness are not separate from awareness. Without awareness, none of the objects would appear.

The victim loop

As with all false mind-created identities, the victim identity is a self-centered loop of thought and emotion. If you
identify as a victim, you entertain thoughts of past in which
life appeared to treat you unfairly. You interpret present circumstances through the lens of the loop, essentially looking
for ways in which life is currently treating you unfairly, all
in an effort to confirm your victimhood. Thoughts of future
are infused with victimhood, such that you project a future
full of more unfair treatment. Constantly viewing the present
moment and the future through the lens of the victim story
strengthens the story. It strengthens the loop—the false "you."

This loop will continue repeating itself until awareness
sees the loop and recognizes that the loop is an object in
awareness. As a thought arises such as, "Life always treats me
unfairly," or "This situation will not turn out well," simply
notice that the thought is coming from within the victim loop
and notice any negative emotions accompanying the thought.
In noticing the thought and emotion, allow attention to gently
return to the space of now and to the space of your inner body
where the negative emotion is arising. Noticing the content of
the victim loop whenever it arises allows your true nature to
be revealed.

Resistance in the mirror of relationship

Each relationship is an opportunity to see whether you are at war with life and others. If a person walks up to talk to you today, it is an invitation to allow awareness to fully welcome that person, to listen intimately to what she is saying, and to be the space in which she is speaking. This allowing is not a doing. It is a present recognition that awareness is always and already open, loving and compassionate. If there is resistance within you to the person or what she is doing or saying, the person is acting as a mirror in which your own resistance is being revealed. This person is showing you your illusion of separateness. You are living in a conceptual dream called self v. other.

When you encounter this "other" today (and the other includes every manifest object that appears in awareness) notice any corresponding resistance in the form of irritation, frustration, unease, uncomfortableness, anger, or resentment. In allowing your relationship to people, situations, and things to be a mirror in which your own resistance is being reflected back to you, the possibility of waking up out of that resistance is available.

Roles

When you identify with a role, you cannot see your own identification. You are that role. Perhaps you are lost in your role as a doctor, secretary, or salesman. Or perhaps you are lost in some other role such as recovering addict, cancer survivor, victim, codependent, or even brother or parent.

Roles are false, egoic identities. When you are lost in a role, the spirit is not free to react naturally and spontaneously to life. You are lost in a past image of yourself. You act and react within the pattern of that past image. You tend to treat others according to their roles and how they relate to your role. If you are a doctor, you see only patients. If you are a salesman, you see only customers. If you are a mother, you see only children. Others people simply reflect back to you your particular role, which strengthens the role. There is no true relationship when images are relating to images.

In present moment awareness, there is freedom from all roles, identities, images, and self-concepts. You are no longer living life through rigid thought patterns of the past. You are free to respond to life intelligently, naturally, and spontaneously. When you notice each role you are playing in the moment you play it, you are present. You are transcending that role. This allows others the freedom to no longer react from their roles. True relationship is then possible.

Financial debt

If you are in financial debt, thought tends to repeat the story of how much you are in debt (past) and whether you are ever going to get out of debt (future). It's a version of the thought-based, time-bound "me."

Practical planning, going to work, and seeking professional financial assistance are all practical steps that can be taken. But the majority of thoughts about debt are unnecessary and self-centered.

You cannot stop these stories by some act of will. That act of will would also be the "me." There can only be a seeing. See the constant referencing of past in terms of how much debt you have. See the constant worrying about future in terms of whether you will be able to pay off the debt. You are seeing that the debt story is a subtle, self-centered victim identity. In the story of debt, it is all about "me." "Poor me!"

What is seeing is those moments is awareness. That is your true nature. Awareness functions intelligently on its own. It doesn't act from within a story. It is naturally at rest and at ease with what is. It knows that you have exactly the amount of money and debt that you are suppose to have right now. Then it goes to work and pays bills. It's that simple.

Romantic love

Romantic love is often based in egoic separation. In the beginning of a romantic relationship, roles are often played. You play the role of the perfect mate in order to get the other person to play the same role. Before too long, the real egoic wanting behind the role playing starts to reveal itself. Arguments start to happen. The arguments appear on the surface to be about mundane, everyday things. But on a deeper level the unconscious beliefs that are operating during these arguments are, "You are not living up to the image I have of you," "You are not filling my inner lack," and "You are not providing the personal gratification I desire in this relationship."

Egoic love is conditional. It is conditioned on whether the other person acts a certain way or says or does certain things that please you or that meet your mental image of the person.

The ego is a set of conditions. See the mental conditions you are imposing on your partner and realize that unconditional love is who you truly are under all these conditions.

Unconditional love knows no lack and seeks nothing from the other. It simply loves. Unconditional love realizes itself automatically through presence, when there is a seeing through of the false roles that are being played, the conditions being imposed, and the desire for personal gratification in the relationship.

The bottomless pit of spiritual self-analysis

It is easy to turn spirituality into nothing more than mental self-analysis, which just keeps the false thought-based dream self alive. You may find yourself thinking about yourself all the time, measuring your progress by comparing where you are today with where you were yesterday and where you want to be tomorrow, and constantly mentally analyzing your interior mental and emotional states. This kind of constant analysis is a bottomless pit of self-centeredness. It never ends. Nothing is ever resolved. One mental point just leads to another mental point and then to another. It's all about "me." It is the dream self (ego) caught on a treadmill that is going nowhere. The mental analysis is happening in an effort to figure out who you are. It is an identity crisis

Presence does not require analysis. In presence, there is no fixation on anything that arises and falls within the space of now. Thoughts are seen to come and go without a need to manipulate or analyze them. In seeing this whole move- ment of the mental dream self, you are witnessing a stream of self-centeredness. Presence reveals your true identity so that mental analysis is unnecessary. It resolves the identity crisis fully and finally. A natural and peaceful inner quietness is revealed in this seeing.

Missing enlightenment

Enlightenment is apparently missed not because it is difficult to obtain. Enlightenment just means presence. Presence seems elusive but it is actually immediately accessible as the very life that is in this moment. Instead of feeling into the simple fact of presence, the mind wanders through time looking for enlightenment, believing that it is somewhere else, in some other time, or in some concept.

Actually, presence is not obtained or missed. It is what you are right now. That is either recognized or it is not. The notions of obtaining it or missing it are ideas appearing and disappearing in presence.

The reason enlightenment *appears* to be missed is because the mind overlooks the simple fact of presence and, instead, gets entangled into a simulated "me" or ego that lives in time and that believes that the past is its identity and the future holds the key to its freedom. That is the lie.

Awakening from that dream means simply noticing what is already here. Everything is already here. The simple fact of presence is already here. The simulated "me" is a movie resulting from identification with thought and emotion. But that movie itself is arising in presence. In realizing that it is simply a movie and not your real identity, identification with the movie dies. Presence (i.e., enlightenment) is revealed to be what you really are. Enlightenment is that simple, way too simple for the mind.

Quietness

When you hear spiritual teachers talk about quietness (or silence), there is a tendency to believe either that you must reach some future state where there is more quietness or get away from your current noisy surroundings.

But quietness is all around you and within you right now wherever you are. It is the "default state" of life. This means that it is always here in between and even during the noise. It is what is here regardless of whether there is sound arising or not. Notice it between the words when someone is speaking and after their sentences. Notice that the words arise from and fall back into the quietness.

Inner quietness never leaves. Notice it when the noise in your head stops. But notice also that the quietness is here even during the noisy thoughts. It gives birth to the thoughts.

In noticing the quietness, your true identity is revealed. No matter what you think about yourself, life, or spirituality, those thoughts arise from and fall back into this quietness. This quietness is a portal to the source of all manifestation. Notice that the mental "you" that you take yourself to be is not separate from that source.

Pointers

Many ideas are used to point to enlightenment, which is an essentially inexpressible realization. You hear words like, "Oneness," "awareness," "consciousness," and "presence." You hear statements like, "Do you see that the 'I' thought arises in the pure awareness that you truly are?"

Those are all wonderful pointers. But there is no such thing as a statement of the truth to which the word enlightenment points. No matter what you say about 'This,' the statement appears from and disappears back into an emptiness that is prior to the statement. The entire planet earth appears and disappears in that same conceptually unknowable emptiness that some call the "source" and others call "God" or "space."

This space is overlooked because it is not an object the mind can grasp. Yet this space is the portal to the seeing called enlightenment. Instead of trying to grasp enlightenment through a formed idea, recognize this formless essence within you. See that this quiet, empty, loving space permeates the universe and every manifest thing.

Ideas are useful for communication purposes but they are as flimsy as a belief in Santa Claus. They can only point to an essence that is not an idea. They are not the essence itself.

The Source

All your life, you have been focused on forms including thoughts, emotions, states, situations, and experiences. Have you noticed the formlessness that is prior to these forms?

People, objects, thoughts, feelings, situations, and experiences arise from and fall back into this formless source. This source is prior to everything that arises including thoughts, emotions, objects, people, and experiences. This source does not leave while the forms are appearing and it remains once the forms disappear. This source contains the abundance you've been looking for all your life. It is already within you. It is what you are prior to what or who you think you are.

The question may arise, "How do I find the source?" The time-bound, thought-based story of you will never find that source. That story is a form arising out of and falling back into the source. This reflection is not inviting you to inhabit this source as if you are a person who is separate from the source and who must find it. This source is what you already are. This reflection is pointing to the *present*, direct recognition of what you already are. No thought will reveal it. Look to presence only.

Enlightenment is missed not because it is difficult to attain. It is your true nature. It is the simple and obvious presence that is here now before that presence focuses on or identifies with the forms that arise and fall in it.

More on "the source"

The mind turns the source into a concept e.g., "God." Thought cannot answer the question, "What is the source of life?" Thought arises from and falls back into that source. Form arises from formlessness. The source is the unknown. Thought is the realm of the known. The spiritual search can continue for years as the seeker keeps trying to know the source (i.e., emptiness, spirit, formlessness, God) through its manifestations (thoughts, questions, religions, beliefs).

In this moment, there is an unchanging, unmoving, formless, timeless awareness in which forms arise, giving the appearance of movement and change. These forms include thoughts, time, sounds, and emotions.

The question, "What is the source," is ignorance. It arises from looking for the truth through a form that is arising— thought. Words can only point back to the formless source. The source must be directly recognized as the very life that you are.

When the "me" story is seen to be just another manifesta- tion, no different than a cloud or a coke can, the temporary nature of it is realized. Attachment to that story naturally dies when the source (i.e., spirit) from which it comes is realized to be your true nature. That realization is only available now because this moment is all there is. Yesterday and tomorrow are just presently arising thoughts—more manifestations. The spiritual search for future awakening is, therefore, a denial of the spirit that is already awake and alive now.

You are not the doer of any action

Within the story of time called "me," the past is who you think you are and the future is who you think you are going to become. But have you stopped to really see that past and future are merely thoughts arising now? Those thoughts are creating an illusory story in which you believe you are the doer of action.

Through present awareness, it is realized that you are not pumping blood through your body, beating your heart, digesting food, or breathing air. You are also not 'doing' thinking or 'doing' emotions. All of this is spontaneously arising in this moment out of nowhere.

In seeing the false self that lives in past and future and mistakenly believes that it is in control, awakening happens. It is realized that life is living itself through the body and mind. There is no separate "you" in control. Only thought creates the story that you are the doer of action. That story references backwards or forwards in time to take credit for actions that spontaneously arose. See that even those referencing-thoughts are spontaneously arising in present awareness.

Notice that you are not doing the laundry, going to work, playing with your children, thinking or feeling. All of that arises spontaneously in this moment out of nowhere. Then notice something amazing. You are not noticing. Noticing is just happening. In this timeless seeing, liberation is available.

Being

"Being" is another word pointing to presence. This is not about a person realizing being. Being just is. This is not about coming to a mental understanding of being. Being just is. This is not about a person doing something to reach being in the future. Being cannot be found or lost. Being just is. This is a present recognition that you are life itself.

The person is just a story of a separate "me" that falsely believes it must do something to find some other separate thing called happiness, love, freedom, or whatever one is seeking. When that story is no longer fed, a natural and effortless being is realized.

In noticing the struggle to maintain pleasure and escape pain, see that the struggle arises directly from the "me" contraction. That contraction is doing anything it can to run away from what is in this moment. It is fighting, complaining, blaming, arguing with others, endlessly replaying the past, and searching into future. All of that arises from the central illusory "me" contraction that believes it is a separate person who must somehow negotiate with something outside itself. All unhappiness and discontent arises from the illusory separation between the subject "me" and some other object called "others," "life" or "my happiness." As being is realized, that illusory separateness is seen through. Being naturally contains the happiness, love, and freedom that is sought.

Ego usurping the search for enlightenment

After years of suffering and searching, you may come upon non-duality or enlightenment teachings that are pointing to the way out of suffering and searching. A burning for truth arises in you and takes hold. You know that, whatever is pulling you in the direction of enlightenment is a force so strong, it must be followed. Most spiritual seekers do not feel as though they have a choice. There is a sense of being drawn towards an awakening.

Trust the force that is pulling you towards awakening. But notice the ways in which the ego likes to usurp that force for its own gains. The egoic drive can usurp the spiritual search and turn it into an addiction to the idea of future enlightenment. You become like a dog chasing his own tail. You constantly think about and discuss enlightenment, comparing one teaching to another, one idea to another, one teacher to another. If this is happening, you can bet that you have created a new story of self out of the search for enlightenment.

Do not make that into a problem. Simply notice when the mind is lost in thinking about enlightenment and how to get there. When a simple, non-resistant openness arises within you to the sights, sounds, feelings, thoughts, and situations of the present moment, enlightenment is possible. All else is ego.

How can I realize enlightenment?

The question arises along the spiritual search, "If I am not the doer of any action, how can 'I' realize enlightenment?" The separate self that you take yourself to be is not your true identity. It is nothing more than a set of images tied together. This set of images consists of thoughts of past (who you believe you are), thoughts of future (who you believe you are going to become) and thoughts that resist what is happening right now.

That set of images creates the appearance of a doer. This is sometimes called the personal will or ego. That personal will believes it took action in the past and that it can take action now and in the future to bring about desired outcomes.

Enlightenment remains elusive when this personal will is trying to bully itself into some future state of freedom. Enlightenment is available when the personal will (i.e., the separate self) is seen to be nothing more than a contraction within the body and mind built around the story of "me" that lives in time.

That thought-based, time-bound self will never realize enlightenment. Instead of trying to do things to reach enlightenment, effortlessly notice what is already being done. Notice the personal will as it arises in each moment. Notice the awareness within the body and mind in which the personal will arises and falls. That which notices is already free.

The River of Life

Notice that life is like a river rushing by and through you. It is constantly moving, yet there is a deeply silent, formless, immovable awareness watching the whole thing. Thoughts, emotions, reactions, cars, books, dinners, pens, pets, jobs, words, relationships and all other forms are moving through this river.

Notice that when thought appears to get stuck on any particular form moving through the river, the dream self is trying to stop the river and gain control. Suffering arises because control is not possible. But notice that when awareness is simply watching this rushing river without getting stuck on any of the forms moving through it, it is like freefalling in space with nothing to hold onto and nowhere to land. In this noticing, there is a possibility of enjoying every form moving through the river without getting stuck on any particular form.

The forms cannot appear without the awareness in which they appear. That which notices the forms moving through the river does not have an independent existence from those forms. As formless awareness and the forms appearing in awareness collapse, it is realized that there is only One Life and you are THAT.

Appearance of Separation

Thought reduces this radiant, mysterious One Life into fragments. Nothing is truly separate. Separateness is just an appearance created by thought. Thought can only think about one thing at a time. For example, think of "pancakes." Do you see that thought can only picture pancakes? It can only see and concentrate on one object or idea at a time. Thought is fragmented. Therefore thought will never see Oneness.

Thought makes the separate thing more important than the whole. Thought is a conceptual, dualistic dream. The main fragment that it makes important is the "I" thought. Everything is seen to center around this idea that "I" am a separate person. Instead of seeing One miraculous life, thought focuses on things like, "I want what I want!" and "Why don't they like me?"

When this "I" thought is seen to be just another fragment, when it is seen that there is no person separate from the rest of life, the entire world of separateness is seen to be merely an appearance. It is realized that there is only 'This.' One Life. When the realization of Oneness has fully surrendered the "me" story, life is lived without a sense of a separate self.

This is not about denying the practical functioning of thought or the realm of the relative. It is about seeing thought's illusory nature.

The world is a reflection of mind

When you see a "tree," notice that you are interacting only with thought. Someone taught you the word "tree." It is not true that you are looking at a tree. The object could have been called a "splunk" just the same. The word is not that which it describes.

When you label a situation as good or bad or believe that a person should or should not be doing something, this is also just thought. There is nothing wrong with thinking. The ignorance arises only when you believe that your thoughts are totally true. Ignorance is failing to see the projector of mind that is continuously placing a conceptual overlay upon reality in an attempt to strengthen a fictitious central "me." Ignorance here is not meant to be derogatory. To ignore here means to "not see."

In seeing the projector of "me" projecting its movie onto the world, the possibility of waking from that movie arises. In this awakening, it is realized that the world is a reflection of mind. Spiritual realization does not come by merely changing the characters and content of the movie that is being projected. The movie is an illusion. Realization is available only through seeing the movie as an object on the screen of awareness. Since it is an object in awareness, it is not what you are. When the movie of self is seen to be an illusion, what you really are reveals itself.

Uncompromising expressions of non-duality?

Some non-duality teachings claim to be "uncompromising non-dual expressions" in some attempt to set themselves apart from the apparent "compromising non-dual expressions." The mind just likes to pick a dualistic position. "Uncompromising" exists only in relation to "compromising." Even the idea, "Oneness," exists only in relation to the idea of "twoness" or the idea of "many." As soon as thought arises, it takes a dualistic position in relation to some other position. Positions exist only in relation or opposition to one another.

The One is uncompromisingly expressing itself as everything from a bird flying through the air, to a toilet flushing, to a preacher preaching the Bible, to an "uncompromising non-dual expression," to a "compromising non-dual expression."

This does not mean that all ideas are equal, which would— itself—be an idea claiming to be truer than other ideas. It is only to point out that the dream self will attach to anything to maintain separateness including the idea that it "gets" non-duality and that the others "don't get it." Every single thing you see, touch, taste, hear, smell, do, and feel is an uncompromising expression of the One.

Only the illusory separate self attempting to set itself apart would be interested in convincing others that its particular expression of "Oneness" is more important than the bird, toilet, preacher, or some other teaching. When the energy of convincing falls away, there is only clarity, peace, and love.

More on dualistic thought and non-dual teachings

Although all thought is dualistic by nature, to deny thought is to deny the very expression of 'This.' Some non-duality or enlightenment teachings point very directly, leaving no room for the seeker to believe that he or she needs more time in order to be free or that there is even a seeker who could do anything to reach enlightenment. Other teachings provide the seeker with methods and practices for recognizing presence. The method may be to watch thoughts and emotions, question thoughts, practice inner body awareness, or follow the "I" thought back to its source until it is realized that there is only emptiness within.

Each of these expressions is pointing to the same Oneness, enlightenment, non-duality, liberation, nirvana, or whatever you like to call it. Yet none of these expressions are the truth. The truth to which all these words point cannot be expressed through dualistic thought.

Keep it simple. Use whatever works. Comparing one teacher or teaching to another is just more seeking energy. When you take a position for or against a teaching, notice that there is always an opposite position. In seeing that opposite positions are dualistic and arise together, you are recognizing your own non-dual nature. It is then realized that thought is not a problem. Although words fail, 'This' loves to express itself in a multitude of ways.

Looking without condemnation and judgment

Notice today whether you are lost in labeling, categorizing, analyzing, and judging everyone you see. When you place condemnation or judgment upon someone, you are not interacting with the person. You are interacting only with your own memory of the person. In placing a memorized concept on the person, you fail to see that what you take to be an "other" is really your own non-dual essence appearing in another form.

Unconditional love can only be realized through presence. In full awareness of the present moment, the past is no longer coming to meet everyone you see. Presence means looking at what is in this moment with fresh eyes, without the condemnation or judgment that arises from relying solely on thought (i.e., memory or conditioning).

When you meet with someone today, simply look and listen without condemnation or judgment. If condemnation or judgment arises, notice that you are looking at the person through a veil of past concepts. Simply look at each concept as it arises, allowing your attention to gently return to that fact that the very presence you are is the same presence appearing in another form that you call the "other." In looking without condemnation and judgment, unconditional love is what is looking. The One is meeting itself as an appearance of two.

The whole story

Non-dual realization is often considered to be the recognition of emptiness (also called pure awareness, space, formlessness or nothingness). That emptiness is your true nature in the deepest sense. The recognition of it is vital to realization.

However, emptiness isn't the whole story. Emptiness can easily turn into a denial of form. It's a trap. As necessary as the recognition of emptiness is, emptiness is moving as, and not independent of, every thought, emotion, experience, and state. This is when the emptiness is seen as totally full. This is when form and formlessness collapse, when the boundary between them is seen as purely conceptual, and all that is left is life living itself simply, naturally, and compassionately through you. This is when enlightenment is not about escaping. It's about seeing that your true nature is "not of this world" which paradoxically allows you to be totally "in this world" in a new way.

Emptiness is the essence of all form. The experience of "nothing arising" is merely a passing, temporary state. Realization is not about fixating in the idea of emptiness, absence, or "no self" or about maintaining a space free of the happenings of everyday life.

Non-duality is everyday life. This book is an invitation first to the recognition of emptiness as the source and then to the seeing that this source is appearing as everything. This is life, vitally full, alive, loving, and free.

No self

The realization of no self is not a position. It is not a philosophy or belief. To speak about it, however, one must enter into the dualistic realm of language. The moment you begin talking about "no self," it sounds like a position. But the realization of no self is the actual seeing that you are only emptiness (i.e., not the mental position or belief that you are emptiness, but rather the actual realization).

Once that emptiness is realized, it is seen that emptiness arises as every mental position but that there is no self to attach to any of the positions. This pointer is not suggesting that you should not take positions. That, in and of itself, is a position. It is simply an invitation to look within, to that which is prior to all positions. It is an invitation to see that there is no self there to attach to any position including the position that there is no self.

Seeing the "me" as resistance

Life is simply happening. It is not happening to you. The "me" story believes that life is happening to it and that it must do certain things and avoid doing other things. Yet doing just arises. The "me" story cannot see this because it is too busy with the story of the doer.

See that the "me" is nothing more than resistance. A circumstance arises and the "me" mentally labels it as bad or unsatisfactory. The "me" may also feel an emotional resistance to the circumstance. The "me" did not bring about the circumstance. It simply happened. The "me" brought about neither the emotional resistance to the circumstance nor the labeling of it as bad or unsatisfactory. All of that arose spontaneously in the moment it arose. Conditioned responses to life circumstances simply arise.

In seeing all of this in the moment it arises, the entire emotional and mental story of "me" is seen to be nothing more than a conditioned response, a sort of involuntary contraction against or reaction to life. In that seeing, the resistance naturally dissipates. What is left is complete openness to what is. In that openness, it is realized that the "me" is not even doing the seeing. Seeing also just happens. It is seen that you are so much more than a self-centered story of resistance.

Inner body awareness

Inner body awareness is a spiritual method. As with all methods, it must be taken in the proper perspective. Methods imply that it takes time to recognize timeless presence. It does not take time. Time is a dream of thought. Spiritual realization is timeless. Any method that makes you believe that you must practice the method for a period of time in order to be free obscures the natural freedom that is here in this moment.

Inner body awareness is not about time. It is about noticing what is already here in this moment. Inner body awareness is an end in and of itself. It is a timeless seeing. Right now, there is a vast space within the body and mind. This is the same space that permeates the entire universe. Turning awareness in on itself within the body and mind allows the vast timeless space to be realized.

Through inner body awareness, there is a direct experiencing of aliveness. Aliveness is felt in each of your limbs and in your stomach and chest as a subtle tingling feeling. As the space in the mind is aware of itself, an inner quietness is found. Thought is realized to be nothing more than form temporarily arising and falling within that spacious quietness.

Inner body awareness is just a tool to reveal that your true nature is empty awareness. Use the tool until it is no longer helpful.

Liberation

L iberation means freedom from your psychological past. The 'person' cannot be liberated because the person is the psychological past.

Some aspects of the past are necessary in this moment. For example, memories related to how to drive your car and how to do your job are practical and are not part of the psychological past (i.e., ego or 'person'). The psychological past is that realm of memories with which you identify and that you call "me." That set of memories can never be liberated. Liberation is timeless, free, unconditioned, loving, light, and open. The psychological past is time-bound, limited, repetitive, self-centered, conditioned, heavy, and closed. To say that the "me" is closed simply means that it is a finite set of ideas in which nothing truly new arises, much like a tape recording or a repetitive loop of conditioning. It is rarely open to the simple wonder and mystery of this moment.

Liberation is the direct realization that you are that wonder and mystery. It is the effortless embrace of life freshly in each moment, without carrying the content of the loop into it. No 'person' can ever do that because the person is that loop.

AUGUST

This is beyond existence and non-existence. It's beyond self and no self. It's beyond subject and object, time and space, past and future. All those words become redundant when the taste of your cup of tea or the tweet tweet of a bird, or the roar of the traffic becomes the most fascinating thing in the world.

— Jeff Foster

Acceptance

Sit still for one moment and notice the timeless, empty, spacious, quiet presence that is here in the room. Even if there is noise in the room, notice that the quietness is surrounding and permeating that noise. Notice this presence within and without the body and mind.

Say the word "acceptance" out loud. Notice that the sound of the word "acceptance" arises and falls back into the quiet presence that you are. The word is virtually useless when you realize that presence itself is acceptance. This presence that is simply here is already fully accepting of what presently is. It does not have to do anything to come to acceptance including utter a word.

Thought does not accept. It measures, judges, blames, complains, analyzes, categorizes, labels, and thinks about life. It is not in the business of acceptance. It is in the business of thinking and talking about acceptance. That is not acceptance. That is thinking and talking. This is not a prescription to not think or not talk. This is an invitation to notice what is totally untouched by thought. All thoughts about acceptance merely arise and fall within this presence. True acceptance is this presence that is always and already naturally and effortlessly accepting of what is including accepting of thoughts about presence.

Who claims to be enlightened?

Who would claim to be enlightened? Who would claim that there is no self, or that all is One? Who would claim to have no beliefs? Only a thought-based, time-bound story of self would claim any of these things, falsely believing that the timeless truth to which the words are pointing can be owned by an entity living in time. In enlightenment, there is nothing to claim and no one to claim it. Enlightenment is seeing through the identification with things including spiritual ideas. Such ideas are of the past. To hold onto them now is to create and maintain a time-bound story.

In the realization that there is nothing to hold onto and no one to hold onto anything, real freedom is available. This freedom cannot be owned by a story of time. The self who loves to hang onto spiritual ideas hates this message. This message threatens its most precious ideas about non-duality or enlightenment. But they are just memorized ideas. In seeing that the person who would try to own these ideas is also just an idea, the possibility for real liberation and love arises. This is a liberation and love that no self can claim to have. It is free of clinging to spiritual ideas including the concepts of liberation and love. This is a presence that uses any and all words to express itself but that is attached to none of them.

More on ideas about enlightenment

Yesterday's reflection stated, "Enlightenment is the death of identification with everything the self loves to hang onto including spiritual ideas." Spiritual ideas are merely stories pointing back to the timeless, empty, awake space in which everything and every story arise.

When it is realized that this moment is all there is, stories continue to arise. The story, "I am enlightened," or "I am unenlightened" may arise. Words such as non-duality, Oneness, and enlightenment may arise to express what is essentially inexpressible. Recognize that whatever we say about 'This' is 'This' appearing as a story about it. The words are never the truth. They are pointers only.

Yet none of these stories should be suppressed or denied. Who would try to suppress or deny them? Only a self with an agenda to change what is would try to suppress or deny anything. Only a thought would seek to deny another thought.

If a movement to suppress or deny a story arises, see it. If a spiritual idea arises, see it. When this seeing happens, an awakeness beyond the stories realizes itself. That last sentence is also a story. It's not the truth. Just see it. Look to where the words are pointing. See that what is seeing is not a story. What is seeing is prior to all stories. In this seeing, everything is allowed to be just as it is, without attaching or identifying with any of it.

Seeking

Seeking arises as the story, "I am not there yet." It also arises as energy in the body that pulls you towards the next moment. Do not try to deny or suppress seeking energy when it arises. Allow awareness to just see it. Awareness has no agenda to get rid of this energy. The mind is what seeks to be rid of seeking energy. The mental strategy of trying to get rid of seeking is just more seeking—more escaping into the next moment.

Ask yourself, "What am I seeking?" The answer may be money, success, fame, love, happiness, peace, or enlightenment. The story goes, "When I obtain whatever object I am seeking, I will be ok." Translated, that means, "When I get whatever it is I am seeking, the seeking will stop." Do you see that, ultimately, you are not seeking some object or future attainment? You are seeking the end of seeking. If you woke up tomorrow and the movement of seeking was gone, what would be left? This moment! There would be a deep sense of contentment with whatever is.

The end of seeking can only be realized now. All desire for future attainment creates a never ending search for something just out of reach. In noticing the movement to escape this moment in search of something else, an opportunity arises to realize that this moment is what you are seeking. That takes no time at all.

Simplicity

Have you noticed how simple life actually is when you are not living it completely through the veil of thought? It is so simple, so effortless. It is doing the laundry, pouring detergent into the washing machine. It is hearing the sound of the door to the machine slamming shut and the cycle starting. It is footsteps to the kitchen, pouring a glass of water, and the feel of cool water flowing down the throat, soothing the body. It is walking to the bathroom, using the toilet and washing the hands. It is the feel of water rushing over the fingers. It is drying off the hands.

It is breathing, smiling, frowning, driving, walking, talking, being. It is noticing thought and then not noticing thought. 'This' is life just living itself spontaneously. No one is bringing any of it about. It is simply happening now. The self that would try to understand this is also just a thought happening now. You do not bring the story of "you" about. It merely pops into your head spontaneously. When this is seen, all sense of being in control is seen to be illusory. In noticing this, the possibility of an awakening into simplicity arises.

Life is so simple, so effortless, so natural. The person trying to live it, trying to control it, and trying to understand it will never see and experience that simplicity.

Are you in control?

Take a look and notice that you cannot know what thought is going to come about until that thought arises. It arises naturally, spontaneously, and involuntarily out of nowhere. "You" did not bring it about. "You" did not even know what was coming until it came.

Do you know what action is going to arise before it arises? Perhaps a thought tells you that you should wipe the kitchen counter. It appears you made a decision and are simply following through with your decision. But didn't that decision arise spontaneously out of nowhere? Did you know that decision was going to arise before it arose?

You believe you are in control. In presence, it is revealed that life is just happening spontaneously. The "you" that you take yourself to be is also just a story arising spontaneously out of nowhere. There is no "you" to choose what is arising.

Watch people when sitting in a room together. Legs are moving. Arms are moving. Heads are turning. But if you ask people whether they are doing those subtle little bodily movements, they will likely not realize those movements were even happening.

If there is no "you" controlling the thoughts and actions that arise or making choices, what does that mean for all your grand plans for the future? See that this reflection is pointing towards a total surrender to what is in this moment.

Apparent choice

Yesterday's reflection stated that there is no "you" in control or making choices. The experience of having no choice can be absolutely liberating. The experience is showing you that life is just happening spontaneously.

Yet, paradoxically, apparent choice arises. Out of nowhere comes a thought that you have a choice between two options: between continuing to replay a past resentment or allowing awareness to see that resentment as nothing more than presently arising thought and emotion.

Notice that even this apparent choice arises spontaneously and involuntarily. Then experience and enjoy the choice. Making choices apparently happens within the dream of the thought-based, time-bound self. Do not try to suppress that self. Just see that it is a dream of time, a dream that you are a person who has control and who can choose to do something now to bring about some future outcome.

Enjoy apparent choice but see it for what is truly is . . . a dream of thought. The dream of self, and therefore the dream of apparent choice, arises spontaneously and involuntarily from the choiceless, timeless, formless presence that you really are.

Enlightenment for no one

With respect to enlightenment, thought says, "I have it" or "I don't have it." Those are dualistic ideas. The mind can get lost not only in the search for enlightenment but also in the false idea that it has attained it. Enlightenment reveals that there is no separate self except as a dream of thought. A self can only consider itself enlightened if it sees others who are not. The idea that I am or am not enlightened is just more separation.

Enlightenment is for no one. It is absolute liberation that no time-bound, egoic self could ever know. No story of self reaches enlightenment. That self is just a story of time, which means a story of mind. That story is doing everything it can to avoid this moment (i.e., to avoid enlightenment). Its main goal is to stay in separation—to be someone in relation to, better than, less than, or more spiritual than the others. It accomplishes this by staying locked in thought, in time.

When that movement of self is seen to be nothing more than thought, something beyond thought recognizes itself. That which wakes up is what you really are. It knows no separation. In this seeing, there is no longer the belief in a separate self who needs to tell stories about being enlightened or not being enlightened.

Spiritual Discourse

When spiritual discourse is stuck on the level of agreement and disagreement, the dream self is attached to spiritual conclusions from the past. When there is agreement, the dream self tends to fall into a false sense of certainty, believing that its ideas must be right simply because others agree with those ideas. When there is disagreement, the dream self feels threatened because it is invested in the ideas that are being challenged. The false sense of certainty felt in agreement and the threat of annihilation felt in disagreement are revealing that you have reduced this radiant, mysterious One Life to nothing more than an illusory separate self created from a set of ideas.

When the truth is expressing itself, it is free, alive, loving, nonattached, and non-defensive. It is observing and expressing what is, not to make an identity or philosophy out of what is observed, but rather merely to express the experience of living, which is impermanent and constantly changing. To hold onto anything that arises and falls, including some past experience or conclusion, is to welcome ignorance, separation, and conflict.

When spiritual discourse is alive in this way, it transcends the dualistic nature of agreement and disagreement. There may still be agreement and disagreement, but the dream self is not involved. There is no attachment to the words. This is when love is speaking clearly and naturally to itself through the vessels known as you and me.

Working and chores

While working or doing some chore around the house that you do not enjoy, notice what is happening. A resistance accompanies the doing. The resistance, when given a voice, says, "I do not want to do this." That story is the cause of the suffering, not the task itself. When that story is noticed, it vanishes. It is then realized that you are not doing the working or the task. These things are doing themselves. They continue doing themselves even when the stories surrounding them are gone.

Resistance or discomfort may still be felt while doing work. There may still be the story that "this should end soon" or that "I should not have to do this work." But there is a recognition in presence that those are only stories. The stories may continue to arise or they may stop completely. Whatever happens is beyond your control. Simply notice that. How can you blame yourself for those little stories if they are seen to arise on their own? When the stories are seen through, the doer is seen through. There is only doing and working—no doer and no worker.

Roles in relationships

We often play roles for each other based on our conditioning including the role of mother, father, sister, brother, wife, husband, lover, customer, salesman, convenience store clerk, doctor, policeman, politician, secretary, friend, preacher, teacher, spiritual seeker, Christian, Buddhist, and Hindu. The list is endless. We are conditioned to believe that we are whatever role we are playing. We are not roles. Roles are rigid patterns of thought. We are much more vibrantly alive than some pattern of thought.

When you are living life through a role, you are attached to the past, to some idea you learned or modeled from the past regarding how to act within a given situation or relationship. Actions are taken according to that conditioned image— that role.

The mind fears that if it does not conform to a certain pattern, role, or image, it will not know how to act or it will not be able to control a particular situation. But the truth is you do not have control. There is no "you" to have control. The "you" is a story of separation fueled by a contraction in the body and mind. The "you" is the role.

There is a presence here, right now, that is not playing any role. It simply is. In recognizing that your real identity is this presence, the playing of roles is seen to be unnecessary.

"You"

Have "you" ever looked at what this "you" really is? Isn't the "you" merely a belief? Granted, it may be a very strongly-held belief. You may believe there is a "you" much more than you believe there is an Easter Bunny. But what is the difference between you and the Easter Bunny? Both are beliefs, aren't they?

In directing your attention to this "you," I am talking about the idea of you, the story of you that lives in time and that has a past and a future. Is that "you" anything more than an idea or set of ideas?

If you walk away after reading this reflection and totally drop the "I" thought as you are cleaning the bathroom, where did that "I" thought go? Where is this "you" during those moments when there is just presence? In presence, your entire past and future vanishes.

The realization of your own absence is the most liberating thing. It reveals that all your regrets, resentments, worries, complaints and anxieties are nothing more than little subplots to a movie called "you." In total presence, the movie and all its little plots are seen to be unreal—merely thought. What is left is your true nature as love, compassion, peace, clarity, and joy.

Teacher and seeker

The dichotomy between spiritual teacher and seeker is false. It is entirely thought-created.

When you read a spiritual book or attend a meeting with a teacher, notice that thought buys into an illusion that the teacher has something that you do not. That very thought-created duality is an obstacle to the recognition of non-dual presence. No one attains enlightenment. Enlightenment is realized to be the natural state when the dream of separation is seen through.

There is nothing to teach. There is only pointing to what already is. The very act of picking up a spiritual book comes from the belief in separation. The belief is, "I do not have what I need." "I am not already whole." "This book can give me something." No book or teacher can give you what you already are. The only thing a teaching can truly do is point to what you already are and to the fact that seeking what you already are is insane.

This is not an invitation to stop seeking or stop listening to spiritual teachers. Only the dream of a separate self would buy into the idea that it somehow has the power to stop seeking. This is an invitation to see life the way it really is. Thought is creating divisions where there are none. In seeing the false division between you and the teacher, between you and this other thing called enlightenment, the possibility of realizing that you are already free arises.

You can't sneak up on 'This'

When the word 'This' is used, I'm referring to that which goes by many names including Oneness, the One Life, non-duality, presence, enlightenment, nirvana, liberation, the Tao, Brahman, God, being, aliveness, wholeness, emptiness, and awareness. 'This' is a realization that reveals that timeless essence is all there is.

You can't sneak up on 'This.' You do not come to 'This' in time. The sense that you are coming to enlightenment or almost there is just part of the story of time (the dream self) that is obscuring 'This.' The very seeking of 'This' makes you believe that 'This' is somehow in the future. But future is just a presently arising thought. It has no reality except in your dream of self.

Instead of doing anything to reach 'This,' notice what is already being done. There is a constant movement towards some future moment. That movement keeps the dream going. It keeps alive the lie that enlightenment is found in the future. It keeps the dream self running on a treadmill.

As long as the belief in some future attainment is operating, this moment will carry with it a sense of lack. In noticing that the effort to do things to reach Oneness or to sneak up on enlightenment is nothing more than a dream of thought happening now, a possibility arises for the realization that what you are seeking is already here. You are already 'This.'

What's going to happen next?

Liberation is not knowing what is going to happen next. Even in the dream of self you don't know what is going to happen next but, within that dream, a story of knowing is told.

Look more closely right now. Sit there quietly in your chair after reading this reflection. Watch an arm move or maybe a finger. Notice your head turn. Notice a thought arise or maybe a feeling. Notice that "you" are not making these things happen any more than you are pumping blood, digesting food, or breathing.

Thought measures 'backwards' to say, "I was just thinking a minute ago," or "I am going to move my arm now." But even <u>that</u> thought arises beyond your control. Even if you are arguing with what is being said here, notice that the argument arose spontaneously and involuntarily.

In noticing that life is just happening spontaneously and involuntarily, there is also a noticing that you cannot know what is going to happen next until it is already happening.

The resistance to life as it is happening is suffering. The recognition that life cannot happen in any other way than it is happening is liberation. Liberation is not about doing anything. It is about noticing what is already being done. This is freedom from the false idea that you are doing it.

Death

The dream self is the movement of mental and emotional energy in avoidance of death. Awareness identifies with thought and emotion in some attempt to create and maintain a self out of past and future. This self seeks permanency. But there is no permanency in time. Time is finite. Time is mind. It is thought. Thought, by its very nature, arises and falls.

Enlightenment is the falling away of the story of "me" living in past and future. In that falling away, what is left is timelessness—the infinite, the eternal. In that falling away, liberation and unconditional love arise. Jesus said, "If you want to find your life, you must lose it." He was not referring to physical death or encouraging martyrdom. He was pointing to the fact that this dream self (which he called sin) is an obstacle to enlightenment or Oneness (which he called God).

When the dream self is seen to be nothing but an illusion, physical death is no longer feared. The fear of death arises only because the dream self believes it is a real entity totally separate from the rest of life—an entity that can die. But your real identity is beyond the cycle of physical birth and death. When the fear of death dies, the fear of living goes with it. That is non-dual freedom.

More present?

You hear teachings talk about the timeless present moment as being the portal to enlightenment. Thought then likes to get involved. It compares the degree of presence yesterday to the degree of presence now. It projects forward into the future to imagine a time when there is more presence. All of that comparing and measuring is time, which means it is thought. There is nothing wrong with thought. But identification with thought is the dream self. The dream self is lost in a story of time. Only thought creates the dream of "more" presence or "degrees" of presence.

When the entire search to be more present— which is a search in time—falls away, presence is realized to be all there is. Even comparing, measuring, and searching arise in presence. There is nothing that happens outside of this timelessness. Thought is merely telling the story that there is a self who is coming to presence. No one comes to presence. Presence is all there is. The story of self is a dream of thought that simply arises and falls within presence. When it is realized that comparing past to future, measuring the "degree" of presence, and searching to be "more" present are all part of the dream of the thought-based, time-bound self, and that even that dream happens in presence, the search is off. It is realized that all there is, is presence appearing as a dream of a separate self.

The doer is a story of lack

The dream self is a doer that is doing things now to achieve other things later. You believe that you must meditate to evoke relaxation or reach enlightenment. You believe you must pray each morning so that God will give you or your loved ones a longer life, better relationships, more money, or a better living situation. You go to spiritual teachers who will tell you how to become more present, surrendered, open, aware, loving, or awakened.

All of this doing assumes that you have control of your life. The idea of personal choice/will creates the story of self in time. The story goes, "I lack something now but if I do this particular thing, I will find wholeness later." The story perpetuates the sense of lack. It traps you into seeking future.

Instead of blindly doing things in order to bring about some later awakening, notice what is already being done. Notice all the ways the doer is busy looking for a later moment. This is not a suggestion to stop doing things. It is an invitation to notice that all doing feeds into the story of self, which is a story that you lack something now but that the future will bring fulfillment.

Enlightenment is simply the realization that there is already enlightenment now under the story of the doer doing things to reach enlightenment.

Chasing after states and experiences

Don't make the mistake of chasing after particular states and experiences. You hear about this thing called non-duality or enlightenment and thought reduces it to a state or experience. For example, you hear about great Oneness experiences in which people see that they are not separate from others, from the floor, or from the sky and you believe you must have that experience.

Non-dual realization is not a particular experience. It is emptiness appearing as every experience and every state.

One way of pointing to it is with the word "opening." Do not envision the opening as a state or experience or something to find or arrive at. What you really are is the present opening through which everything arises and falls including thoughts, emotions, beliefs, experiences, and states. The opening never changes. It does not come and go. It is stateless and experience-less.

In realizing that what you really are is this opening, it is seen that every thought, emotion, belief, experience, and state that comes through the opening is not in fact separate from the opening. You are both the opening and that which comes through it. The opening and that which is coming through the opening constitute one present reality happening.

The mirror and its reflections

Non-dual awareness is like one mirror. The mirror has no concept. It has no view. The mirror knows no separate people or things. The reflections of the mirror give the appearance of separate people. Yet those separate people only exist as separate, and only know themselves to be separate, in relationship to others.

Dualism is a play of mental opposites. There is no "me" without a "you." No right without wrong. No black without white. No success without failure. No good without bad. No positive without negative. No one can be "spiritual" unless there are others who are "not spiritual." A belief cannot be true unless other beliefs are untrue.

There is only the One appearing as many. Only thought creates the notion that there are separate things, separate people, and separate ideas.

Spiritual realization is a seeing beyond the dream of separateness/dualism. This realization is calling awareness out of its mental attachment to our separate philosophical, religious, cultural, national, political and personal divisions. Suffering and searching exist when thought buys completely into the dream of its own reflection. The "person" believes she is totally separate and then longs for wholeness, not realizing that she is that wholeness. In seeing the separate person as a reflection, the possibility of recognizing Oneness (the mirror) arises. This is not about denying the reflection (i.e., the separate person). It is about seeing that it is ultimately a dream of thought.

Exposing the seeking game

In playing the game of spiritual seeking, you believe that—through control, effort and practice—you will come to some later point of enlightenment, happiness, love, success, or contentment. But the hidden gem in seeking is the opportunity to expose the seeking for what it truly is—a game of mind.

Instead of blindly following each movement of seeking, expose the game. Allow awareness to see it without judgment. See what is really happening. The thought-based self is playing the game of looking for spirit in form (i.e., things). Ordinary, everyday present awareness is already formless spirit. The dream self is lost in a dream of temporary 'somethings' (i.e., temporary thoughts, feelings, ideas, religions, beliefs, states, experiences, jobs, relationships). It goes from one something to the next something in search of spirit. This is about the possibility of seeing that control, effort, practice, thoughts, feelings, ideas, religions, beliefs, states, experiences, jobs, and relationships are temporary 'somethings' arising from the formless, changeless nothingness of spirit that is the source of all.

In exposing the seeking game, there is no more avoidance of present awareness. No more escaping from the present experience to some fairytale experience in the future. The possibility arises for seeing that, in the timeless presence that you really are, nothing is appearing as everything. Spirit is manifesting as every form—every 'something'—including every false idea about future awakening.

The dream of choice

The seeker asks, "Should I engage in spiritual practices to bring about enlightenment?" The teacher responds, "Who is going to do that?" This can frustrate the seeker unless it is realized what is really being said.

The dream of self is a dream of time. There is a belief in a separate person with a past and a future who can choose to take action now to bring about some later event. Within the spiritual search, choice is based in personal motivation: "What can I do now to achieve something later?" The dream self falsely believes it is in control. It's all about the "me" and what it can get.

Enlightenment is the realization of no self, which is a realization of timelessness. When time is seen to be nothing more than a mental stream of thoughts called past and future arising now, the "me" is seen to be a temporary thought form arising from that formless, timeless awareness. Choice is seen to be a dream of time, meaning an aspect of the dream of self.

Should you engage in spiritual practices? In seeing that all spiritual practicing emanates from a central illusion of time and control, the possibility for liberation from that dream arises. Engaging in spiritual practices in the blind pursuit to bring about some later event called enlightenment just strengthens the dream of time and control. It strengthens the dream of self.

One present play

Life is one present play of appearances: sights, sounds, smells, thoughts, feelings, experiences, states, and other things. Mentally labeling these as separate things solidifies the false assumption that there actually are separate things happening at different times and in different places.

See that there are not two here. There is only one present play of life. To the mind, there is a "you," sitting in a chair, listening to a bird chirping outside. With that seemingly harmless interpretation, the mind has created a false appearance of separate things happening in different places. It has divided this one present play into parts: a separate "you," a chair, listening, a bird, chirping, and outside. This is what the mind does. It filters the present experience dualistically. This reflection is not about getting rid of the mind. It is pointing to simple, clear, empty non-dual awareness prior to the mind's dualistic interpretation of the present experience.

The separate "you" is an idea happening in awareness. The notion that there is a chair is also an idea. The notion that there is something here called listening that is separate from what is being heard is also an idea. The notion that there is a bird "outside" is an idea. Ideas are not aware. Only awareness is aware. In looking only with present, spacious, non-conceptual awareness, what seemed to be separate things happening in different places is seen to be one present play. Just 'This.'

Thought is similar to a sense

You experience the present reality of life through the sense of smell. Yet it would be ridiculous to suggest that you should close off all other senses and only smell the present reality.

You experience the present reality of life through the sense of sight. Yet it would be silly to suggest that you should close off all other senses in favor of sight only.

You experience life through taste and touch. Yet it would make little sense to choose taste or touch as a way to experience the present reality to the exclusion of all other senses.

Experiencing the present reality of life through only one sense is a partial view of reality.

Thought is similar to a sense. When thought is taken to be reality rather than just another way of experiencing the present reality, the being dream of a separate self arises. You totally believe the whole story of thought, including its interpretations, beliefs, ideas, religions, philosophies, judgments, opinions, and personal motivations. The exclusive experiencing of life through only the 'sense' of thought presents a partial view of reality.

There is something here, call it awareness, that is aware of thoughts as temporary appearances in reality. This awareness knows that thought is a limited, partial view of life. In seeing thought as similar to a sense, there can be a waking up out of the exclusive, partial viewing of life through thought.

Reaching a state of no thought?

You listen to a spiritual teacher talk about having a quiet mind. That sounds wonderful. So as you set out to reach a state of no thought or less thought, the seeking begins . . . .

Only thought would seek a state of no thought. Thought gets busy looking for something other than simple, ordinary, spacious, timeless awareness. Thought is seeking the end of itself. Thought cannot bring the end of thought.

The point of seeking, if there is any, is not to reach some later state of quietness or no thought. It is to expose the seeking energy. See that the very idea that you must reach a state of no thought is a thought arising now. That thought is apparently obscuring the quietness that is already here.

In the spiritual search, if there is a genuine looking, it can be seen that "you" are merely a thought arising now. The notions of future enlightenment, peace, silence or stillness are also just presently arising ideas. The idea of "you" is chasing other ideas. In noticing this seeking energy, it is realized that every thought arises right now from quietness. You are this quietness that is appearing as every thought. In this seeing, there is no longer a desire to be rid of thought. There is only what is, whether it's a moment of pure awareness without thought or a moment of incessant thinking.

The timeless unknown

It is sometimes said in non-duality meetings or books that there is nothing you can do to bring about enlightenment (i.e., Oneness) or that there is no one there to do anything. The words non-duality, Oneness, and enlightenment are just empty images pointing to the fact that life is already happening. It's already happening now. There is no path to what already is. The person who would set out to do something is a dream of thought, a dream of time, arising in the unknown, the timeless.

Within that dream, the notions of choice, control, and cause and effect arise. But when the dream is seen through, what is realized is what already is. No choice and no control. How can one control or bring about what is already happening? What is realized cannot be grasped or explained by the intellect because the intellect is merely an expression of it. Clear concepts and unclear concepts are both 'This.' There is nothing that 'This' is not.

'This' is the timeless unknown from which time and knowing arise and fall. It cannot be realized through thought and time because thought and time are just temporary images arising and falling. They are part of the dream. Yet 'This' is so immediately here. It is absolutely real. It is all there is. You are not a person who is separate from it and who can then somehow find it. You are it. Now.

Duality and Non-duality

The human mind is dualistic.I only know a "me" if there is a "you"—an "us" if there is a "them."I know myself only in relation to the other.I make the other wrong so that I can be right.I judge others to know who "I" am.When I say, "She is dumb," I am comparing myself to her in some way—as either dumber or smarter.

My philosophical conclusions exist only in relation to other philosophical conclusions. I have no view unless there is an opposite view. There is no political party without opposition.No Christian without a non-Christian (Muslim, Jew).No enlightened being without a non-enlightened being.

Non-duality is not about strengthening the dualistic mind or further defining a me against you.It is about seeing through these false divisions and judgments.

For the most part, my thoughts of others have nothing to do with them.They are mostly about me.These are 'my' thoughts, interpretations, and philosophies.The "me" is kept alive by comparing who I am, what I do, and what I know to who the others are, what they do, and what they know.

When this mirror of relationship is exposed, the separate self is revealed to be a phantom.Everything from war to the simplest of disputes with my spouse about taking out the trash is seen to be a dream of separation, entirely created by dualistic thought.

The Absolute and the relative

Some non-duality teachings say there is nothing you can do to bring about enlightenment and no one to do anything. They say that there are no seekers or teachers. It is all a dream of thought. That is true.

Other teachings say that there are methods that may help to bring about awakening including inquiry, noticing or watching thoughts and emotions, or keeping attention in the inner body. That is also true.

How can both be true: that there is nothing you can do and that there is something you can do? In the relative sense, which means within the dream of thought and time, there appears a person who engages in practices and who appears to be making progress towards awakening.

In the Absolute sense, there is only timeless awareness. There is no control, no choice, and no cause and effect. Everything is happening spontaneously and involuntarily in presence. There are no separate people doing anything. From that perspective, it is seen that the relative arises as a dream of thought in the Absolute. Time arises from timelessness. Form arises from formlessness. The dream of a separate self arises from Oneness.

A good spiritual method will help dissolve the belief that it is possible to do something in time to reach timelessness or that a separate self can reach Oneness.

Cravings

Many come to the spiritual search because of addiction. They are looking for the end of the cravings that lead to obsession and self-destructive habits.

Cravings are forms that arise from a formless, spacious awareness. Cravings do not start out as thoughts. They begin as little energy movements arising right out of this formless realm. These cravings, if they are not seen the moment they arise, turn into little mental stories about needing ice cream, beer, or some other substance or activity to satisfy the craving. These movements can grow from mental stories into full-blown obsession very quickly if they are not seen by present awareness.

When cravings arise fully in present awareness (including inner body awareness), they are seen not to be monsters in control of our lives. They are energy forms with a temporary life span. They come and go as part of the present play of life. They only stick around and turn into obsession when awareness fails to see them when they arise. In failing to see them, awareness becomes entangled into these forms. That entanglement creates the illusion of a separate self based in lack whose story is "I need something to make me feel complete."

Notice that present awareness is already perfectly complete as it is. Present awareness allows everything to come and go and sees that cravings are awareness appearing in form. That seeing alone provides a natural healing.

Stories of future fulfillment

Thought tells unconscious stories about future fulfillment. The stories may be: "If I meditate, I will become enlightened in the future and will experience great liberation, love, and peace just like my teacher;" "If I can just get my wife to change, I will be fulfilled in this relationship;" or "If I work really hard, I will be successful at my job and find happiness."

Do you see what thought is doing? It is trying desperately to move away from this moment into something else, something better. This is the cause of unnecessary searching and suffering.

In waking up from the dream that paradise exists in the future, you realize you are living in paradise right now. This moment is it! Thought may say, "But it does not feel like paradise!" The reason it does not feel like paradise is because thought is still operating on an unconscious assumption that only the future will bring fulfillment. Dig into that assumption. Is it true? Where is future? Is it hiding behind the trashcan? Is it in your backyard? Is it on the moon? Have you ever touched anything called "future?"

Have you ever really left the presence in which these words are being read? As you sit here right now, is future anything more than a presently arising thought? If not, then you know that your notions of future fulfillment are nothing more than mental storytelling. That seeing is awakening.

The abundant emptiness

Within the body and mind, there is an empty, undivided, changeless awareness. This awareness never enters the time stream. It never visits the past or future. Is it the space in which the images of past and future arise and fall.

You can get a felt sense of empty awareness right here, right now. Feel the space within your feet, legs, stomach, chest, arms, neck and head. Realize the emptiness of this space. A thought may arise, "I cannot feel the space." Notice that thought come and go. What is left is the space. A feeling may arise and fall. What is left is the space.

When this space realizes itself, you know what you really are. You see that you could not possibly have been thought or emotion, both of which are temporary forms arising and falling. When this space fully realizes itself, it is empty and yet that emptiness is entirely full. It is abundant. This is not something words can express. It must be experienced directly.

SEPTEMBER

Time is in the mind. Space is in the mind. The law of cause and effect is also a way of thinking. In reality all is here and now and all is one. Multiplicity and diversity are in the mind only.

—— Nisargadatta Maharaj

Being

What you truly are under all the thoughts of what you are is being. "Being" is a word similar to awareness in that it points to the felt sense of "I AMness" prior to the "I" thought. If you cannot sense that being now, there is a story of a separate self obscuring it. Some pointers direct you to question the story until it is seen through. You can also just stay with the sense of being under the story. Relax as the natural and effortless being that you are. This felt sense of being is always and already here, no matter what is happening.

Thought may tell the story, "I'm driving to work right now." Being, however, is not driving to work. It is simply being. Thought may tell the story, "I wish my spouse would do what I ask him to do." Being is not in that story. It is just being. Thought may tell the story, "I'm seeking enlightenment." Being is not seeking enlightenment. Being just is.

In realizing being, you know exactly what you are. Stories may continue to arise. They may quiet down. Regardless of whatever stories may or may not be arising, there is always being. There is always this "I AMness" before, during, and after the stories "I am this" or "I need that" arise. Being is timeless. This timeless being manifests as time and thought, but is ultimately free of its manifestations.

Be present?

In enlightenment teachings, you may hear the phrase, "be present." But if you look around, 'you' are the present moment. 'You' are not separate from it. 'You' are life itself. The only thing obscuring this realization is mental and emotional activity that continuously tries to move away from this moment into a dream of past, future, and resistance to now. The notion that you are separate from life is a creation of thought.

The personal will who tries to 'be present' and bring about a personal awakening is the dream. Instead of doing anything, including trying to be present, gently notice what is already being done. A dream of self is already being told. Thought is replaying the past, searching into future, and resisting what is in this moment, all for the benefit of a "me." That mind movement is a dream of control. It is a dream of personal will. Suffering and searching arise when you buy into the illusion of control and personal will.

When the personal will is seen to be a dream of thought, it dies on its own. That is true spiritual awakening. You realize there is nothing to seek. Paradise is already here, now. It has always been right here, right now under the dream that there was a "you" who was somehow separate from it and who needed to do something to find it.

Who are you defending?

In your arguments, debates, disagreements and disputes with your spouse, family member, friend, boss, or someone from another nationality, religion, or philosophy, who are you defending? Have you really asked this question? Have you really looked?

Thoughts arise involuntarily and spontaneously in response to other thoughts. During the heat of conflict, emotions such as anger and anxiety arise involuntarily and spontaneously in conjunction with those thoughts. The energy behind these emotions creates an unconscious contraction around the thoughts. This creates the sense of a separate self invested in the thoughts. In being right, you make the other wrong. By weakening the "other," you strengthen the "me."

When awareness notices this mental and emotional frenzy while it is happening, the illusion of self is exposed. What is being revealed is that, beyond that mental and emotional energy, there is no "me." It is the energy of attack and defend that makes it feel as if there is a separate self there.

The imagined, thought-based self is constantly creating and defining itself by defending its thoughts and attacking the others, and comparing and contrasting itself to the others. Yet that separate self exists only in relation to the other. Both "self" and "other" are thoughts. They are images in the mind. The notion of "self" arises only when the notion of "other" arises. In this seeing, conflict is seen to be illusory. In reality, there is no one and nothing to defend.

If you can see it, it isn't you

The dream self is created from identification with objects that arise. For example, you might think, "I am angry," or "It's a dreadful day." But look more closely. If you can see a thought, is that thought you? If you can see an emotion, is it you? You are the seer, not the objects seen. That which is seen is an object that arises and falls—a temporary form. You are that which is looking at those objects as they arise and fall. Even the notion that there is a seer as a separate identity is an object (an idea) in awareness. In looking inward, there is no separate entity there. There is only awareness recognizing awareness. Awareness is not an object. Your true identity is pure seeing itself. This can be fearful if there is a desire to hold onto some identity. But it is absolutely liberating if you see that even that fear is an object in awareness.

Suffering happens when you believe that you are your thoughts and emotions. In reality, you are not angry. Anger is arising. It's not actually a dreadful day. The thought, "It's a dreadful day" is arising in awareness. This is not about denying or suppressing thought and emotion. It is about seeing them for what they really are.

Unconditioned presence

Perhaps you've lived your life not realizing that prior to all the conditioning and conditions, there is an unconditioned presence that is totally and vibrantly free and loving. Maybe you've been locked in roles, job titles, beliefs, religions, or thought-based identities. This unconditioned presence is what you are—right now—before you think about who or what you are.

Thought might respond, "There is nothing here." The mind is so busy looking for something other than simple presence, so busy thinking about life and complicating it, that this unconditioned presence is missed.

Thought places conditions on your experience: "If my wife would stop nagging, I would be happy." "If my boss would appreciate me more, I would be satisfied with this job." Do you see the game the conditioned mind plays? Don't judge these thoughts. To condemn thought is just more conditioned mind. Thought says, "If I could only quiet my conditioned mind, I would be at peace."

Don't make an enemy out of thought. Notice that the conditioned mind is doing exactly what it is supposed to do. It is thinking. Simply notice the space in which all of that is happening. Notice this unchanging presence that is always and already here 'under' all that conditioning. This presence is unconditioned because it has no interest in placing conditions on your experience. It is naturally and effortlessly at one with what is—regardless of what the conditioned mind is doing.

Liberation

If unconditioned presence is what you really are, does this mean that you must seek some state in which you are totally calm and aware of everything? No. This is not about reaching any state or experience. Everything—every state, experience, thought, emotion, and reaction—arises from and falls back into that unconditioned presence.

The word liberation points to a shift in which life is simply happening and there is no self trying to control it. This includes not trying to control states, experiences, thoughts, or emotions.

There can even be a tendency to get stuck in awareness, believing that you are supposed to be in a state in which you are aware of everything. Is that even possible? Isn't it still control?

Liberation is childlike. It is life living itself in whatever way it happens. It is life being calm. Life being obnoxious. Life being quiet. Life being loud. Life being aware. Life being unaware. "You" are the unconditioned presence through which all of that happens.

When everything is allowed through that presence without resistance, the self that is trying to control or maintain states, experiences, thoughts, and emotions is seen to be an illusion. This seeing brings a natural equanimity, peace, joy, and love. But those attributes are not in any way contrived or brought about by a person's effort. This shift happens only when the self trying to manipulate the experience of living is seen through.

Chasing awareness

The word awareness is sometimes mistakenly associated with a state found in time. This is the "I got it/I lost it" syndrome. The "I got it" sense happens when there is pure awareness without much conceptualization (i.e., "I am present"). The "I lost it" sense occurs when there is the experience of being lost in thought or emotion (i.e., "I am not present"). This can create a cycle in which you are chasing the state of awareness and trying to quiet thought and emotion. This is still control and tends to keep the search going as you continuously fuel the idea that there is some state that you must find, maintain, or recreate.

Instead of treating awareness as a state that can be found or lost in time, notice the timeless opening in which all states happen. Temporary states of thinking and not thinking, feeling and not feeling, and seeing and not seeing arise and fall within that opening. The opening does not come and go.

In noticing that your true nature is that opening, the movement of chasing states and the notions of "I got it/I lost it" tend to relax naturally. In this opening, anything can happen. There is no "you" there resisting or controlling or trying to maintain or recreate anything that comes through the opening. There is only the opening and whatever is coming through it.

Aliveness in the body

Noticing what is happening in the body does not simply awaken you to the life all around you. It awakens you to the realization that you are life itself.

The aliveness in your body is there to wake you up out of the dream of a separate self. Feel the sensations throughout the body no matter what you are doing. Notice that there is always a sense of aliveness within. Aliveness cannot be found in time or manufactured. It is what is already happening within the body right now.

If anger or fear arises, notice it without judgment. If judgments about these emotions arise, simply notice them also. Notice that these thoughts and emotions are harmless when they are seen the moment they arise.

This is not a prescription to engage in a spiritual practice. This is an invitation to notice what is already being done. Are you 'doing' emotions? They are arising involuntarily and spontaneously, aren't they? If you had a choice, would you choose fear or anger?

Are you 'doing' aliveness? The aliveness in your body, from your feet to your head, is just happening. You aren't bringing it about. Simply notice the aliveness that is already happening. Notice that this aliveness is everywhere, not just in the body. In that noticing, life is waking up to itself as One Life.

The dream you are projecting

Thoughts constitute a relative, dualistic dream being projected outward and placed over reality. When you believe that your president is a lousy leader, that your grandma ought to take better care of herself, or that some other religion is wrong, the dream is dreaming itself. 'Your' thoughts aren't objectively true. They are just thoughts. You are carrying around a sort of virtual projector, projecting a movie of personal opinions, beliefs, ideas, philosophies, and conditions. The basic plot of the movie is that life should be different than the way it is. That plot keeps the idea of a separate you alive. Beyond that movie, there is no separate you.

You are totally innocent of this. Great compassion for yourself and others arises when it is realized that "person" is merely a thought dream and that this dream arises beyond your control.

When this involuntary dream is seen, it loses its momentum. It is seen by no one. One could say, it is seen by awareness. Awareness is just a word describing the intelligent, empty space in which the dream arises. When that space is realized, an unnamable, unconditional, loving presence is seen to be your natural state. Even the story that there is awareness aware of the dream is seen through. In liberation, all stories lose their heavy meaning, even the story of being, Oneness, liberation, or any other word used to describe it. Life simply lives itself.

Allow?

In these reflections or other pointers, you may hear words like, "allow thoughts and emotions to arise and fall." But do you even have control in allowing thoughts and emotions to arise? Allowing still implies control, doesn't it? It implies that there is a person who has control over what arises. Is that true? When you see the word "allow" used in these reflections, the word is pointing to the natural and effortless noticing of what is already happening. The word has nothing to do with personal will or effort.

Thoughts are arising. Emotions are happening. There can only be a seeing that this is already the case.

When you hear, "allow this situation to be as it is," what that really means is notice that this situation is already happening in exactly the way it is happening.

In that way, noticing is allowing life to be just as it is. Even when there is no noticing, that inattention is also just happening. Life is living itself, whether there is an awareness of what is happening or not. In that seeing, seeking, resistance, and suffering end. Yet if seeking, resistance, and suffering arise again, notice that these movements are also just happening beyond 'your' control. That is what is meant by the word "allow."

Silence

Silence is the natural state. That does not mean that we have to remain quiet all the time or that we must try to avoid sound or bring about a quiet mind. We don't have to do anything to recognize silence as the natural state except notice that silence is always and already here. It is already the natural state. It is everywhere. It is all around you. It is within you. You are it.

No sound is separate from the silence that gives birth to it. If you cannot sense the silence, just notice what is here. If sound arises, notice the sound. Notice that it arises and falls naturally without any need for you to judge it, welcome it, escape it, or reject it. Notice the silence that is here before the sound arises, while it is arising, and after it falls. If loud music is playing, notice the music and notice the silence that surrounds it. Conversations, music, explosions and other sounds arise from silence. These things are silence in another form.

The next time you hear a sound, notice that you are the silence that is listening to it. You are the silence that is here before the sound arises, while it is sounding, and when it is gone. There is nothing that you need to do to recognize silence as the natural state except notice that your very essence is silence.

The felt sense of being

Most people live their lives through thought. They take themselves to be that thought stream. When "enlightenment" is mentioned, the natural tendency is to search for it through presently arising thoughts about future attainment or to attempt to grasp it intellectually. Both avenues will fail miserably. Enlightenment is not found in thought. Enlightenment is just a fancy word for the realization of a felt sense of being. This permanent being is who you really are, beyond any temporary thought that arises and falls.

Do not get stuck in words like "being." As with any word, being is just another idea in the thought stream. Although the word being is an idea, it is pointing to a felt sense of aliveness within the body and mind. Being is so simple it is often overlooked by a mind searching for a future state or for conceptual understanding. The clearest conceptual understanding about being is not being. Being is not for the intellect to grasp. It is what you are before the attempt to search for it or grasp it intellectually arises.

Using the words "felt-sense" may lead the mind to believe that being is like an emotion. It is not. Emotions come and go within being. Being is the unmoving, unchanging, timeless 'felt' sense of being alive within the body and mind. It is that simple. Making enlightenment more complicated than that is just more searching and more intellectual grasping.

Being and seeing

Yesterday's reflection said that making enlightenment more complicated than simple being is just more searching and intellectualizing. How is that reconciled with pointers inviting you to see or notice what is arising? Aren't those pointers complicating things?

The invitation to see or notice is not about doing anything. It is about noticing what is already being done.

What is 'being done' is a story of self that lives in time. That story arises and falls in little subplots such as, "Why did that horrible event happen to me in the past?" and "I hope to accomplish great things in the future." That is a story of mental images. It is not who you really are.

Enlightenment is a shift into the realization that timeless being is what you really are. This truth sets you (the story) free. This is why it's called liberation.

The invitation to 'notice' is an invitation to see what is absolutely true beyond that story of self. The invitation is not directed to the story. It is an invitation to being itself, which is beyond that story, beyond time.

In this realization, 'you'—the story—do not reach enlightenment *in time*. Enlightenment is realized to be being itself. It is what has always been here under the story that 'you' were coming to it. Pointers to "notice" and "see" are invitations to realize this truth right now—to awaken to this timeless being.

Free will

In treating the question of free will as a philosophy, the mind tends to pick between two dualistic positions: there is or is not free will. But when the question of free will is taken to be an experiential question, you move beyond philosophy into the possibility of awakening.

Look at what is actually happening now. Thoughts and emotions arise spontaneously and involuntarily. Legs and arms move on their own. Do you notice these occurrences before they happen? How could you notice something before it happens?

When the mind-made story of "me" is active, it is telling a story of control. It is constantly commenting on what is going to happen next, believing that there is a "me" taking action. But when that story is seen, it tends to vanish like a cockroach scurrying away as the kitchen light comes on. Action is then taken but without the story of "me" pretending to bring it about.

Look to see whether even the choice to drink tea or coffee arises spontaneously and involuntarily in the mind. Before the choice arose, there is no sign of the idea of coffee or tea. Then, all of a sudden, the choice arises. Did you bring that choice about?

Don't think about free will. Just look. The answers are not in philosophical conclusions. They are revealed in this experiential seeing. They are revealed in presence.

Seeking

Seeking happens in so many subtle and not-sosubtle ways. It happens when you repeatedly attend spiritual meetings, read spiritual books, meditate for hours, or engage in other spiritual practices unceasingly.

It also happens in little, subtle ways throughout the day. For example, you are doing the dishes and there is a movement within you, perhaps a thought or feeling, towards something other than what is happening. That movement creates a pull towards some future moment. That is just as much seeking energy as engaging in routine spiritual practices each morning. The "me" movement is looking for something other than what is in this moment.

There is nothing wrong with seeking energy. It is not something to try to remove. The very movement to get rid of seeking is seeking. Whenever we desire this moment to be other than the way it is, that is seeking.

In simply noticing seeking, the energy tends to dissipate on its own. When seeking arises, notice the little voice that says it shouldn't be there. Is that true? Seeking shouldn't be here? If it's here, it is here. Why argue with that? Seeing seeking energy and the little accompanying "spiritual ego" voice that judges the seeking is all that needs to happen. The truth takes over from there.

Awareness and thought

It can be incredibly liberating to realize that you are not thought. All 'your' life, 'you' believed every thought racing through the thought stream in the mind. Then you hear a teacher that points you to pure awareness prior to thought. From that pointing, there can be a freeing realization that thought is not who you are. It merely arises and falls within who you are.

But liberation invites a deeper realization than mere identification as awareness. Notice that the distinction between thought and awareness is a thought-created division. Is there really something here called "awareness" totally separate from something else called "thought?" Only thought creates that rigid division. Until thought rises up to make that distinction, there is only 'This'—One Life happening now as one continuous flow.

Although realizing that you are pure awareness can be liberating, it can also trap thought into searching for a purer and purer state of awareness—a state that is free of thought. But only thought would seek to get rid of thought. Chasing a deeper state of awareness is a thought-driven search.

In the realization that all distinctions are illusory, including the division between awareness and thought, liberation arises. Life lives itself—simply, vibrantly, lovingly, spontaneously and effortlessly. Everything is allowed to be just the way it is, including thought.

Chasing states

In these reflections, the natural state is sometimes referred to as "the opening." Who you really are is the opening through which everything happens including thoughts, emotions, reactions, pain, frustration, states of calm awareness and states of total confusion.

You've been told that you must reach some state called "enlightenment" in which you are totally calm, peaceful, and loving. This tends to send the mind on a chase into future. Emotionally painful states are labeled bad. Calm or pleasurable states are labeled good. The chase involves seeking the good and avoiding the bad.

When the mind is chasing some ideal "good" state, it avoids what is actually occurring when pain, frustration, or confusion is occurring. This fuels the chase towards the ideal state and keeps the search going.

Pointing to your true nature as the "opening" allows a seeing that anything is possible in this opening. A state of pure, calm awareness or a state of great fear may happen in the opening. Whatever is happening is allowed by 'no one.' There is no one there deciding which state is good and which is bad. Without the labeling of good v. bad, the chasing tends to stop on its own.

If the mind renews the chase again towards something other than what is happening, notice that the chase is happening in that opening. As this is seen, there is nothing left to chase. There is only 'what is.'

What do 'you' really want?

What do you really want? Whatever you really want is reflected in your life right now.

You may say you want freedom or peace. Look more closely. Are you surrounded by material things or constantly worried about debt? Are you seeking to be right and to have your ideas prevail in conversations with others? Are you looking for others to be different than the way they are? Are you always seeking something other than what actually is in this moment? Are you constantly looking for validation, attention, praise, acknowledgement, and love?

The mind is deceptive. It makes claims about wanting peace or freedom. Despite its claims, what you really want is showing up in your life right now.

Once you see what your life is actually telling you about what is really important to you, the possibility of seeing self-deception arises. Enlightenment is a demolition project. It reveals that the self is nothing more than a set of stories.

No matter how strongly you claim to want freedom or peace, the circumstances in your life reveal the actual stories you are buying into. If you are worrying about money, arguing with others, seeking praise from others, or constantly wanting to be right, those are the things most important to you. Those are the things you really want. What you want is reflected in your life right now. That seeing allows true freedom and peace. All else is self-deception.

Do emotions go away?

During the spiritual search, there can be an erroneous belief that, in enlightenment, feelings go away and nothing is felt. This is a false myth.

In the so-called egoic state, the dream self tends to avoid and escape emotions. You take drugs, drink alcohol, eat too much, work too much, engage in activity that keeps the mind stimulated, strategize about the future, exert control, complain, blame, or otherwise think or act your way out of feeling emotions directly. The movie of self is directed at avoiding what is in this moment. It is only natural that the movie would imagine enlightenment to be the ultimate method of escaping emotions.

Enlightenment is a natural state in which emotions are felt directly and immediately in the moment they arise. There isn't a "you" choosing to feel emotions. They simply arise fully in awareness. You no longer feed the story of time, which is the story of self. Feelings are not accumulated along a time-bound storyline. They are allowed to come and go freely. There is no person there attempting to avoid, escape, or analyze them.

In awakening, anything is possible in the opening known as "you." There can be awakeness to a moment of emotional explosion or to a moment of no feeling whatsoever. Everything is allowed. Nothing is pushed away.

Seeing the dualistic mirror of relationship

There is only 'This'—Oneness appearing as two. It appears as separate people. But this is just an appearance. The "me" exists only in relation to the "other."

Notice what the dualistic mind is doing. Thought creates a "self" by comparing and contrasting itself to the "other." In your outward judgment of another, the mirror of relationship creates an inward self-definition. When you say, "she is wrong," you are impliedly strengthening the "self." You can only know that she is wrong if you are right. You can only claim to be attractive in comparison to others that you deem unattractive. You can only claim to succeed if others fail. You are only poor in comparison to those that are rich or not as poor as you are. You can only be a victim if others are perceived as being treated more fairly by life. You can only claim to be enlightened if there are others who are not enlightened.

The spiritual search is a search for your true identity. But you cannot realize your true identity through the dualistic mind. You will only find this mirroring effect—this dualistic comparison and separation. The dualistic mind will only give you a mental image that has relevance only in relation to something else.

This is not a prescription to stop judging others. This is an invitation to see the dualistic mind at work. That seeing reveals your true identity beyond the separate self.

Fixation

Enlightenment means not fixating in any realm of experience. The main fixation in the so-called egoic state is with the experience of being a separate self. There is a fixation with this "I" thought and with all thoughts related to it. This is the cause of suffering and the reason people begin searching for release.

In seeing the fixation with the "I" thought and all its stories, a release from that fixation happens. But fixation can return, and often does, 'after' an initial awakening. The mind likes to fixate in a realm of experience. So it fixates in some of the by-products of awakening such as joy, peace, and love. When a moment of fear or confusion arises, the question is, "Where did my peace go?" The searching begins again.

There can also be a fixation with mental interpretations of enlightenment—fixations with words like "no self" or "Oneness." Enlightenment is not a religion or philosophy. The intellect will never grasp 'This.' If you find yourself arguing with someone over teachings or anything related to enlightenment, you can bet that there is some mental fixation happening.

In the realization that everything is impermanent and that there is nothing to hold onto, the movement of fixation tends to fall away. Everything is allowed to be within the opening known as "you." Even if seeking or fixation arises again, it is allowed to be.

'This'

The person who sets out to do something in order to realize 'This' is the very obstacle to realizing 'This.' This is not a prescription to do something or do nothing. It is an invitation to notice the many ways in which the person efforts to move away from the utterly obvious simplicity of what is.

In this moment, there is no such thing as enlightenment or a path to enlightenment. There is no person who is liberated or almost liberated. Those are just presently arising thoughts. They are little stories the dualistic mind tells. In the moment when those stories are believed, awareness is making a self out of thought. There is nothing wrong with that. Everything arises in and as 'This.'

Look around and, instead of seeing anything called liberation, Oneness, enlightenment, 'This,' or any other story, notice the space, the flowers, the buildings, the desk, the floor, the arm, the pets, the people, and the sky. Notice the breathing, laughing, crying, complaining, hurting, talking, and walking. Life is much simpler than a story of thought that tries to describe it.

Forget words like "enlightenment" and "nonduality." They are just stories. They are no more meaningful than the toilet flushing or the dog barking. Whatever is presently happening is where the real meaning in life is. To not see this is to miss life itself. But 'This' includes missing 'This' also. There is nothing that is not 'This.'

Nothing is opposed to anything else

Thought divides reality up into me v. you, us v. them, this religion v. that religion, this belief v. that belief, and a host of other divisions that are not real. These divisions are creatures of thought. Nothing in reality is opposed to anything else.

In non-dual teachings, one often hears that awareness is your true nature and thoughts appear and disappear in awareness. This is only a pointer. It is not the truth. There is no such thing as a statement of the truth because all statements appear in dualistic language and therefore create the appearance of two. This creates the false notion that reality can split itself apart from itself. In this false dualism, it appears that something is opposed to or separate from something else. Even the notions of true v. false are created entirely by thought.

Nothing is opposed to anything else. There is no real division between awareness and thought. When there is a belief in this division, there is often the corresponding belief that one must stay in awareness and deny thought, as if thought is opposed to awareness. In reality, thought is not independent of awareness. In buying completely into the mental division between thought and awareness, it appears that there are two here. This creates the sense of "I got it" when pure awareness is being experienced and the sense of "I lost it" when thought is arising. This is a trap.

The insanity of seeking

Imagine two fish debating about what water is. Imagine two birds trying to come to some conceptual understanding of air. Imagine the ocean trying to grasp what wetness is. Imagine a dog believing that he must travel a spiritual path to find "dogness." Imagine two aliens on another planet trying to understand what life is. Do you see the insanity of all this? The same insanity is inherent in the search for enlightenment. Enlightenment just means presence, being, or aliveness. The words are not the thing they describe. Those words are merely pointing to the very life that you are right now.

Your entire search for enlightenment is happening in enlightenment. Your entire search for presence is happening in presence. Your search for being is happening in being. The search for life is being conducted by life itself. You are that which you are seeking. You are looking for God with his eyes.

As this is realized, and it can only be realized now because life is only now, it is seen that no word, idea, philosophy, belief system, or pointer could ever get you any closer to 'This' that you already are.

'This' is so simple, obvious, and immediately close that it is missed as soon as you go looking for it or as soon as you start trying to find it in thought.

Non-duality is love

What is this which is beyond the dualistic opposites of right v. wrong, positive v. negative, pleasure v. pain, form v. formlessness, One v. many, awareness v. thought, this position v. that position, this belief v. that belief, this idea v. that idea, duality v. nonduality, this person v. that person, this group v. that group? There is a field in which that dualistic game is playing out. You are that field. Thought just likes to stick with one particular position within the field. That is the nature of thought. It knows nothing of this field. It only knows its position. The dream self is nothing but a thought-based entity. Therefore, the dream self is essentially only interested in its own dualistic position.

In noticing when thought gets stuck on a position, something beyond dualistic thought recognizes itself. One could call it love. But this is a love beyond the dualistic opposites of love v. hate. This is a love that embraces the whole. It embraces the dualistic interplay. It knows that the truth is not in a dualistic position. The truth cannot be known through attachment to some dualistic idea (and all ideas are dualistic).

Although the dualistic mind tends to see many paradoxes and contradictions in this message, love sees no paradoxes or contradictions. Love sees that the truth is shining through in this message in a way that thought cannot understand or express.

Walking

The simple act of walking is a portal to 'This.' As you walk down the street or even to the bathroom, simply notice what is already happening. Legs are moving. Arms are swaying back and forth. The head is turning to look at things.

Notice that each movement is happening on its own. Notice that walking is just happening. The story of you that lives in time (i.e., the thought-based self) is not doing the walking. Each leg is placing itself spontaneously in front of the other, without the need for any command from that thought-based self. There is no voice telling you to put each foot in front of the other.

While walking and noticing the miracle of life living itself through the arms and legs, notice that the entire story of self that lives in time is totally absent. There is only 'This.' Walking. That's it. Where are all the worries, problems, and details of this life of yours? This is showing you that your entire story of self is completely made up and that it is possible to live without that story. This is showing you that the story is self-centered. It is creating a center called "me" that believes that it is in control. The simple act of walking and noticing that the "me" is not doing the walking reveals that there is no center to life. There is no self. There is only 'This.'

Oneness

What is this boundary between you and God, between you and enlightenment, between you and happiness, between you and the other, between you and Oneness, between you and peace, between you and the rest of life? Have you ever asked yourself whether it is absolutely true that there is a line separating you from these other things? Are these lines not created by thought? Where do these boundaries exist? If they exist only in thought, what is left when they are seen through? The separate self is a thought-based entity, created by belief in these boundary lines.

In the willingness to allow the question, "What is absolutely true?" to destroy every thought-created boundary line, something arises beyond the idea of a separate self. Fidelity to this truth dissolves all the false beliefs that have created these boundaries.

Oneness is not anything "you" as a separate entity could ever realize or find or get closer to. Oneness is not a philosophy. It is what you are. It is all there is. How can you get nearer to 'This,' when 'This' is what you already are? 'This' is realized in your absence, which means in the absence of the false belief that 'you' are somehow separate from the rest of life, from what you seek, from Oneness itself.

Seeking in all aspects

Seeking doesn't happen only in the context of enlighten-ment. It is your constant companion. Notice the ways in which you look for some future moment, avoiding what is in this moment.

When you are brushing your teeth in the morning, are you thinking about when you will be done so that you can brush your hair or get to work? When you are driving to work, are you thinking about arriving at work or what you will do tonight after work? When you arrive at work, are you thinking about lunch, the finishing of a project, or the end of the day?

When you are doing chores around the house, are you thinking about getting the chores done? Does your day feel like one entire movement forward? If so, all of that is seeking energy. Seeking energy is not good or bad. It is just not true that something should be happening other than what is hap-pening. Suffering arises when we live in illusion.

There is an old Zen saying, "Before enlightenment, chop wood, carry water . . . after enlightenment, chop wood, carry water." So what is the difference? The difference is that, in enlightenment, the dream self who believes it must constantly think about what is going to happen next falls away. Life is lived much more easily--without the false idea that you have control and that something must be happening other than what is happening.

Complaining

Complaining, either to others or only in thought, is one of the ways in which the dream self keeps the dream of separation going. Complaining about someone or something makes the dream self feel morally superior. Whenever thought makes the other wrong, the dream self sees itself as right.

The attempt to stop complaining assumes that you have control. But "you" are just one of the many thoughts occurring spontaneously and involuntarily within the dream. The very movement to stop complaining is a movement of the dream self trying to get rid of itself. Do you see the futility of that?

In judging the voice in your head that is complaining as bad, you are seeking a future moment where there is no complaining. That very movement is seeking. It is a denial of what is. If complaining is arising, that is what is arising. Period.

Noticing the complaining voice (as well as the voice that says that complaining should not be happening) is enough. That noticing tends to allow the complaining to die on its own. But if that complaining voice dies out, "you" did not kill it. If the voice returns, "you" did not bring it back. There can only be a seeing of what is coming and going beyond your control, which is to say that there is no self who has control. The noticing being referred to here comes from beyond the dream of self.

Totally natural and effortless

Liberation is totally natural and effortless. If life is not being lived naturally and effortlessly, it means that the story of the doer, which could also be called the story of the controller, is there. The doer believes that success depends upon doing things and controlling outcomes. It believes it must do something in order to achieve some later result. This is what makes life appear to be a struggle and a search.

In liberation, it is realized that the doer is a fiction of thought. The story of self is seen to be an illusion.

The question inevitably arises, "What can I do to realize a liberation that is natural and effortless?" The very question is a trap. It arises from the story of self, the doer, who is efforting to do something in order to gain something else. The story of self is asking how it can get rid of itself. It is asking how it can control life. But only that story would ask the question.

Noticing the ways in which the doer believes it can do something to come to liberation allows the doer to be seen as a false entity. What is left is liberation. Liberation allows even the story of the doer to arise, knowing that the story is not true.

OCTOBER

There are no correct experiences to have. The well-being we have sought by trying to rearrange thoughts, feelings and sensations is always and already present as the seamless flow of everything that arises.

— John Astin

Resentment

To say that you are a person who is resentful is a story. In the story, 'you' are the main character who gets to focus on 'your' pain and 'your' story of how someone in 'your' past did 'you' wrong. It's all about you. The story of resentment makes you feel morally right and justified in your pain, which in turn keeps the sense of separation and self-centeredness alive.

Enlightenment is not about "letting go" of resentments. Enlightenment is seeing things the way they really are. When resentment arises, that is what is happening. Any movement to get rid of resentment is seeking. Dreaming that you are a person who is resentful and who is going to get rid of resentment in the future perpetuates the dream self and keeps resentment around. The dream self is not interested in being resentment-free. It just wants to be separate. To accomplish this, it keeps the story of time alive. That includes the story of making resentment into a problem to get rid of over time.

In noticing the emotional pain and mental story of resentment as it arises, there is a seeing that you do not bring resentment about. Therefore, you are not in control of when it leaves. In that noticing, resentment is allowed to be exactly as it is without any movement to get rid of it. It tends to diminish on its own when it's brought into this light.

Unconditional love

Unconditional love is not based on what the other person does or does not do. It is not based on whether someone lives up to some image you have in your mind. It is not based on whether you get a return on your investment in a relationship. Those are conditions.

Love is who we are. It is what life is. You cannot give love. To love someone is not to give them anything but to recognize the love that is already there. To pretend that you have something that others need, including love, is arrogant. This pretense fuels separation. It is spiritual violence.

To seek, expect, or demand love is not love at all. It is egoic neediness. Love wants nothing because it lacks nothing. Love does not seek love. It places no conditions on life and others. It simply recognizes itself everywhere, in everyone. It does not buy into the illusion of separation.

Unconditional love is not something that thought could ever show you. To realize it, find out what is prior to that thought-based story of "me" in the mind. What is reading these words—not the thoughts that arise to agree or disagree with what is being said—but rather the simple presence itself? What is resonating beyond these ideas? That presence is love. Realize that what you truly are, beyond all mental conditions, is unconditional love.

Gratitude

Gratitude arises when the preciousness of 'This' is realized. 'This' is life happening right now in whatever way it is happening. Perhaps 'you' are sitting on a chair, just reading these words. That is all that is happening and it is perfectly enough. Sitting. Breathing. Looking. Reading. Thinking. Feeling. That is all there is. Suffering and searching arise when the belief in a separate, thought-created "me" starts telling the story that something other than 'This' should be happening.

Once the search for something more starts up, true gratitude for 'This' cannot be seen. Gratitude is not something we find in the future. Future is just a thought arising now. Gratitude is not thought. You can think about gratitude, but it would still just be a thought about gratitude entertained by a separate self. True gratitude arises naturally in presence. Gratitude is realized to be your very essence when the search for something more than 'This' is seen to be a thought-based illusion.

When 'This' is seen, the simplicity and preciousness of life is seen. In this realization, it is not that 'you'—as a separate entity—are grateful for other people, things, and situations. In true gratitude, there is no self attempting to gain something from other people, things, and situations. There is only gratitude. Gratitude for 'This' in whatever form it takes right now. Simple gratitude for aliveness itself.

The simplicity of 'This'

In the search for something more than this moment, the simplicity of 'This' is missed completely. Look around. Sense the being—the felt oneness with life. Thoughts may be happening. Perhaps a feeling of anxiety briefly arises and falls in awareness as you read this reflection. Maybe there is the sound of a dog barking, a clock ticking, or a child laughing in the other room. That is all that is happening. Isn't it beautifully simple? Spiritual awakening is that simple. It is to realize 'This' fully and to allow the search for something more than 'This' to die naturally in that seeing.

Isn't the search for something more a dream of thought arising now? Can you grab the future and control it from where you are sitting now? You cannot touch the future because it is nothing more than presently arising thought. When this is seen fully, the search is seen to be an illusion.

How can you need something other than 'This?' 'This' is precious. 'This' is all there is. Spiritual awakening is about the truth. The truth is that 'This' is life, happening now. 'This' is it. It is that simple. 'This' is when whatever is presently happening— whether it is the sound of dishes being washed or a plane flying over heard—is the most fascinating thing because it is all that is happening. It is truth.

Awareness is great as a pointer, but lousy as an identity

The word "awareness" points to an immediate, timeless, formless non-conceptual seeing. All concepts arise in this seeing. "You" are merely one of those concepts arising in this seeing. Your entire story of self, as detailed and personal as it feels, arises as a set of concepts in awareness.

Although it can be liberating to see that the separate self is a concept and that who you really are is closer to this awareness, there can be a subtle fixation with the notion of awareness even after the initial seeing. The word "awareness" is great as a pointer, but lousy as an identity or philosophical fixation. If the word "awareness" is taken as more than a simple pointer, there can be a subtle fixation with passively witnessing. An unconscious belief arises that there is something here called "awareness" or a "witness" watching something else called "thought" or even "life." This is still dualistic.

When the word "notice" is used in these reflections, it is not an invitation to passively witness life. It is a call to love—to the unknown. Spiritual liberation cannot be known through dualistic concepts. Liberation cannot be realized when there is a fixation in some realm of experience. Liberation arises naturally when the dualistic boundaries between self and other, awareness and thought, and form and formlessness are seen to be illusory. You are not the witness of something separate from you called "life." You are life itself.

Seeing beyond dualistic emotions

A negative emotion is an alarm bell revealing that there is attachment to some story in time happening. If resentment, sadness, guilt, or shame arises, notice that a story of past is happening. If anxiety or fear arises, notice that thought is telling a story of future. When anger or frustration arises, notice that there is a story of resistance to now happening (e.g., the driver in front of you is not doing what you want her to do).

Awakening presents the opportunity to see that these stories are arising now. You aren't actually visiting the past or future. There is simply thinking arising in timelessness. Suffering is an illusion of thought.

Liberation is not about removing emotions or thoughts. It is not about destroying the ego. Only ego would seek to destroy ego. Liberation is about seeing how attachment to these stories in time creates suffering.

In seeing that this thought life is keeping a dualistic, time-bound, self-centered story alive, the possibility of liberation from suffering arises. In that seeing, attachment to these stories and their accompanying emotions dissolves on its own. Liberation is not about replacing the negative stories and emotions with positive ones. It is about seeing what is actually happening in 'your' mental and emotional world. Peace, love, and joy arise in that seeing. These attributes of peace, love, and joy exist beyond dualistic emotions.

Love just is

Thought takes dualistic positions. It says: "This is about Oneness." "This is not about Oneness." "There is a God." "There isn't a God." "Spiritual realization is about awareness." "Spiritual realization is not about awareness." "There is a self." "There is no self." "There is choice." "There is no choice." "This is about Jesus." "This is not about Jesus." "My life is good." "My life is bad." "This teacher has it." "This teacher doesn't." These are all dualistic stories.

Thought cannot see non-duality. The function of thought is to take dualistic positions. Thought can even take a position on thought. "Thought is bad" is just another dualistic position.

Oneness is not a position. It is not anything to argue about. It is nothing at all. It cannot be grasped. You can't get it because you are it. It is a seeing that life is impermanent. There is nothing to hold onto. No experience. No concept. No belief. No philosophy. No expression. Nothing, nothing, nothing. To the dualistic mind, that may sound like nihilism. But again, the dualistic mind will never see 'This.' When non-duality is realized to be this seeing of what the dualistic mind is constantly doing, an opening can happen. The attachment to all positions dies. Love is what is left. This love takes no position on non-duality. It is not for or against it. It sees no other so it allows everything. Love just is.

The dream self is a virtual reality

The dream self is like a conceptual overlay placed on reality. Thought interprets reality through concepts, most of which act to confirm the central "me" concept. "I" exist only in relation to the "other" thing, person, event, etc.

The dream self is a conditioned existence. In some computer games, participants wear stereoscopic goggles that produce images of a virtual reality. Similarly, in the dream of self, conditioning creates a virtual reality that says: "This is a chair" or "My husband should listen more." These are thought-based interpretations of reality based on memory. The dream self is essentially the past coming to meet the reality of now.

When the past (memory) meets the present, life feels dead. Thought gives the false impression that you can know life by labeling and judging it. But life is not conceptual. It is an actuality. The depth and miracle of life is veiled when life is lived only through the goggles of the dream self, the playing of one mental image after another.

Liberation is like taking the goggles off. It is seeing reality the way it is, including the thoughts that are arising. Life is not conceptual. When this is seen, what is left is a love of reality. This love is not dependent on thought. For example, your love for your husband has nothing to do with whether he does what you "think" he should do. This is unconditional love.

Raw sensitivity and openness

In allowing the body and mind to be absolutely open to the experience of sensitivity in the present moment, the truth reveals itself automatically. Every notion of separation, every fixation, attachment, and identification gets swallowed by that openness. Love just eats the 'self' away. Bit by bit, the 'you' that you take yourself to be is devoured.

Many experience a contraction against that degree of sensitivity. They would rather hang out in or try to recreate some experience, identity, by-product of awakening, fixation or position that this is somehow about awareness, or Oneness, or some other insight that pops up along the way. But 'This' degree of openness cannot be pinned down. It swallows even your insights.

In this raw openness, you see that what you thought or felt to be true in the dream state was just fear, masquerading as a separate self. You see that, even after an awakening experience, little pockets of resistance want to come back to know something. But there is nothing to know. That is what pure love reveals.

When this love burns up every mask you've tried to hide behind, there you are standing naked in a truth that cannot be expressed. It cannot be held onto. This is raw openness, the kind that no fancy Advaita inquiry or pointer can touch. In this openness, there is nothing to find—nothing to add and nothing to subtract. There is only 'This' meeting itself.

The ordinary and the extraordinary

The mind believes that enlightenment is something other than this present experience. It keeps looking for the next moment. It can't believe that enlightenment could be as simple as taking out the trash right now. Yet it is. Enlightenment is overlooked in each moment simply because we are expecting something extraordinary somewhere else, in some later experience.

Then one day, after all that movement towards some other moment in the future, the mind utterly fails. It sees that it cannot know. It gives up. It doesn't give up because some guru said that enlightenment happens when the mind gives up. It gives up because it sees that no matter what the question, the answer will not be enough.

When the mind fails, it is like falling into a ditch. A hand reaches to the water and mud. "What is this? It's like I've never seen this before. . . " All of a sudden the water and mud appear alive for the first time. "That's me. I am that water! I am this mud!"

Joy, love, wonder and innocence arise. The person who was looking for enlightenment drops away completely and all that is left is what was always here . . . this ordinary life in this moment. But now, because there is no one living it, and no one looking for some later moment, it is extraordinary.

The simple recognition of what is

In the search for 'enlightenment,' a natural tendency of the dualistic mind is to analyze a teacher's words. The mind looks at information and compares it to previously learned information and then analyzes whether the new information is consistent with its stored memory. But this analysis is the seeking. The self—attachment to stored thought—is seeking to confirm itself, its own ideas.

'This' is pointing to something so obvious that, once it is realized, the tendency of the mind to attempt to grasp 'This' dies. Pointers are intended to allow the mind to unravel its fixations and relax into the simple recognition of the space of now and everything that arises and falls in it—to the sound of a car going by, the sensation of breathing, a feeling arising and falling, a thought coming and going, the wiggling of a toe, or the sound of a friend's voice. It's that simple.

Even in that realization, the mind may continue to fixate. It wants to hold on tightly to its own interpretation of 'This.' Instead of seeking 'This,' it believes it has attained it. It starts to believe that its pointers are true and that others' pointers are not. It turns away from the simple recognition of what is and, instead, tries to own 'This' on a personal level. No one owns 'This.' 'This' is simply what is.

Perfect order

The "me" is looking for the right experience, the right state, or the right thought. It believes that if it can rearrange the thoughts, experiences, and states into the right order, it will find spiritual awakening. It is this resistance, avoidance, seeking, and control by the "me" that gives the appearance that awakening is not already here.

There is no right experience, state, or thought. Stated another way, the right experience, state, and thought is found in what is presently happening. Every experience is exactly as it should be because it is exactly as it is. Every state is exactly as it should be because it is exactly as it is. And every thought is exactly as it should be because it is exactly as it is. The "me" that would try to rearrange this furniture and pretend that something that is happening should not be happening is the only obstacle to awakening.

In seeing that this "me" is nothing more than a movement of mind, it is seen that even that movement is exactly as it should be because it is exactly as it is. In that way, even resistance, avoidance, seeking and control are exactly as they should be because they are exactly as they are. There is nowhere to escape to, nothing to avoid, nothing to get to, and nothing to attain. There is only a simple love of what is. That is perfect order.

Your demand on life

What is it like to live with no demand for this moment to be different than it is? In order to answer the question with total honesty, something deeper than thought must look. Thought—when there is identification with it—demands that life be other than the way it is. Thought is the demander. The demander cannot answer this question of what life is like to live without the demander.

To answer the question, there must be a looking at what the demander is doing in the present moment. Thought looks to a person or situation but does not see what is really there. It brings all sorts of images from the past and places those images on the person or situation. It cannot see the person or situation clearly. It sees only images. Thought also resists what is happening now and demands that something else happen. Demand brings the energy of conflict and separation to life. Love seems obscured by this energy.

Unconditional love is what is left when your demand on this moment is gone. That does not mean that thought stops completely. In seeing what thought is doing, and how it is demanding life to be other than the way it is, life lives itself. Thought may still arise. Action may still be taken. There may still be a movement to change a situation, but the action is taken from love itself, not from the demander.

When the two become one

We come to the spiritual search because a lot of thinking is happening. The mind is lost in the story of "me" and everything that is happening to "me." It can be confusing and painful. Then a spiritual teaching points us to an inner non-conceptual awareness. An incredible peace and freedom is realized when there is a shift from attachment to everything to a realization of pure awareness or emptiness.

We can get stuck in pure awareness though. We can find ourselves in the realization that nothing is happening. We realize a beautiful nothingness. And yet . . . isn't that just another point of reference, another dualistic point which is opposite of the point of reference of everything? If we identify too strongly with the notion of being no self or pure awareness, we are stuck again. The dualistic mind has found another position. It is dwelling in the idea of absence.

Liberation is no longer mentally fixating on one idea within a set of polar opposites: non-conceptual awareness v. concepts, emptiness v. form, nothing

v. everything. This is when thought and awareness dance together in one seamless dance, when there is no preference for either. Nothing is seen to be appearing as everything. This is when there is a collision of emptiness and form, of nothing and everything, and all that is left is the love and mystery of what is.

Enlightened person?

In presence, there is a natural detachment from stories. Resistance to life seems to die away. It is realized that the ego (i.e., dream self) does not exist except as a movement of thought and emotion that is resisting life, creating an imaginary self that is separate from the imaginary others.

As the old stories fall away in presence, watch the 'ego' find a subtle new avenue of resistance. For example, you may find it increasingly difficult to have conversations with people whom you deem to be "lost in stories" or "not present."

Look at what is happening. The mind has found a new story. This is completely unconscious. The story, if made conscious, would be something like this: "I am present. I have awakened. These others are not present. They are asleep." Do you see the separation this subtle story engenders? Your new identity could be called "enlightened person" or "the one who is present." This story is as false as any other.

Notice your resistance to the others whom you deem to be lost in stories. Allow that noticing to wake you up out of this subtle story—your point of reference as someone who is "present" or "enlightened" in relation to the others.

Silence and noise

Silence is a word that points to the endless, peaceful depth of the universe. In the dream of being a separate person, the mind appears noisy. It stays busy rehashing the past, arguing with what is happening now, and searching for some future moment. When you look within in an absolutely honest way for this "I" that is making this noise, all that is found is silent emptiness. There is no noisemaker. There is only the noise.

When the dualistic mind first hears that there is no separate self—that there is only this silent emptiness—it may continue making noise. Let that happen. Do you have a choice anyway?

This is not about stopping the noise. Only a thought within the noise would think of stopping the noise.

Look into the deep well of silence that is always and already here, both within the body and mind and without. This silence can never leave you because it is, at the most fundamental level, what you are. In this looking, the noise is seen to arise from and fall back into this silence.

When this silence is realized, you finally know exactly what you are—but you know that words can never truly express it. Nonetheless, words continue to arise from it. This is when there is no desire to stop the noise. There is a seeing that the noise is a perfect expression of silence.

Space as a pointer

The word space is a nice pointer. Look with awareness into your inner body. Let awareness feel the inside of your toes, your calves, your knees, your legs, your groin, your stomach and chest, your arms, your shoulders and your head.

Notice that your inner body and mind is one undivided awake space. Notice that the only 'thing' that makes a distinction between the inside and outside of the body is thought. Thought creates an imaginary, solid boundary between "you" and "life." When thought is looking, there is a boundary. When non-conceptual awareness is looking, it sees no solid boundary. The space in the room or area around the body is the same space as within the body.

As this awake space sees that there is no separation between you and life, Oneness is revealed. This awake space is directly aware of what is, before thought registers or records experience and places it into concepts. Before the thoughts "arm," "body," "me" and "space" arise, there is only the direct, undivided presence. There is only this direct experiencing.

In this direct experiencing, thoughts arise. Emotions arise. These 'things' appear from this space and are therefore not separate from it. Only thought creates a distinction between space and form, between thought and awareness. In seeing that this interplay between space and form is one seamless dance, all there is, is the present play of life—a total mystery.

The Unknown

In spiritual seeking, the conceptual mind searches for meaning or release from suffering. Ultimately, the mind is looking for an answer to the question, "Who am I?" When the conceptual mind is involved in this seeking, questions beget answers, which beget more questions, and so forth. The final answers to life's questions always appear out of reach, somewhere else, at some other time.

When it is seen that thought cannot solve this identity crisis, a fresh opportunity arises. This is not necessarily the end of thought, just the end of seeking a sense of self in it. The space within you that is already totally connected to this moment sees every attempt by the mind to "get it." In that seeing, there is a falling into a vast, spacious, silent unknown.

"Non-duality" is that unknown. It points to the realization that no dualistic answer can solve this great mystery. The mind freefalls unable to land solidly on any position. In this freefalling, nothing needs to be solved. The questions die in the seeing. It is revealed that there is only 'This'—the present play of life—and that this present reality is the answer. What joy! It is realized that the answer was always 'This.' The conceptual mind couldn't see it. It was too busy looking for some future 'This' or some idea of 'This.' Ideas are never the actual 'This.' They are second hand knowledge.

Action

Yesterday's reflection discussed the great unknown— a realization in which the "one who knows" is seen to be an illusion, leaving only 'This." The thought-based self that reads that last statement may believe that, in allowing the great unknown to be realized, it will be paralyzed into inaction or an inability to use the mind for practical purposes. This is a common misunderstanding.

For example, take the act of fixing a computer. When there is a belief in the thought-based self 'doing' the fixing, frustration can arise very quickly. This frustration is then held onto—played out in a story of time. Pretty soon the mind is complaining within a dream of time. It might say, "My son should have fixed this yesterday" or "I will never get this damn thing fixed!" Do you see the story of separation and suffering in that dream?

When the thought-based self is seen through and life is lived in the unknown, there is no one doing the 'fixing.' There is still conceptual knowledge being used to fix the computer. Action is still taken. But there is no one demanding life to happen in a certain way. If frustration arises, it arises to no one. There is no carrying that frustration over into a story of time about how the computer should have been fixed yesterday or about how it may take days before it's fixed. There is only 'life' fixing a computer.

One seamless dance

In enlightenment pointers, you hear about a realization into your true nature as formlessness (sometimes described as silence, space, emptiness, consciousness, awareness, nothingness, or spirit). When thought looks for formlessness, it can't find it.That is because thought is form.Practices, inquiry, and a host of other methods tend to keep the mind lost in form.

Of course, enlightenment is not about stopping thought. Only another thought would seek to do that. Enlightenment is about seeing. Seeing happens only now. Every attempt to move into some future moment of 'seeing' is actually just thought arising now.

Sit in your chair, walk around, or go outside. It doesn't matter. Just notice what is already here. There is already space all around the body. That same space is within the body. 'You' don't sense it? It can't be found through thinking about it. It is already here, before concepts or images about it arise. Notice that silence is already here. It gives birth to every sound. 'You' don't sense it? Silence can't be found through thought. Stop looking there.

'You' are the conceptual movement of mind known as "me" that believes it must do something to realize true nature. But in seeing what is already here, true nature is revealed effortlessly. True nature is this movement of form (i.e., thought, objects, time, sound) dancing with this formlessness (i.e., space, awareness, silence). True nature is this one seamless dance happening now.

When two dreams meet

When thought looks out into the world, it projects a dream in which it is believed that people should do what you want them to do.It's all about control. Each body/mind that believes itself to be a separate person is projecting such a dream.When two dreams meet, there is potential for conflict.

The illusion of control may manifest, for example, when your co-worker fails to tell you about an important phone call. Suddenly, you find yourself angrily telling her how incompetent she is. Your spouse nags at you to fix the broken mailbox. In response, a thought arises that your spouse should not be nagging.

Is it true that life should be different than the way it really is? If your co-worker forgot the phone call, that is reality. If your spouse is nagging, that is reality. In your dream, something other than reality is supposed to happen.

While arguing with reality, the present moment is being filtered through thoughts about the other person rather than how the moment actually is. Stated another way, you are looking at the other person through the veil of time—through past conclusions about who they are or future ideals regarding how you would like them to be.

When reality does not match your dream of thought, conflict arises. Love is then conditional. When you meet someone without the veil of time, you meet them in unconditional love. Love is meeting itself.

Form and formlessness, flipsides of the same coin

We come to the spiritual search fixated on form (i.e., identified with thought, emotion, the body, relationships, vices, jobs, etc). In listening to nonduality teachings, we become aware of a whole realm of existence that we didn't see—the formless realm (i.e., space, silence, peace, awareness, emptiness). We can then become fixated on that formless realm. The mind becomes fixated on finding or maintaining the experience of formlessness.

Liberation is not fixated on either realm. Form and formlessness are flipsides of the same coin—two ways of looking at one present reality called life. 'This.' 'This' is not something one needs to search for in time. It is always right here. Open your eyes. What is here right now is an interplay of form and formlessness. Thoughts arise in awareness. Sound arises in silence. Buildings, plants, cars, bodies, lamps, oranges, and staplers arise from nothingness and dissolve back into it.

To be free of fixation with either realm is liberation. This is when making a distinction between form and formlessness no longer makes sense. 'This' is when the notion that there is something here called "form" and something else called "formlessness" is seen as purely conceptual— redundant even. It is realized that life is not conceptual. It is actual. 'This' is when life is seen as a beautiful, unknowable mystery continuing to unfold in whatever way it is unfolding.

Formlessness

Yesterday's reflection stated that liberation is no longer being fixated on form or formlessness. However, because we come to the spiritual search fixated or identified with form, pointers to formlessness can help to loosen up identification with form.

Realizing formlessness takes no time because it is timelessness itself. It is NO-thing. In this timeless space of now—right where you are sitting—there is space all around the body, around the fingers, hands, legs, and chest. There is space in the room. If you go outside, that space is infinite, reaching outward in every direction.

That same space—sometimes called awareness— is within the body and mind. It is the non-conceptual awareness that is always looking. It sees immediately 'what is' before thought arises to label what is. This is presence. It registers every experience directly before the mind places labels and divisions over the experience. Yet, it is not an IT—not an object—but rather that which sees all objects.

Close your eyes and notice that there is no boundary between the space "within" your body and mind and the space "outside" of your body and mind until thought creates a boundary. When that thought (and every thought) is seen to be a temporary image, it is allowed to die. That is the death of identification with form, and the realization of formlessness.

Positions

We come to the spiritual search with a solid, dualistic belief in a separate self. We hear pointers like "no self" and "you are pure awareness" from spiritual teachings. These help the mind relax out of its dualistic position that there is a separate self. From that relaxation, it is seen that you are not a mind-made story. You are not a separate self.

This can be an incredibly liberating realization. Yet, even with a little glimpse into this seeing, the dualistic mind has a tendency to try again to locate an identity, a conceptual dualistic position. It tends to want to rest on the position that there is "no self" or that there is only "awareness" or "oneness." But the intellect cannot grasp enlightenment. No word is it. Ultimately, 'This' is not any dualistic position. It is more like a great unknown in which love flourishes naturally.

What is awake to all dualistic positions? What is awake to the positions of self v. no self, choice v. no choice, separation v. oneness, awareness v. thought, spiritual v non-spiritual? The question "What is awake to all positions" is not meant to help you locate yet another position or identity, but rather to simply see that there is a field in which all positions are seen, any and all positions can be expressed and appreciated, yet no position is held onto. That field is "love." Love is not a position.

Emotions

A common misconception about enlightenment is that "negative" emotions go away. It is true that, in this realization, awareness is no longer attached to thoughts of past and future. Thoughts still arise but they aren't blindly believed. So "negative" emotions that arise in conjunction with the mental story of "me" tend to arise less.

But emotions still arise. Enlightenment does not exclude anything—including any emotion, thought, experience, or state. It is the opening in which everything is happening. It is a seeing, not a denying of what is. Ultimately, it is pure awareness being completely open to whatever emotion, thought, experience, or state is happening at the moment.

When emotion arises, it arises to no one. The emotion does not attach itself to a time-bound story of "me." It isn't accumulated and held in the body. It comes and goes.

Enlightenment just means presence. In presence, emotions may be more painful than ever. Thought is no longer being used to justify, rationalize, and blame. There is no more escaping. The raw emotion is felt directly. There is a total freedom to feel but there is no identification with what is being felt. For example, there is no longer the story, "I'm angry." There is only anger, coming and going to no one. When there is no accumulation of pain and stories, there is a freshness in each moment, an openness to whatever arises next.

Questions dissolve

Non-duality is a shift in perception. It could be described as a wider view of life. In the mind-identified state, awareness is focused narrowly on forms including mainly thought. The mind tends to see forms, shapes, people and things in the foreground while ignoring the vast spacious, formless background in which the forms appear.

In the shift in perception, the space and silence seem to shift to the foreground and form tends to shift to the background. Thought is still there. Emotions and other forms are still there. But awareness is no longer intensely focused on the forms.

This is a natural relaxation. It is seen that suffering and searching arose merely because awareness was contracted into or focused into the forms and ignoring the space and silence.

Instead of asking yourself, "How can I make this shift permanent?" simply notice that the question, and every other question, is a form in the foreground on which awareness is focused. In noticing the space and silence from which that question arose, the question seems to answer itself. It is not that you find some great conceptual answer to your question though. Instead, the question just dissolves away into the spacious nothingness that gave birth to it.

I got it, I lost it

You are sitting on your porch and it is seen that all there is, is 'This.' There is no one there measuring whether this current experience is good or bad or better than some other past or future experience. In that moment, time stands still. The utter beauty and simplicity of 'what is' is realized. The story of self falls away. Then you go about your day and notice at some point that the peace left. The dream of self is back.

The sense of "I got it" is identification with a particular experience. It is the false belief that reality is supposed to look a certain way and that, when that certain way appears, you've somehow "got it." The sense of "I lost it" is when the mind believes it has to get back to that experience once the experience is gone. This is a trap. All experiences are temporary. To continue looking for some past experience is to keep the search alive.

Enlightenment just means the recognition that whatever is appearing now is a perfect expression of awareness. The dream self can never recognize this because its only goal is to keep the time-bound story alive—to keep the search going. See that the trap of "I got it" and "I lost it" is the mind's way of keeping that search going. That seeing allows the oscillation between "I got it" and "I lost it" to fade.

The child and the bug

A child looks at a bug with total curiosity. He isn't thinking about the bug. He has never seen a bug before. He has never learned the word "bug." He can't call it an "arachnid" or some other classification either. He hasn't learned those words. He simply looks deeply at this strange and wonderful creature. No thought comes to the looking. There is only the looking. In that looking, there is no child. The idea "I am a child looking at a bug" doesn't even arise. It's a story, totally irrelevant to the looking. The story is a second hand account of something too intimate for words.

In *that looking*, before thought labels the experience and files it away as 'something known,' there is an immediate presence that simply sees. This presence is not at all conceptual. It is the unknown. There is no word for it. Even the word "presence" is a story seen by this looking. It is what allows the bug to be seen. It is what allows the word "child" to be seen. It is what allows everything to be seen and to just be.

In realizing that this essence that is looking is what you really are, all suffering ends. Presence simply looks with innocence and intimacy. Concepts still arise. But you now know exactly what you are. No story will ever suffice again. This presence is your true identity.

The child and the bug (seeing through the story)

In yesterday's reflection, we spoke about the child and the bug. As the child looks at the bug without the story, "I'm a child looking at a bug," the strict division between the child and the bug vanishes. This is not to say that the apparent form of the child's body and the form of the bug's body disappear. Oneness is not a seeing that everything is one homogenous thing without textures, lines, and surfaces. The division vanishes because it is realized that, ultimately, thought is creating the division.

The concept "child" or "I" does not come into existence except through thought. The concept "bug" does not arise until thought arises. When the story "I'm a child looking at a bug" arises, separation arises with it. The dualistic mind is placing a conceptual story on something that is happening in the actuality of now.

In looking without the veil of thought, the separation between these two things—the child and the bug—is seen to be illusory. When this separation is seen through, there is only this looking. The division disappears.

This is ultimately what "non-duality" is pointing to. It is describing a way of being in which the stories we tell—which are always second hand accounts of what is actually happening in the space of now—are seen through. When the stories are seen through, the divisions that arise with those stories are seen through.

The child and the bug (denying the story?)

Yesterday's reflection pointed to the fact that separation happens merely because thought is believed. The story that there is a "child looking at a bug" creates a virtual reality in which it is believed that there is something called a "child" totally separate from something else called a "bug." This is what people experience when they tell the story that they are a separate person who needs to find some other thing called enlightenment, Oneness, or nonduality. The searching arises when the story arises. The search creates the separate self.

Does this mean that stories can or should be controlled or stopped? Only the story would seek to control the story. Simply see what is happening in this moment. Life is living itself. There is a presence that is awake to what is happening before thought provides a commentary. Stories arise beyond our control. When we seek to control the stories, we are seeking some illusory future state of "no thought." We are denying form.

When the stories are seen to be feeding the separate self, attachment to the stories dies. Life is no longer seen as a story in which you lack something called happiness, peace, or enlightenment that can be found in future. When there is no longer attachment to that story, the story may or may not continue to arise. In any event, it is realized that whatever it is that 'you' are, you are already complete.

Path v. no path

Non-duality teachings state that there is no path to 'This.' To the self, there appears to be a path. The spiritual seeker "thinks up" and maintains the self each time the "I" thought is believed. That seeker can even experience the sense of moving closer in time to 'This' as she measures and compares the degree to which there appears to be a self now to the degree to which there appeared to be a self in the past. The path arises only through that measuring and comparing.

Before the shift in perception called enlightenment, the mind interprets 'This' in terms of a separate self living along a time-based path. In the shift in perception, the self and the path fall away "together" because the path is the self.

Is there a path or not? When the mind interprets life from the relative perspective, there is a self, and therefore a path. When the mind interprets from the absolute perspective, there is no self, and therefore no path. See what the dualistic mind is doing? It is looking for a place to land in that dualism of path v. no path. It believes that if it finds somewhere to land conceptually, it has the truth. But the truth is not conceptual. It is actual. It is life itself, appearing in whatever form it appears right now. The "truth" is in every experience and every perspective.

NOVEMBER

The unknown is not measurable by the known. Time cannot measure the timeless, the eternal . . . . But our minds are bound to the yardstick of yesterday, today, and tomorrow, and with that yardstick, we try to inquire into the unknown, to measure that which is not measurable. And when we try to measure [the unmeasurable] we only get caught in words.

— Krishnamurti

Truth is every experience and perspective

Yesterday's reflection stated that truth is not conceptual, but rather actual. Truth is "life itself, appearing in whatever form it appears." It is in "every experience and every perspective." That seems very abstract to the intellect. It is not something the intellect can grasp. 'This' is so simple and obvious that it is overlooked in each moment.

To see what is being pointed to here, once must simply notice. To say that truth is in "every experience and every perspective" is simply to say that there is only One life happening now. Life never happens outside of the space of what we call "now." Nothing is appearing as everything including every experience, thought, feeling, belief, state, and perspective.

When there is a sense of a separate self, nothing is pretending to be a separate person. When seeking happens, nothing is appearing as seeking. When a clear concept arises, nothing is appearing as a clear concept. Nothing also appears as a totally unclear concept, a squirrel, a toothbrush, anger, humility, and a Wall Street investor. There is nothing that 'This' is not.

When the mind stops believing that something should be happening other than what is happening, and when emptiness is realized, it is seen that you are life itself, appearing in all forms, all experiences, all states, and all concepts. The simplest word for this is presence.

Waking up to the mystery

Thought cannot really see the beauty and mystery of this life. Take, for example, a walk through the forest. In that walk, you are witnessing total wonder, an alien world that cannot be known through thought. Yet the mind comes to label everything that is seen. It believes that in calling one aspect of it a "tree," it now knows what is there. It believes that those 'things' falling to the ground are "leaves." It believes this whole scene is a "forest." Thought creates a world of totally separate things. The bare naked Oneness of life is overlooked in that labeling.

In the mind-identified state, the moment a thought is placed on something, the looking stops. The mind falsely believes it knows simply because it has a label and category for everything. The world looks entirely conceptual. Childlike curiosity, innocence, and wonder are veiled by the world of the known. Life is reduced to a set of memorized concepts. You aren't looking, listening, feeling and experiencing life directly.

Waking up doesn't mean that you stop thinking. Waking up refers to seeing that our thoughts about reality are not reality. They are interpretations, coming from a mind conditioned by memory. In looking freshly at what is here, in noticing our labels for everything as they arise (instead of totally believing those labels), waking up to the mystery is possible.

Your thoughts about others

A simple dispute with your spouse reveals so much about how the dualistic mind works. In those moments when a dispute is happening, "you" want to have your point of view prevail. "You" want your loved one to validate (agree with) your thoughts, feelings, and experiences—to buy into your dream that reality is whatever you think and feel it is.

For example, you say, "Honey, I would like you to change, to be more open and caring, to listen to me more." In that moment, you are interacting with your thoughts about your spouse, some future ideal you have in your mind about how he is supposed to be exactly the way you want him to be. This makes love conditional. You are resisting what actually is. If your spouse isn't listening, that is what is actually happening.

Does this mean that you should never suggest that your spouse change? Presence is not a prescription to do or not do something. It is about seeing that your thoughts about others are your dream. Whether you leave the relationship, stay in it without trying to change your spouse, or continue trying to change him is ultimately irrelevant to this seeing. In your dream, your spouse should be more like your thoughts of your spouse rather than who he really is. It's like saying, "This desk should be a turtle." It isn't reality.

The word is not that which it describes

By reading the word "muffin," are you able to taste a muffin? If this reflection uses the word "playground," do you find yourself swinging on a swing set? Words are not that which they describe.

There is a tendency to buy into spiritual concepts—enlightenment, non-duality, presence, Oneness, awareness, God, and even the word "spirituality." But these words are only pointing to awakening to the actuality of life beyond your concepts about life. Suffering and searching happen only because the mind is identified with concepts, mainly the idea of a separate self based in lack. There may be a tendency to even buy into what this reflection is saying as if it's the truth. The mind just wants to land on some conclusion about 'This.'

But to really see and know 'This,' there must be a direct, immediate experiencing of the life within you and before your eyes. To bite down on this thing we call a "muffin" is to really know what a muffin is. To swing on a swing set is to directly and immediately experience that to which the word "playground" is pointing.

Similarly, when it is realized that spiritual concepts are only ever pointing to the direct and immediate experiencing of actual life right now, an unconditional love of what is arises. No concept could ever be that love. Love is actual. It is the essence of life itself.

Don't believe what 'spiritual teachers' say

There is ultimately no such thing as a spiritual teacher or spiritual seeker until thought arises to tell that story of separation. The mind projects thoughts onto reality. We call this a 'building,' that a 'teacher,' this a 'Republican,' and that 'enlightenment.' That is a dream of thought. Nothing wrong with it. No need to deny it. It's beautiful. But separation isn't ultimately true.

Notice the tendency to believe what so-called teachers say. Enlightenment is not a belief. It is not an idea that you memorize and carry around like a belief in Santa Claus. If you believe what teachers are saying, you will likely miss what is being pointed to. There are many expressions of this inexpressible realization. Getting caught up in comparing and contrasting the messages only keeps the mind in the false notion that 'This' can be grasped intellectually. The words are pointing beyond adherence to the words, to the immediate experiencing of what you are and what life is beyond your ideas about that.

"You" are a set of past thoughts, beliefs, opinions, perspectives, and feelings to which awareness has attached. When that separate self is seen through, there is only 'This'—a totally alive mystery. The portal to 'This' is now. In this moment, the past is seen to be nothing more than presently arising thought. There is no way to teach what is. All spiritual teachings are past thoughts. Second-hand knowledge.

Autumn

The fresh morning air being breathed into the lungs effortlessly, leaves falling from trees onto the driveway and the grass, a chilly wind blowing through the hair. Isn't autumn beautiful? But isn't the word "autumn" just another leaf falling from a tree, another temporary form arising and falling in 'This'—the utter mystery we call life . . . .

Enjoy the trees, the leaves, the driveway, the grass, the wind, the hair, and the thought "autumn." These 'things' are coming and going. Nothing to hold onto, not even the word "mystery." It arises and falls. Nothing is yours. "You" are just one of the forms arising and falling.

To a mind looking to hold onto these forms, what is being said here can be frightening. Actually, it is totally liberating. Each moment is totally fresh and new. The past is gone. Notice the mind's tendency to hang onto some past moment. Notice its tendency to search for something in the future. The past and future are just thoughts, just leaves. There is nothing to grab onto. Nowhere to land.

Instead of grasping onto the temporary forms, ask yourself: What is here? What is it that is always looking at the coming and going? When a concept arises as if to answer that question, know that even that concept is coming and going. That is the mystery.

Free to feel

When there is identification with thought, the mind is trying to figure life out conceptually. It creates belief systems out of fear of the unknown. It defends its beliefs and tries to convince others that its beliefs are right. Identification with thought creates and maintains separation.

What the dualistic mind is ultimately doing is defending and strengthening a "me" that is based in fear. The mind rationalizes, justifies, blames, analyzes, and judges life as it is happening in some attempt to gain control and knowledge about what is happening. The mind believes that, in controlling, resisting, and knowing, the "me" will survive.

The "me" is a dream. It stays alive only through constant identification with thought and emotion. The incessant mind activity keeps feelings from being felt directly. For example, in the moment a fearful thought arises, the actual fear in the body isn't felt. When the fear isn't felt, it fuels more thoughts about the future including about what will happen or how a scenario will turn out.

In liberation, identification with thought is gone. The "me" illusion is seen through. Therefore, the incessant movement to rationalize, justify, blame, analyze, believe, and judge dies. There is a freedom to feel directly whatever emotions arise without having to "think" them away. When there is a freedom to feel emotions directly, those emotions do not accumulate over time. They come and go freely. There is no "me" to hold onto them.

What is the separate self?

The sense of being a separate self is more than a creation of mere thought. Thought seems to play a vital role in separation. For example, you cannot think about a "me" without shutting out the rest of life. You can't think about blue jeans without shutting out airplanes, oranges, and everything else in life. In thinking, the mind entertains a highly fragmented view of reality.

But the sense of being a separate self goes much deeper than just thinking. It involves not only identification with thought but also with emotion. The entire body and mind contracts around the belief in being a separate person. The sense of being a separate "me" is felt to the very core of one's being. This contraction is experienced very acutely during seeking towards future goals, arguing with those we love, defending our beliefs and viewpoints, and replaying the mental story of "me" repeatedly in whatever form that takes (i.e., victim, seeker).

Even though the sense of separation is held very deeply in the body and mind, simple presence breaks it up and reveals it to be an illusion. In the moment this "me" energy rises up to negotiate with life and others, to defend itself and attack the other, to search for something outside itself to bring happiness, notice that you are witnessing an illusion. It's a powerful illusion, but nonetheless still only a belief, similar to a belief in the Easter bunny.

Form is none other than formlessness

Awareness is who you really are prior to form (i.e., concepts, content). Awareness is naturally spacious and non-conceptual. Identification with form happens when there is no realization of this simple formless awareness. Thought is believed totally including all the divisions and boundaries that come with it.

Once this simple awareness is realized, thoughts continue to arise. There is still content, personal history, and a body/mind but there is no longer identification with these 'things.' You stop believing your thoughts simply because it is seen that thought (form) is none other than awareness (formlessness). This is seeing through the dualism of awareness and thought. There are not two here. Thoughts that used to seem so important are now seen as just as empty as the awareness from which they emanate.

What is being said here is purely conceptual. There is nothing to believe in these words. Believing these words would be identification with form. The experience of liberation is much simpler than any explanation of it.

This is about seeing the true nature of reality. Once it is seen that your fundamental nature is emptiness, you see that all form is essentially empty. All divisions and boundaries are seen through in this realization. That is Oneness. Divisions and boundaries are essentially thought-created. In this seeing, love naturally arises. Love sees no real boundaries and yet it respects apparent boundaries.

Lack and wholeness

The sense of lack comes directly from the belief in a separate self. The separate self longs for wholeness. It seeks wholeness through career, education, relationships, substances, shopping, sex, and even spiritual searching. This separate self is perfectly designed to keep the sense of lack alive. Each time it goes looking for wholeness, it strengthens the idea that there is a separate self that lacks something.

Notice that a false idea is playing itself out over and over in the mind. The idea is that there is an "I" separate from wholeness that will find something, some future moment, or some other person or situation that will make "me" whole. But the "me" can never feel whole. It is, by its very nature, separate.

Notice the mind desiring others to be different, refusing to feel emotions and instead seeking ways to escape them, and searching for love, praise, acknowledgement, happiness, wholeness, peace, or freedom "out there" or "in the future." The notion that wholeness is "out there" or "in the future" is just thought arising now.

What is noticing is an unwavering presence to what is—to all these mechanisms that keep separation in place. This presence sees through the belief in the separate self. This presence is, by its nature, already whole. There has always been this wholeness, but it was being obscured by the story of a "me" looking for it.

Fear of death

Objects appear in awareness. These objects include experiences, states, feelings, paths, practices, and concepts. Awareness is not any of those objects. You can never find awareness because "you" are a mental object in awareness.

Suffering and searching happen because there is identification with objects in awareness. As awareness mistakes itself to be an object (i.e., a separate person), it sees this separate "me" entity as finite and subject to death. A fear of death arises with that mistake. Awareness grasps for some state, experience, thought, feeling, path, practice or other object to solidify the separateness and survival of the "me." The separate self will never rid itself of this fear of death because it is an illusion built from that fear.

Awareness is already free of the fear of death. It was never born. It is that which is looking at the "me" story including its fear and grasping. In seeing that who you really are is this awareness, the grasping stops. With no more illusory "me" grasping at objects, each and every experience, thought, feeling, relationship, and other object is allowed to be exactly as it is. There is no longer a searching for fulfillment, survival, and identification in objects. It is seen that what you truly are is this awareness and that this awareness (i.e., nothingness, spirit) is appearing as every object (i.e., every thought, feeling, experience, state). In realizing this Oneness, the fear of death dies.

The seamlessness between awareness and thought

Yesterday's reflection, as with many non-duality writings, made a distinction between awareness and thought—between nothing and everything. The mind falsely believes it knows what we are talking about when we locate a NO-thing called "awareness" in relation to a something else called "thought." But is the distinction absolutely real?

Don't think about what is being said here. Thought will always create distinctions. Just look. Where does a thought begin? It appears to arise out of and vanish back into this NO-thing we call "awareness." But where is the actual, solid line between thought and awareness? Can you see the very point at which this NO-thing called "awareness" turns into this other thing called "thought?" Can you see the very point at which this thing called "thought" dies into "awareness?"

This reflection is not inviting a philosophical view or an attempt to grasp non-duality intellectually. Instead, this is an invitation to notice the seamlessness of life. Thought bleeds seamlessly out of awareness and falls seamlessly back into it. The line between thought and awareness can never really be found. This One Life is apparently moving in and out of form in a mysteriously seamless way. The mind's idea that it "gets" non-duality simply because it has located a NO-thing called "awareness" and a something else called "thought" is ultimately just another dualism. There is nothing to get. Life is simply living itself seamlessly, way beyond what the intellect can grasp.

The seamlessness between nothing and everything

Yesterday's reflection spoke of the seamlessness between awareness and thought. Look around. This seamlessness is everywhere. There is space. Out of apparent space comes matter—planets, stars and other celestial bodies. When those planets, stars, and bodies dissolve, there is only space. There is a nothingness we call the "sky." Out of that nothingness come clouds. When those clouds dissolve away, there is only this nothingness called "sky." There is awareness. Out of that awareness comes thought. When that thought is gone, there is awareness. There is silence. Out of that silence comes sound. When the sound is finished, there is only the silence. There is nothingness. Out of that nothingness comes form including the body, mind, personality, history, and story of "you." When form vanishes, all that is left is that nothingness.

Non-duality is not intellectual, scientific, or philosophical. It is an invitation to see what is actually happening. It is a timeless noticing of what already is.

There is nothing to hold onto because everything is impermanent. Total surrender to what is by no one. When there is no longer identification with the temporary forms, your true nature is realized to be this nothingness. This nothingness, this spirit, is what you really are, beyond your name, body, intellect, and story—all of which are temporary forms. Then look a little closer. That nothingness is appearing seamlessly as everything. It is totally full. That is love.

Seeing through the dream of self

What is the dream self? Is there anything other than awake emptiness looking right now? The dream self is a movement of grasping towards thoughts, feelings, experiences, beliefs, knowledge, conditioning, and interpretations (i.e., temporary forms). This movement is a contraction in the body and mind designed to maintain an illusory separate entity known as "me."

When this assumed center is seen through, there is only this immovable, changeless, timeless awakeness. The dream self is occurring in this awakeness that is looking now.

Mental interpretations that tell you the world and others ought to be different are just part of 'your' dream. Your ideas about yourself and life are seen to be empty. They are manifestations of this empty awakeness.

This doesn't mean that forms stop arising when 'This' is seen or that you stop thinking, feeling, or experiencing. There is no "you" to stop or start doing anything. Doing arises involuntarily from awakeness. Temporary forms are not the enemy. Non-duality is about seeing through this dream of self that is grasping onto these temporary forms in some attempt to solidify a central illusion called "me." Being an illusion, this "me" can never reach awakeness. Awakeness already is. The dream of self is seen to be nothing more than a grasping towards temporary forms that are apparently arising from and falling back into this awakeness.

Openness

Non-duality is experiential. It is not about conclusions, although conclusions naturally arise as a result of interpreting experiences. So if liberation, no self, no choice, or any other experience is happening, watch the mind return to make a conclusion about it. It wants to believe it "gets it." It wants to place the experience of life into a conceptual category and then preach to the others about the validity of its own conclusions. It brings the experiential nature of non-duality into a dualistic conclusion. When there is identification with that conclusion, the separate self is rearing its head once again under the guise of "enlightenment."

Throughout our lives, the mind analyzes and categorizes everything. From the time we are children until we die, it grasps for conceptual understanding. It wants to place life into neat little packages. But non-duality is not a neat little package. It blows open all packages. It is openness itself—the ongoing discovery of life as it unfolds in this timeless space.

As a sense of presence, no self, or no choice is realized, notice the mind's attempt to place the vast landscape of experience into a neat dualistic conclusion. Life is not a conclusion or concept. To even say, "It's all One" is a packaging of sorts. When this openness that you truly are remains open to what is happening and the mind is no longer fixating on its interpretations, liberation is realized.

The dueling dualistic mind

Notice what is happening when you believe strongly in a particular viewpoint. The dualistically opposite viewpoint is often repressed. All points of view, because they arise from the dualistic mind, are ripe for separation and conflict.

If you say, "I know my view is correct," this belief carries with it unconscious doubt. If you knew with absolute certainty that your view is correct, there would be no need to defend it. That knowing would not carry with it unconscious doubt. The belief that something is a certain way carries with it an unconscious, unexamined doubt that it is not that way. This is why you find yourself defending your views. You are not so much defending the view as you are defending the dream self that is attached to it. Identity is lurking in our viewpoints.

Your arguments with others really have nothing to do with them. You are pushing for your point of view to prevail. Only non-dual awareness sees this dualistic "duel" as it really is. Thought cannot see what is happening here. Thought is dualism. In the moment you see your point of view being held tightly and defended, notice that there is fear and doubt in you. Fear and doubt arise directly from the dream of self. When this game being played by the dualistic mind is seen, all viewpoints are seen as dualistic. They exist only in relation to their opposites.

Oneness meeting itself everywhere

Yesterday's reflection stated that all views are dualistic. This is, itself, a dualistic view. A view can be clearer or truer than another view, but only relatively or dualistically. The view that "all is One" is only pointing to the absolute. It is relatively clearer than some other view. Oneness cannot be expressed.

Yet Oneness is expressing itself in every view and everything. Nothing is appearing as everything— as an ant crawling across the sidewalk, the sand blowing in a desert, and a mother kissing her baby's forehead. It is appearing as your "correct view" and as the "wrong view" held by someone with whom you are debating. There is nothing that 'This' is not. In seeing that you are not this dream self, but rather 'This' that we call Oneness, it is realized that Oneness is meeting itself everywhere. It is appearing as two.

In this seeing, dualism arises but there is no longer identification with it. You are not seeking an identity from any dualistic view.

This non-dual seeing is not some grand enlightenment in the future. "Future" is a thought arising in the non-dual awareness that you are right now. It is a dualistic view that exists only in relation to its opposite—past. Simple presence reveals an awake space in which everything is arising. The absolute is therefore right here, right now. It can be known only through direct experience, not through dualistic views.

The direct taste of what is

No matter how clear the non-duality expression, it is only pointing to the richness of what is in the present moment.

Imagine sitting with your back against a tree reading a book about orange groves. The book is clear in its description of the look of an orange grove and the taste of an orange. But no matter how many clear words are used, they are still only a second hand account of the real thing.

The same is true for non-duality pointers. The words can be helpful to point but the pointers are ultimately seen to be false, a second hand account of life is that already happening.

Awakening is akin to standing up from that tree, putting the book down, and realizing you have been unknowingly sitting in an orange grove the whole time. The sweet smell of oranges flows through the whispering breeze. The bright oranges hang from the tree, nestles in leaves, while perfect white orange blossoms scatter themselves everywhere. As tongue and mouth taste the sweet, succulent orange, you see that no words could ever describe that. It must be tasted directly.

This is what non-duality is. It is not conceptual or intellectual. It is the direct taste of what is. Simple presence. Words can only point you there and show you that you have been avoiding this direct taste for years by thinking about life instead of realizing you are it.

Thought is not the enemy

There can be a tendency to fall into the trap of believing that thought is the enemy. But only thought would formulate such a belief. In that case, thought is deciding that thought is the problem. This can keep the mind spinning for years in a spiritual search.

Thought is a beautiful tool, useful in many practical ways. But when you are looking for your sense of self in thought, suffering and searching occur. The spiritual search is essentially an identity crisis.

Thought separates the whole into illusory parts. According to dualistic thought, there is an "I" separate from and having a relationship with everything else. That is what thought is supposed to do. Thought will always tell you that you are separate person who must reach, maintain, recreate, or negotiate with something else to be happy and complete.

In seeing that there is a non-dual awareness that is already awake to the space of now, the identity crisis solves itself. To put it conceptually, this non-dual awareness is already whole, undivided, and full of love and warmth. As this awareness "moves through" the prism of dualistic thought, separation is created. Separation is not ultimately real. It allows practical functioning in the world to happen. In recognizing that your fundamental nature is this light of awareness that is always and already changelessly present, thinking continues but is no longer identified with.

Notice what you really are

Before you tell the next story, complain about your boss, argue with your kids or your spouse, notice what is really here in the space of now.

The mind comes up with all sorts of stories: "I am happy," "I am angry," "I am right," "I am spiritual," "I am not spiritual," "I'm a father," "I am really good at my job," "I am unemployed." Whatever comes after the words "I am" is just a story. That story constantly changes. There was a different story there when you were twelve years old. There will be a different story there on your deathbed. But the felt sense of "I amness" or being never changes. It is what you really are. How can you be a story, a constantly changing set of images?

Before the story arises that you need something other than what is happening right now, notice the presence that is already here and totally complete in and of itself. Once it is seen that this timeless presence is what you really are, the search for something else is over. Presence already contains all the love, freedom, peace, compassion, and joy you've been looking for "all your life" in these stories. You missed it because you took the stories to be true. You took yourself to be a story.

Hope is a postponement of awakening

Hope is a postponement of awakening. The body and mind projects a future story in which it is believed that you will be freer, more peaceful, or more content. This projection creates a vacuum in this moment, draining the natural energy that is available through presence.

Hope is one of the great myths of spirituality. You may experience resistance to this message because hope provides perfect ego food. Embedded in hope is a story of getting better or becoming more fully yourself. This is attractive to the dream self. But the moment the mind and body projects this story of future happiness, it sustains the belief that you are not already there. The search for something more solidifies the lack within, which perpetuates the drive towards future, which in turn solidifies lack. This is the cycle of seeking.

In seeing hope when it arises, there is the opportunity to see it for what it truly is. It is a postponement of life itself. Life has never been anywhere but right here in the space of the timeless. Future is merely a thought arising in this space. This seeing reveals that the entire search for something more is the problem, not the solution. When the illusion of hope is seen, notice that the space in which it arises is what you really are. Hope obscures this natural state, which is—by its very nature— already totally complete.

Intimacy with life

A thought is a mental interpretation using concepts learned in the past. When we use the word "presence," we are not pointing only to a mental interpretation of what is happening now. Your thoughts about what is happening now have little to do with what is actually happening. They are your thoughts, your dream. When we use the word "presence," we are pointing to a non-scripted, non-conceptual awareness that is awake to what is happening right now including awake to the thoughts about what is happening now.

Presence means awake to the timeless space in which interpretations happen. This awake space looks at a plant and sees a mystery. This awake space is naturally intimate with that plant. The word "plant" is a second hand account of the actual plant before your eyes. No word can reveal the true depth of what is here in this mystery we call "life." The awakeness has no name for that plant. Only the thinking mind names it, gives it a story, and makes it into a separate object living in space and time.

Thought is beautiful. But thought is from the past—memorized concepts that separate you from what you are viewing. This awake space is intimate with what is actually here now. To live in presence means to live in intimacy with the actuality of life, including even the mental interpretations once they are seen as not ultimately true.

For or against

Some try to think themselves into freedom or happiness. The idea is that, if "I" keep thinking, I will come to some final conclusion about myself or life. A mind engaged in this thinking game may take a position in favor of thinking and against a message about pure awareness.

Others realize that there is a pure awareness here that is beyond thought. The mind may return to take a position in favor of awareness without thought.

Still others experience a liberating seeing that what we are is an opening in which there can be either thought or no thought. The mind may even take a position in favor of that experience.

Thought likes to conclude that its particular experience is "it." It looks for agreement in the world with those who mirror back its conclusion and disagreement with those who don't. The dualistic mind knows only for or against. Its subtle goal is to reinforce a "me" that is right in relation to the others that are wrong. This is how non-duality turns into fundamentalism.

Sooner or later it is realized that there is no single experience of life that is "it." 'This' is arising as every experience and every dualistic conclusion. In this realization, the mind still does what it does. It plays in dualism. But it is realized that what we are has nothing to do with a particular experience or dualistic conclusion.

'This' is every experience

Yesterday's reflection stated that 'This' is arising as every experience and every dualistic conclusion. Stated another way, nothing is appearing as everything.

The mind creates dualism. It has an experience and then it makes a judgment about that experience. For example, the experience of peace is considered to be spiritual. The experience of frustration or seeking is considered to be not spiritual. These dualistic conclusions keep the mind searching, looking for a particular experience(s). The mind seeks the positive and avoids the negative, seeks peace and avoids non-peace, seeks success and avoids failure. It is always looking for something to move towards and something else to move away from.

In continuously going to the mind, life seems like a never-ending succession of chronological experiences that are supposed to magically bring about the ultimate experience.

Notice what is already here. There is only this timeless presence before you begin dreaming about a past or future experience. Within this timeless space, dualistic interpretations arise: thoughts, feelings, experiences, states, time, positive, negative, success and failure. It is the mind engaging in its dream of becoming, its dream of a separate me that will one day capture the experience of awakening. When it is realized that presence is already awake to every experience, and that every experience is 'This'— even the experience of seeking—the search is over.

Problems arise from the script

Problems appear to be "out there" in the world. It appears that your spouse won't do what you wish and that this causes you frustration. It appears that you are unhappy because you don't have enough money in the bank. It appears that you are lonely because you don't have a mate.

As long as you perceive problems to be "out there" in the world, you unconsciously feed those problems. Nothing is actually happening to you. Life is simply happening, whether you consent to it or not. When you internally consent to it, it appears that things "out there" are going well. When you internally reject what is happening, it appears that things "out there" are not going well.

If your spouse acts a certain way, that is a fact. It is only your mental and emotional script that says she should be other than the way she is. If there is no money in the bank, that is a fact. Only your script says it should be otherwise. If you are not in a relationship, that is a fact. Only your script says it should be otherwise.

The source of your pain is never outside "you." "You" are a script created by identification with thought and emotion. The life that you call "yours" is merely a script being projected outwardly by this inward mechanism. When that script meets timeless awareness, it is seen to be unreal.

Unconditional love

At the deepest core of being is unconditional love. This is unlike the love associated with the dream state in which there is a belief in a separate person who loves certain things and people and doesn't love other things and people. There is always a seeking towards personal gratification in that egoic love. The "me" is out to get something. To even want love in return is still seeking gratification for a personal self.

This love has no personal ambition, personal motivation, or personal agenda. It isn't seeking control. It isn't even seeking love or any other reward in return. This love simply looks at the world and sees itself. It moves to include because it doesn't recognize exclusion as ultimately real.

The unconditional love of being knows no separation. Yet it doesn't even hold tightly to "no separation" as a position. This love isn't interested in positions. In each position taken in relation to your spouse, your boss, your friend or your enemy, love seems obscured by an illusory "me." Love isn't actually obscured. Love is what you are. It is the position that creates the sense of separation. The separation is not real.

This love simply is. It simply loves. No amount of effort will show you that. This love swallows the whole notion that there is a "you" that must somehow do something in order to find something separate called love.

Family

When the process of separation first began at an early age, family members were the first "others" against whom we defined ourselves. Our stories involving them often carry issues of control, pain, abandonment, identity, abuse, resentment and a host of others. These relationships are also our first taste of truly unconditional love. Is it any wonder why family gatherings during holidays often bring out the unseen, conflicted past in us?

There can be no 'doing' in order to deal with these feelings and stories. The mind has been engaged in a lifetime of doing—coping, escaping, seeking, avoiding, rationalizing, attacking, defending, and hiding. Every movement to do something about thoughts and emotions that arise in family relationships is an avoidance of what is.

These thoughts and stories cannot survive in the light of awareness. You are not "the little sister who resents mom and dad." That is a story. Simply notice it. Your thoughts about family members have little to do with them. They constitute your dream. Notice them.

When these stories and feelings remain unseen, we are not relating with family members. We are relating to our own dream of thought. The past in us is being projected onto the present moment. When we see ourselves as stories who must negotiate with other stories called "family members," separation is believed. Conflict happens. The past continues to create a veil over what is. Love feels obscured.

The false witness

You are sometimes invited to witness form. Forms include things that have solid appearances and temporary life spans including thoughts, emotions, states, experiences, bodies, trees, clouds, pickles, planets, and so forth. Although form comes and goes, that which is witnessing form does not. The silent witness within you, sometimes called "awareness," is often your first taste of the realization that the time-bound, thought-based story streaming through your head is not actually you. You are also not any particular emotion, experience, state or other form. It appears that you are the formless awareness that is aware of form.

Yet awareness implies a you that is separate from what it sees. That witness is the last remnant of the dream of a separate self. It is the sense that nothing is happening or that life is happening but who I am merely witnesses it. As long as there is a separate entity, including even a witness, duality remains. You are still separate from life.

As the witness is seen to be an illusion, liberation and love arise. It is seen that the idea that there is an awareness here aware of something else is just that— an idea. With no more witness or identification with awareness, Oneness is realized. The line between nothing and everything is seen through. You are no longer noticing life. You are no longer an idea. You are life.

Are there two here?

Looking out into the world, everything is happening in that seeing space. To point to your natural state, we use words that describe the absence of something including timelessness, formlessness, silence, non-conceptual awareness, and selflessness. Don't get caught up in the words. They are merely pointing you to this seeing space, the space in which time, form, sound, concepts, self and everything else arises. Simply look at what is here: space, quietness, thoughts arising, feelings being felt, cars going by, birds chirping.

"Your life" is a dream being projected onto this seeing space by the dualistic mind. When you say, "This is an awful day," or "My kids are not acting right," the dream is dreaming itself. The mind just plays a game of "for or against" whatever it sees. By being for or against what is seen, the "you" illusion stays in place as the center of life. "You" are continuing to be projected out into this space you call "your life." Simple presence reveals everything that needs to be seen. It reveals that you don't have a life. You are life. You are inseparable from this moment, from this space, and from everything that is arising in it. You are inseparable from life. The mind is creating division. It is creating this as opposed to that—you and the world. Beyond this dualistic dream, are there two here?

Presence and doing

What is it like to not attempt to change, fix, create or recreate any experience for the benefit of a "me?" When an experience arises—whether pleasurable or painful—it is simply allowed to be. This allowing happens by no one. Stated another way, this allowing happens naturally and effortlessly from the simple recognition of presence beyond the time-bound, thought-based story of the doer that falsely believes she is in control.

You are this presence, not the time-based story that is making effort to gain a future benefit from her actions. Presence sees that every experience is— by its very nature— temporary. Every past experience has now gone. Presence is always here. Instead of trying to find out who you are through particular experiences, recognize that presence is arising as every experience.

Presence does not have a self-centered objective. It isn't seeking to add something to itself through experience. Presence just is. Its very nature is to allow. It even allows all doing to happen.

Doing that arises from presence has a different feel altogether than doing that arises from the "me" energy that has an agenda to get something in return for its actions. Doing that arises from presence accepts what is naturally and effortlessly and then responds naturally and effortlessly. It has no selfish agenda because it recognizes no separate self.

DECEMBER

The same awareness that's present when you stop thinking is also present in every thought. By the power of sustaining awareness for short moments, many times, confidence in awareness is nurtured until awareness becomes permanent and automatic at all times and in all situations—including the times when many thoughts are arising.

— Candice O'Denver, Great Freedom

Doing without the doer

Right before you are about to do a difficult task or chore, notice what is happening in the body and mind. The story, if made completely conscious, would look something like this: "I don't want to do this. This will be bad. Maybe if I can get done quickly, I can do something that will feel good." This story is not usually that conscious. It's more like a subtle undercurrent of mental and emotional energy in the form of resistance to what is.

When that story is seen, it is realized that the doer—and the burdens that arise with the doer—is not ultimately real. It is merely this resistance energy. This is not about getting rid of the doer but rather noticing that it arises and falls in a larger space called presence. This presence is what you really are. Then action is taken by presence, not by the doer lost in the duality of good v. bad.

The doer is a dualistic movie. Psychologically speaking, good v. bad are not "out there" in the world. They are stories the body/mind is projecting outwardly. The dualistic self only knows how to be for or against something. It cannot just be with what is. Only presence can. Presence is naturally accepting of what is. Doing without the doer is the ultimate freedom. It is so free that when the story of the doer arises, it is allowed completely.

Inquiry

There is disagreement among writers and teachers in non-duality as to whether self-inquiry has any value. Some say it can reveal enlightenment. Others claim it is a useless activity because there is no self to do the inquiring. Instead of believing what writers and teachers say, see for yourself.

As a thought arises today, look for the source of that thought. Allow the spacious awareness within you to find out who is thinking. Allow the question, "Who am I?" to rest in awareness. In response to the question, another thought may arise. Perhaps the thought that arises is your name. But what is the source of that thought? The mind will merely provide thought after thought in response to the question, "Who am I?" Do you see that there isn't even a mind? There are only thoughts, one after another. How could you be a thought or set of thoughts? Thoughts come and go. What is it that never comes and goes?

When spacious awareness looks for the source of all these thoughts it meets itself. Spirit becomes aware of itself—hence the words "spiritual realization." Where you thought there was a solid, separate self, there is only awareness. Awareness does not come and go. This awareness reveals that what you are—life itself—is so vast and loving, it cannot be known directly through thought. See this for yourself.

The separate self is in competition with the other

You can repeat the phrase "no self" a million times and never see that to which presence and non-duality pointers are pointing. "No self" is not a mental conclusion. It is a seeing.

Awareness sees that you—as a separate, thought-based entity—do not exist except in relation to the other. This is the mirror of relationship. "You" are a mental movement kept alive by constantly being in competition with the "other."

Thought is constantly comparing "you" to the "other." You are fat only in relation to those who are skinny. You are a good person only if there are others who are bad people. You are unenlightened only if there are others who are enlightened.

This constant mirroring in relationship keeps the mind locked in separation. The one mirror of awareness has split itself into a million reflections. The whole goal of the reflection known as "you" is to be better, worse, or otherwise separate from the "other." Without an "other" to which to compare yourself, who would you be? Do you see the selfcenteredness inherent in the mirror of relationship? It is all about you. When it is seen that the reflection known as "you" stays alive through constant comparison and competition, that self is seen to be false. The "other" is also seen to be a phantom. What is left cannot really be expressed. Love is as good a word as any.

Alignment with what is

When a problem arises, notice what is actually happening. There is some event happening externally—"outside" the body/mind. Simultaneous to the event, thoughts and emotions arise internally (i.e., within the body/mind) to interpret the event as negative. The unconscious story created by these negative thoughts and emotions, if made conscious, would be: "I am against this event."

Many people lives their lives reacting to one problem after another. For them, life is a series of problems. They live at the mercy of internal reactions to external events. They see themselves as separate from what is happening externally. They remain in a perpetual state of resistance to what is.

To live in presence means to be awake to the internal reactions—awake to the internal resistance to external events. This awakeness notices thought and emotion the moment it arises. In that awakeness, it is seen that problems and suffering do not originate from the external event. Problems and suffering arise from identification with the internal reaction to the event (i.e., identification with the thoughts and emotions that interpret the event as "negative").

In this seeing, the internal body/mind becomes naturally aligned with external events. This is what it means to be in total acceptance of what is. When the internal body/mind is in alignment with what is happening externally, the dualistic line between internal and external fades away. That is Oneness.

A quiet mind

A quiet mind can become a goal for the dream self on the spiritual path. Goals arise from thought. Thought thinks that if it can bring about the end of thought, quietness will be realized. Can you see the futility of thought trying to end thought? It's like a hamster running in a wheel, believing that if she just continues running, she will stop the wheel.

If thought quiets, it is not the result of working towards a future goal. It is not something achieved by a "person." The "person" is the dream self (the doer). The dream self is identification with thought. Its dream is a dream of time (namely past and future). The dream self believes that if she just continues seeking quietness in the next moment, then seeking will end. It's as futile as the hamster on the wheel.

If thought quiets, it happens naturally through presence—through seeing the dream self's incessant tendency to achieve future goals, including the goal of quietness.

As identification with thought relaxes, the dream self dies. Timeless awareness wakes up to itself, beyond the dream of time and goals. Awareness contains a natural quietness. The natural quietness of awareness reveals that this moment is perfectly enough. Seeking ends in that seeing. Thought continues to arise, but it is no longer a problem. It is seen to arise from quietness. It is none other than that quietness taking form.

This that is awake

If you want to know who you are, look within and ask: Where is the self beyond thought? Is there a "me" that is not created by thought? No matter what conceptual answer you place upon the question, the answer will be just another thought. Even without direct experience, common sense tells you that you are not a thought or set of thoughts.

Only the time-bound, thought-based self would want to get rid of itself. This is not about destroying ego. It is a seeing. See that who you take yourself to be is determined by thoughts of past. Who you want to become is determined by thoughts of future. Even the thoughts that interpret what is happening now are often an avoidance of what is. When you resist what is happening right now through interpretation, thought is chasing some future mental ideal or an image learned in the past about how life is supposed to look and be different than the way it really is.

What is right here, right now and merely awake? This that is awake has no agenda to change what is. That which is looking is not a thought (or even an emotion). It simply looks. It simply is. No thought is needed to know it directly. This is what you really are. Thoughts merely arise in this that is awake.

The past

Many come to the spiritual search identified with a painful past. It's like living in a movie that you take to be real. In this movie, life as it presently appears is colored by the content of the past. If you are a victim, present circumstances give the appearance that you are continuing to be victimized. If you believe your life is incomplete, present circumstances are interpreted to be "not enough." If you were abused, neglected or mistreated in the past, it is likely that those patterns are repeating themselves now in some way. You believe whatever your thoughts tell you.

This past identity perpetuates itself through present mental and emotional interpretations. Reality as it really is now is veiled by this movie.

The question is, "How can I be free of the past?" "You" cannot be free because you are the movie. There is a presence already here—reading these words right now—that is beyond identification with the time-bound, thought-based movie of the past called "you." By noticing the movie of past as it arises to interpret the present moment, this presence is realizing itself. It is seeing that what you are is this presence. You are not a movie, interpretation, memory, or emotion. Those are objects coming and going in presence. Noticing the movie reveals that it isn't real. What is left is the utter simplicity, love, freedom, and freshness of what is in this moment.

Forget the past?

Yesterday's reflection stated that your past identity perpetuates itself through present mental and emotional interpretations. Does this mean that liberation is the total forgetting of something called the past?

There is no way to touch the past right now except through thought. When images arise and fall and there is a sense of being in the past, you can see that you are not really in the past. Thought is arising now. Memory.

Liberation means no longer identifying with memory. It is not about totally forgetting the past. Totally forgetting the past is amnesia. To totally forget the past would be to suppress thought completely. Even if it were possible to suppress thought completely for a while, it would merely be a state. States are temporary. They come and go in presence. Thought is not the enemy. Only thought would seek to suppress itself.

When there is no longer identification with thought, however, it is seen that the past is not who you are now. Thoughts of the past may still arise. Memory still serves its practical function. But there tends to be a natural quieting of the mind when there is no longer identification with thought. The past no longer burdens you. You are free to live in the freshness and simplicity of this moment, liberated from the heavy burden of the mental and emotional contraction called "me and my story."

The future

Who you really are is searching for itself in a movie called "future." In this movie, life as it presently appears is not good enough. No matter what experience, state, thought, emotion, event or other thing is happening, there is an unconscious sense that some future moment will be better. Reality as it really is now is veiled by this movie in which it is believed that you are not already fully yourself and that something needs to be found in the future or "out there" before you can be fully yourself.

In the spiritual search, the question, "How can I be free of the future?" arises. It is the wrong question. It assumes again that you need to find some future state in which you are free. "You" cannot be free because you are the movie of time playing in the mind. Every step taken towards some future happiness sustains the belief that you are not already there.

There is a presence already here now that is awake to the search for future. Future is nothing more than thought arising now. By noticing the movie of future as it arises, this presence realizes itself. Who you are is this present awareness and the movie is merely playing within that presence. The movie is not you. When you stop trying to find yourself in the movie, what is left is the utter simplicity, love, freedom, and freshness of what is.

The body and emotions

Much of what we talk about in presence pointing has to do with identification with thought. Yet the sense of being a separate self is an entire body/mind affair. The dream self does not reside merely in thought. Even if we see that thoughts are objects arising from non-conceptual awareness, that seeing does not necessarily free awareness from egoic identification. The experience of resistance also involves an emotional contraction felt in the body.

Notice that emotions correspond with thoughts arising from the "me" story. When anxiety is felt, it is the body's way of revealing that thought is entertaining some story about how the "me" is threatened by a future event. If resentment is arising, it is an invitation to see that thought is telling the story that someone in the past treated the "me" unfairly. All dualistic emotions correspond to dualistic thoughts. In looking at the space of now, there is no past or future. These stories, and the emotions that accompany them, constitute a dream called, "I am a separate person." In noticing these emotions, it is seen that they arise in (and as) awareness. Emotions are forms. Form is none other than formlessness. Emotions are expressions of the awareness from which they arise. This awareness is your true nature at the most fundamental level. Once that is seen, it does not mean that emotions stop arising. It means that there is no longer identification with them.

What you see is your dream

No matter what your particular story is—whether it is victim, seeker, doctor, addict, Christian, Muslim, Democrat, spiritual person, scientist, or social worker—that story is seeking confirmation of itself. You are looking out into the world through a particular lens based on what you already believe to be true and who you believe you are.

When a Democrat looks out into the world, he sees the world as Democrat v. Republican. He is seeking confirmation of his political identity. When a Muslim looks out at the world, he sees a Muslim world, created by Allah. He sees Muslims v. non-Muslims. The same is true for every identity. The world is, at least in part, a creation—and therefore a reflection—of your own mind. This is a closed-circuit system, perfectly designed to keep your story in place.

This is neither good nor bad. It's just not real. Your view of the world has more to do with your story than with what is real. You are co-creating reality by looking through a lens designed from ideas with which you identify. Non-duality is pointing to what is here beyond your personal story. Through presence, you see what truly is. There is an emptiness here that is already totally at peace, wise, loving, and liberated. It is not an idea. It isn't seeking to confirm a limited, self-centered view. It arises as everything. That is Oneness.

The simple joy of being

This moment contains the simple joy of being. All that is happening now is sitting, reading these words, thoughts and emotions arising, light in the room, and sound and silence. The dream self is the mechanism that is looking for something other than what is happening now. It believes that it is going to reach some future state where something extraordinary will happen. Yet, in the next moment, the same things will be happening. Sitting (or standing), thoughts and emotions arising, light, sound and silence. Thought looks at what is presently happening and says, "But there must be something more... " There isn't anything more. The search for something more is only a thought arising now.

Being is not a past or future state. It is not an experience that you once had or must reach in the future. Being is the present experience in whatever form it appears. It is what you are.

When you believe you lack something, you are back into a time-bound dream called "me and my life." If you can see that the lack is not real and that it comes directly from the belief that you are not 'there' yet, seeking ends. The simple joy of being reveals itself in that seeing. Everything you ever wanted is already here. You are life. In the search for a future, better life, the simple joy of being is overlooked.

Seeing through thought

Thought creates apparent duality. It arises as simultaneous and mutually-dependant opposites including right v. wrong, good v. bad, you v. me, us v. them, positive v. negative, success v. failure, agreement v. disagreement, happy v. sad, self v. no self, spiritual v. unspiritual, enlightened v. unenlightened. Do you see the incredible limitation built into dualistic thought? Thought can only land on one side or the other. It cannot hold two opposite views. Thought will only show you a partial, fragmented, dualistic view of life.

Oneness can only be revealed through non-dual, formless awareness. Non-dual awareness is not a thought. It is what is looking right now before thought fragments your present experience into apparent dualism.

In reading that last paragraph, it may sound as if you need to reach a state of no thought before Oneness is realized. No. Once you see that who you are is this non-dual, empty awareness, you see that every dualistic thought is also empty. You (empty awareness) are appearing as every dualistic perspective. Formlessness is form and form is formlessness. Dualistic thought is seen through. "Seeing through" thought means that thought no longer creates a rigid sense of separation. There is no longer identification with any view that appears in the realm of dualistic opposites. Thought loses its power over you. Each dualistic view is seen to be ultimately as empty as the awareness from which it comes.

Trying to be present

Trying to be present implies that there is a person separate from presence that can somehow become more present.

Presence is not a doing. It is being what you already are. Presence is what is sitting in the chair, breathing, holding this book, and looking at these words. It takes no effort to be what you already are (or even to do what you are already doing). Pointers to presence are simply inviting the noticing that life is already happening spontaneously and involuntarily. You are that life.

In trying to be present or to arrive at a future awakening, you are entertaining a mental dream arising in the very presence that you already are. Notice that your effort to be present arises in presence. When the word "notice" is seen here, there is a tendency to make that into an effort. The idea is, "If I just continue noticing these thoughts and emotions, I will become more present and awake." But the effort to notice thoughts and emotions arises in presence. There is nothing you can do to become present. "Noticing" is merely a word inviting you to see that presence is what is already noticing. Your true nature is the very presence that would set out to find itself. When you see the futility of trying to be what you already are, effort and seeking ends. What is left is what was always and already here—presence.

More on trying to be present

Yesterday's reflection stated that presence is not a doing. It is being what you already are. The mind may hear that statement and then tell the story, "I am already enlightened." But that would be just another story told by the dream self, a result of identification with thought. Thought is memory, the past.

The seeing that is referred to here reveals that there is no "me." You are not any thought including the thoughts, "I am enlightened," or "I am not enlightened."

Although yesterday's reflection stated that there is nothing you can do, there can be a noticing of what is already being done. The "dream self" is a term describing the habitual tendency to define a "me" from thoughts of past and to look for personal fulfillment in thoughts of future.

There is an awareness that is already here now that sees the "me" for what it is—a time-bound, thought-based dream. This awareness naturally and effortlessly notices the dream self whenever it arises. That seeing is all that is needed. If noticing is being made into an effort, then you know the "me" has hijacked the noticing. Effortful noticing comes from the dream self—the story of "me" that believes that it will gain future enlightenment through noticing. That is just another thought arising now. No "me" becomes enlightened. Enlightenment refers to the natural presence that is awake right now to the dream self.

Awareness and thought

Your present experience can be broken down into two apparent aspects: awareness and thought. Awareness is your essential nature. It is a wide open, empty, peaceful, loving, intelligent awake space that is inseparable from this moment. Thoughts are temporary images that come and go in an endless succession. Thought is usually some dualistic interpretation about how the past is incomplete, this moment is not good enough, or the future holds the answer.

Awareness identifies with the thought stream, fixating on one thought after another. This creates the illusion of suffering and searching. It is a trap to seek the end of suffering and searching through more thinking. To thought, there is no end. There is only another thought.

If you can see the futility of this self-perpetuating cycle, there is the possibility of recognizing that your present experience already contains your essential nature as awareness. The thoughts merely come and go in awareness. Don't try to suppress them. Let them come and go. Noticing them provides the opportunity to see what is really happening. That which is noticing these thoughts is awareness itself.

In your present experience—no matter where you are or what you are doing—the simple recognition of your essential nature as awareness shows you the rest you have been seeking. In resting as awareness, you see that thought is not a problem. It is merely an expression of—and therefore not even separate from—awareness.

Sudden or gradual enlightenment?

It seems counterintuitive to say that realizing your timeless true nature may happen gradually over time. Certainly, once the dream self is seen through, what is realized is that the entire of story that there was a "you" coming to something called "enlightenment" is seen as just that . . . an illusory, thought-based, time-bound story. The story arose in awareness. There was identification with it. When it is seen through completely, what is left is only the timeless seeing called enlightenment, presence, or non-duality.

Many who teach or share in the area of enlightenment, presence, and non-duality report that, at some point, there was a moment of initial awakening from the sense of being a separate self. In these reports, the sense of being a separate self is seen through instantaneously and what is left is an indescribable freedom.

Be that as it may, many others report a gradual unraveling or "waking up" that appears to happen over time. There is a sense that one feels lighter, freer, and more peaceful at one point in time than he or she did at an earlier point in time. Of course, only thought would make such a measurement. Nonetheless, it may take time for the self-sense to be seen through completely. Instead of becoming fixated on whether enlightenment is sudden or gradual, simply notice what is in this moment. This moment is the portal to this timeless seeing.

This is not about suppressing thought

Presence is not about suppressing thought. It is about no longer identifying with it.

The dream self is a thought-based, time-bound fiction. In the dream, it is all about "me" including my life, my past, my future, my goals, my lack, my troubles and complaints, my experiences, my friends, my spouse, my job, my feelings, and my spirituality. In this self-centered story, you are not only the main character, you are the only one that really matters. To a certain degree, other characters have meaning only with respect to how they relate to your story.

This self-centeredness is created and maintained through identification with thought. You identify with thoughts of past that tell you who you are. You identify with thoughts of future that tell you whom you will become. Your identification with thoughts that resist what is happening now keeps you feeling separate from life.

This dream is one big avoidance of your true nature as timeless awareness. Awareness is outside of the time-stream. It is awake now. It is the very presence that is looking at these words.

Once this awareness is recognized, identification with thought dies. Thought is then seen to be helpful and even beautiful. It is used for practical purposes, to take others' perspectives, to further non-self-centered goals, and to care for all sentient beings. You see that you are not a separate person. You are life. Life takes care of itself.

More on suppressing thought

Here is an imprecise analogy (all words are dualistic). Awareness is like a pure white light behind thought. The "thinking mind" is like a prism that disperses the light into apparently separate colors. When life is lived solely through thought, everything appears to be totally separate. From that perspective, there is a "you" that is separate from life and therefore inherently incomplete and lacking. This causes conflict, suffering, and searching.

When it is recognized that your true nature is the pure white light (non-dual awareness), peace of mind is realized. That does not necessarily mean that thought stops arising. It may quiet or it may continue moving. It doesn't matter either way. You have realized what you really are.

Some fall into the apparent trap of trying to suppress thought and "stay in awareness." This can result in a bias against thinking or even hostility towards, or mistrust of, intellectuals and intellectual pursuits. To deny the intellect is to deny awareness itself. In realizing that your true nature is awareness (the white light), you see that awareness is appearing as every thought (every color). When this is seen, you no longer seek a sense of self in one thought or the other. You are not trying to convince everyone that your color is the right color. Yet thought is not denied. The rainbow of colors is enjoyed and appreciated. The colors are none other than expressions of the light.

This is not about suppressing emotions

The illusory separate self is a mental and emotional construct that exists only when awareness identifies with its dream of time. The "me" is a time-bound, mental story of past, present, and future. This mental illusion is supported by identification with negative, dualistic emotions that arise in conjunction with thoughts. For example, the feeling of resentment is inextricably tied to the thought that the past should have been different. The feeling of fear is inextricably tied to the thought that the future will turn out badly. Outside of identification with these thoughts and emotions, there simply is no separate self who suffers.

In noticing the emotions that arise in conjunction with these thoughts, it is seen that there is no "you" that is resentful or fearful. There are only emotions arising in timeless awareness.

Does this mean that the goal is to suppress all emotions? No. Once it is seen that emotions are temporary, dualistic forms that arise and fall within awareness, it is also seen that awareness is arising as those emotions. There is no separate self there. There is only emptiness appearing as every "thing." In this case, the "thing" is an emotion. That seeing naturally and automatically frees awareness from the false notion of being a separate self who is suffering.

Weaning off of spiritual concepts

The mind has a tendency to get hooked into spiritual concepts like enlightenment, presence, awareness, no self,
and non-duality. It's a lot like a heroin junkie with a needle in
his arm. It feels good for a while, but in order to be free, he
must wean himself off the drug.

Imagine you are playing with a dog and you throw a bone
across the room. Then you point to the bone in an attempt to
get the dog to fetch it. Instead, the dog just runs up to your finger, sniffs and stares at it. The more you point to the bone, the
more interested the dog becomes in your finger. That is what
it is like when the mind gets hooked into spiritual concepts.

Liberation is freedom even from attachment to words like
liberation, enlightenment, no self, presence, awareness, and
non-duality. Once it is realized that these words are pointing
to the actuality of life spontaneously happening right now,
you see that the words were not what they were describing.

There is nothing you can do to wean yourself off these
concepts except notice what is already being done. The mind
is already hooked into concepts. Noticing the tendency to
repeat certain spiritual phrases and mantras allows a natural
weaning to happen. Just notice, the seeing takes over from
there. That seeing allows all words to be used without attachment to any of them.

Will belief bring peace of mind?

Presence is beyond belief. Belief is married to doubt. Therefore, belief will never bring peace of mind.

In presence, there is no doubt because presence does not arise from thought. It does not arise from belief. Belief is the past—a memory of some conceptual framework that you are carrying. People tend to believe what makes them feel good unless they want to feel bad in which case they will believe what makes them feel bad. Presence is beyond the dualistic opposites of good and bad. Good and bad are concepts that arise in the presence that is awake now.

With belief, there is always something to defend. As soon as your belief is threatened, the doubt comes screaming to the surface. You have to defend your belief and attack the others' belief in order to maintain your false sense of certainty.

Presence reveals your true identity. There is no doubt in presence. There is nothing to defend. Presence is so simple, so immediately accessible, that it is overlooked the moment awareness goes into thought for understanding.

When awareness stops looking to the mind for a sense of self, and there is an openness to the simple I AMness that is present right now before you try to understand life and who you are through concepts, peace of mind is realized.

Belief and conflict

Yesterday's reflection stated that presence is beyond belief. Thought may then ask, "How can I get rid of belief?" It's the wrong question. The dream self cannot be rid of belief. It is based on beliefs. The dream self is just that . . . a dream of thought, which is past (i.e., memory). It is not just the belief in being a separate entity. It includes all the beliefs that solidify that sense of separation. Whether you see it or not, if you believe you are a separate self, you are looking at reality through a conceptual lens. The beliefs you are carrying in memory are coloring everything you see now.

A Christian sees through a Christian lens. A scientist sees through a rational, scientific lens. A Democrat sees through a Democratic lens. Your story of self has no interest in getting rid of itself. Its goal is to keep separation alive.

This is not about getting rid of anything anyway. It is about seeing. If you cannot see how belief is limiting your view of reality, just wait. Sooner or later, conflict will arise. You will find yourself defending some belief and attacking the other's belief. Conflict reveals where you are stuck within a limited conceptual framework. Your sense of self is invested in the belief you're defending. Love and peace are revealed through that seeing. Love and peace are not beliefs. They are natural attributes of presence.

This is not about suppressing belief

The last two reflections have stated that presence is beyond belief. But this is not about suppressing belief or anything else for that matter.

As awareness is realized to be your true nature, you can longer rely on beliefs for comfort. You start to see that beliefs are temporary forms and that all form is essentially empty and dualistic. This sounds like bad news to the dream self. But it is great news. Once you are free from adherence to rigid beliefs that separate you from others, the possibility of unconditional love and liberation arises.

In a way that seems almost paradoxical, this unconditional love and liberation does not dismiss or disregard the beliefs of others. Nothing is appearing as everything. Therefore, the empty presence that you are, once it is realized, respects and loves all form because it sees itself in every form. At the same time, this unconditional love and liberation helps to relieve unnecessary suffering in others when there is an openness to that relief.

Presence sees through all separation. It is not in conflict with the others. So there is no need to reject what others believe. There is nothing to defend and nothing to attack. That kind of deep acceptance has the capacity to allow presence to be realized in anyone you meet. It has the capacity to help others see the ways in which their belief systems are causing suffering, separation, and conflict.

When Oneness becomes a fundamentalist belief

The last few reflections have discussed how beliefs often fuel separation and conflict. These reflections are not meant to encourage you to suppress belief. Form is none other than formlessness. To suppress belief is to deny the empty awareness from which it arises. Nothing is appearing as everything including every belief, idea, and view. What is being pointed to here is the seeing of how the dream self is born from identification with beliefs, creating illusory conflict and separation.

The view that "all is One" is a correct view relatively speaking. Stated another way, it is clearer to say "all is One" than to say "there are four." But form is relative. Views are clear *only in relation to* other views. That is the nature of dualistic language. The non-duality to which the word "Oneness" points cannot be expressed. In failing to realize the inexpressibility of non-duality, the mind can turn Oneness or any other spiritual conclusion (i.e., "no self") into a fundamentalist belief.

How will you know your spiritual conclusion has become a fundamentalist belief? You will find yourself in conflict with all others who do not agree with your particular conception of Oneness. You will stop listening and learning, believing that you own the truth.

The pure seeing of identification with belief in Oneness allows identification with that belief to dissolve naturally. What is left is genuine Oneness, free from the "me" who would own it.

Is all judgment wrong?

When one gets a taste of the "I-don't-know" mind— the very emptiness that is his true nature—there is a tendency to believe, on an unconscious level, that all judgment is wrong.This, itself, is a judgment claiming to be right, of course.In that sense, it is a performative contradiction to make a judgment that "all judgment is wrong" or that "no judgment is clearer than any other judgment."Can you see the delusion in that?When this happens, you know that not-knowing or emptiness has embedded itself as a fixed position.It is no different than any other narcissistic position.It is ego 101:"I'm right, and everyone else is wrong!"That is the very nature of the dream self—identification with thought.

Being free of fixed positions does not mean that you have no view. Views arise all the time. Nothing is appearing as everything, including every view. Buddha talked about "right view," which is the realization of your fundamental nature as emptiness and then the deeper seeing that form is none other than that emptiness. In that seeing, thought is not seen as wrong or bad. It is celebrated, played with by no one. The arising and falling of thought is the magnificent display of emptiness taking form. Some views are seen as clearer than other views. But when it's seen that all views are empty, there is attachment to none of them.

Recognizing present awareness

Recognizing awareness takes no time. If you are looking for it in time, you are overlooking it completely. It is always and already present. The future is merely thought appearing as an object in awareness. People spend decades, even lifetimes, meditating, praying and engaging in spiritual practices, looking for awareness, not realizing that awareness is what is looking. It is the awake space in which all objects—including meditation mats, thoughts, prayers, spiritual practices and books— arise and fall.

The white space of this page is like awareness. These words are objects appearing and disappearing in the white space. Although the words can be helpful to point to the white space, the space itself remains unchanged and untouched no matter how clear, unclear, spiritual or unspiritual the words are.

No matter how many thoughts you have about awareness and no matter how many practices you do in order to find it, awareness is the timeless, formless, empty, unchanging awake space in which all of that happens.

As you stand up from this reflection and continue searching for awareness, notice what is already looking. Notice the space in which all of your seeking energy arises. Each emotional and mental movement towards a future moment of awakening arises in the awareness that is already present. Once you recognize awareness, you see that it is synonymous with "spirit." The spiritual search in time is a denial of spirit, which is already here.

More on recognizing present awareness (the body)

You may believe that you are solely the body that sits there reading this reflection. But at different ages— 10 years old, 20 years old, and your present age— there is a different body. Science informs us that the entire body—including organs, skin, and the skeletal structure—completely recreates itself, down to the last atom, every four or five years. Identification with a body is identification with an illusory, temporary form. The body that appears now is not who you ultimately are.

As you read this reflection, can you sense what is looking? What is looking is awareness. The body is merely an object appearing in this spacious, empty awake awareness. Awareness itself is not an object. It has no features, no qualities, no beginning or end. It is neither old nor young, fat nor thin, tall nor short. It is simply awake.

Recognizing present awareness releases false identification with the body. It reveals your true nature as emptiness. That recognition frees you automatically from the false suffering associated with identification with the body including the self-centered stories surrounding age, beauty, illness, and death. This does not mean that you should ignore the body. The body is a relative form. Form is emptiness and emptiness is form. You are emptiness, manifesting as that temporary body and as every other body and form. In recognizing that you are life appearing as all these forms, life naturally takes care of itself.

More on recognizing present awareness

You may believe that you are your story, that your past defines you, and that the future contains the conclusion of your unresolved past. Although it is true that there is a relative, conceptual story that arises as the dream self, it is not who you really are. Both past and future are nothing more than limited, fleeting, time-bound concepts arising in present awareness.

Living life only from the story is like carrying on your shoulders a TV screen that shows only temporary images of past and future. It is a lie to say that you are that set of images. Who you are is the changelessly present awareness in which the images arise and fall. You are the actuality of life, not a series of concepts on a screen.

There is actual life here—vibrant, awake, intelligent, loving, peaceful, mysterious, abundant life. In order to realize this actuality, do nothing except notice the present awareness that is already here. It is the empty, awake, radiant space of now in which your story of time arises and falls. No matter what grand or awful story you are calling "your life"—including your past or future or even about what is happening now—that story is only a set of images. That conceptual story cannot see the actuality to which these words are pointing. This is not about denying concepts. It is about seeing that present awareness is non-conceptual.

More on recognizing awareness

The last three reflections have discussed recognizing present awareness. Remember that we are only pointing to an inexpressible realization. When we speak of it, thought is used. Thought divides up this One Life into pieces. It makes it appear as if there is something here called present awareness (i.e., formlessness or emptiness) that is totally separate from something else called thought (i.e., form).

When you recognize the present awareness to which the last reflections are pointing, it is seen that form is none other than formlessness and formlessness is none other than form. Thoughts arise from awareness. They come and go. What is left when thought disappears is awareness.

Recognizing present awareness is not about denying thought, emotions, the intellect or any other form. It is about seeing that there are not two here and then living from that seeing. It is about no longer identifying with the forms but letting them arise and fall naturally and completely. This seeing could be called a living realization. It is the pure freedom of realizing that you are emptiness and the pure and unconditional love of realizing that the emptiness is none other than form. This living realization is an indescribable way of being in the world that is no longer fixating either in awareness or thought. It is a flow of life that is completely natural, loving, and peaceful.

Formlessness is revealed in the death of each form

The formless is that which does not die because it was never born. Yet it is who you are in the deepest sense. You are the emptiness coming into form in all its beautiful varieties. When each form dies, there you are—the emptiness that gave birth to it and that is here in its absence.

The body that you have now is not the body you had five years ago. But the awareness that looks at the body is changelessly there regardless of the body (form) that comes and goes. The thoughts that arose yesterday are now gone. There are new thoughts today. But the awareness that sees those thoughts come and go is always here. In fact, every body, experience, situation, thought, state, and emotion—in short, every form—has come and gone. A million deaths have happened and yet here you are still! What has been here all along simply looking at, and appearing as, that coming and going?

As each thought, sound, emotion, state, experience, and other form dies, notice the quiet, still emptiness that is left. The death of each form is revealing that you are not that particular form. You are the essence of life itself coming into each and every form. That is not some religious belief or fairy tale. This is a living realization for you to know directly. You are 'This.' You are beyond the cycle of birth and death.

Index of entries

January

March

April

May

June

July

August

September

October

November

December

ABOUT:
Scott Kiloby

Scott Kiloby is an international speaker and the author of *Reflections of the One Life: Daily Pointers to Enlightenment, Love's Quiet Revolution: The End of the Spiritual Search, Doorway to Total Liberation: Conversations with What Is,* and the companion book to this one, *Living Relationship: Finding Harmony With Others.* He is also the creator of an addiction recovery method called Natural Rest. His book on this method is called *Natural Rest for Addiction: A Revolutionary Way to Recover Through Presence.*

Scott travels all over the world giving talks in which those attending experience nondual presence. In these meetings, every position and belief gets challenged. This leaves those attending completely open to allow the present moment to unfold in a new way, free of identification with thought. The point of the meetings is to allow people to go home and discover for themselves the freedom Scott's message is pointing to.

Scott is simplifying and demystifying the message of enlightenment or non-duality. He reaches out to people who are suffering or seeking or cannot seem to find fulfillment in this life, no matter where they go or what they do. He communicates that freedom is available and that it is actually contained in their very presence, yet it is overlooked.

Scott has opened the Kiloby Center in Palm Springs, CA, where he and his facilitators work with people on addiction, anxiety, depression and with those who are interested in experiencing non-dual realization. If interested, visit:

www.kilobycenter.com.

Connect with Scott's work:
www.livingrealization.org
www.livingrelationship.org www.kiloby.com
www.doorwaytoliberation.com
www.twitter.com/Scottkiloby
www.facebook.com/kiloby

www.kiloby.com
www.livinginquiries.com (For more info on the Unfindable and other "Living Inquiries")

www.kilobycenter.com (Scott's recovery and retreat center in Palm Springs, CA)

www.naturalrestforaddiction (Scott's addiction work)

TESTIMONIALS

"It may be that from your perspective, you don't see all of the enormous value and benefit you bring to so many. I have partaken of countless pages of writings, videos, audios, etc. but what you have shared with the world is in a whole different league. It's an actual, applicable, practical, doable, experience-changing offering."

"After a lifetime of moving from one spiritual belief system to another [in non-duality teachings], I've discovered a genuine, non-dogmatic invitation to wake up from the dream of seeking and instead to live in the powerful presence of what is. Scott is one of the most down-to-earth, accessible and honest teachers I've met. Working with him continues to alter my experience of life profoundly. I'm able to glimpse a quality of Being that has nothing to do with circumstances."

"*Living Realization* is truly different: it is as much of a 'how-to' manual as is possible with this kind of material. Despite the limitation of words, the paradox of duality, and the futility of trying to explain 'how' to realize no-self, the approach of LR succeeds more than any other book I've encountered (including Scott's other books). Finally, a clear writing which guides the reader to let go of and see through the reader... step-by-step."

"Our group finished the book *Living Realization* today. That last chapter is a very clear summation—quite powerful actually... thank you for your willingness to be the vehicle for this clarity on awareness and inseparability. You are one of the few that is able to see this and explain it. The Middle Way is so freeing."

"When I read your book, *Living Realization*, I could *not* skip over any part of that book. I mean, I would've liked too. It is so packed full of wonderful stuff. I've read fifteen books in the last fifteen weeks and there was nothing in there that I didn't think was useful. It was one of the most enlightening books I've ever read…really. I think it's a masterpiece!"

"I have been meditating and reading books on non-duality and Eastern philosophy for many years. The writing of Scott Kiloby is the most direct, articulate and carefully worded expression of liberation from suffering that I have encountered."

ADDITIONAL TITLES:
Available from the Kiloby Group

Living Relationship: Finding Harmony With Others
Scott Kiloby

Love's Quiet Revolution: The End of the Spiritual Search
Scott Kiloby

Reflections of the One Life: Daily Pointers to Enlightenment
Scott Kiloby

Natural Rest for Addiction: A Revolutionary Way to Recover Through Presence
Scott Kiloby

Doorway to Total Liberation: Conversations With 'What Is'
Scott Kiloby

AVAILABLE AT:
www.barnesandnoble.com
www.livingrealization.org
www.amazon.com